Canada Among Nation

TOMLINSON

Canada Among Nations
2011–2012

Canada and Mexico's Unfinished Agenda

EDITED BY ALEX BUGAILISKIS
AND ANDRÉS ROZENTAL

Published for the Norman Paterson School of
International Affairs, Carleton University
with The Centre for International Governance Innovation

by McGill-Queen's University Press
Montreal & Kingston • London • Ithaca

© McGill-Queen's University Press 2012
ISBN 978-0-7735-4011-8 (cloth)
ISBN 978-0-7735-4012-5 (paper)

Legal deposit second quarter 2012
Bibliothèque nationale du Québec

Printed in Canada on acid-free paper that is 100% ancient forest free
(100% post-consumer recycled), processed chlorine free

This book has been published with financial support from
the Norman Paterson School of International Affairs, Carleton
University, and The Centre for International Governance Innovation.

McGill-Queen's University Press acknowledges the support
of the Canada Council for the Arts for our publishing program.
We also acknowledge the financial support of the Government of
Canada through the Canada Book Fund for our publishing activities.

Library and Archives Canada has catalogued this publication as follows:

Canada among nations.
Annual.
1984–
Produced for the Norman Paterson School of International Affairs
at Carleton University
In cooperation with The Centre for International Governance Innovation.
Publisher varies
Each vol. also has a distinctive title.
Includes bibliographic references
ISSN 0832-0683

ISBN 978-0-7735-4011-8 (bnd)
ISBN 978-0-7735-4012-5 (pbk)

1. Canada – Foreign relations – 1945–   – Periodicals. 2. Canada –
Politics and government – 1984–   – Periodicals. 3. Canada – Politics
and government – 1980–1984 – Periodicals. I. Norman Paterson School
of International Affairs.

FC242.C345   327.71   C86-031285-2 REV

This book was typeset by Interscript in 10/12 Sabon.

Contents

Preface

FEN OSLER HAMPSON
AND PAUL HEINBECKER

The present volume of *Canada Among Nations* is the twenty-sixth in the series. This annual publication continues to be a widely read and cited source on Canada's role in the world. The series is used extensively in courses on Canadian foreign policy and international affairs in colleges and universities throughout North America, and it counts the public policy community, members of the media, the business community, and the interested public among its avid readership.

The purpose of the series is to provide a better understanding of important developments in Canadian policies and the environments that shape them and, in the process, to promote a more informed public debate about appropriate policies and priorities for Canada.

This year the volume focuses on Canada's relations with one of its key North American partners – Mexico. In a departure from previous editions which have focused on thematic issues, this book specifically targets the Canada-Mexico relationship. The ensuing chapters examine the evolving and multi-faceted bilateral relationship; explore the as yet unrealized potential for "trilateral" co-operation with the US; and identify and assess new opportunities for joint collaboration in regional and global forums and on emerging issues such as security, energy, and climate change. We can think of a no more able editorial team than Alexandra Bugailiskis and Andrés Rozental who have organized this year's volume. Both are distinguished senior public servants in Canada and Mexico respectively who have devoted much of their professional lives to advancing relations between our two countries. They have assembled an extraordinarily impressive group of contributors from government, academe, the media, and the wider policy world in Canada, Mexico, and the United States. The result is one of the most definitive studies of the Canada-Mexico relationship in the twenty-first century. The essays provide a rich historical examination of this evolving relationship, with sound analysis and advice on current policy challenges and recommendations on a roadmap to the future.

The essays in this volume, while rigorous and comprehensive, are written in a manner that is accessible to a wide audience. The authors gathered at Woerner House in Waterloo to review drafts of their chapters in the spring of 2011. We are grateful to the Centre for International Governance Innovation for hosting the workshop which provided useful feedback to the authors on their first drafts and helped shape the volume as an integrated whole.

As the general editors of the series, we would like to thank Tom Bernes, David Malone, and Rohinton Medhora who continue to lend their strong support to the series and this volume in particular. We also would like to thank Kevin Arthur, Sofía Barrón Esquivel, Anne Blaney, John Cadham, Simon Palamar, and the Department of Foreign Affairs and International Trade (DFAIT) officials in Ottawa and in Mexico for the extraordinary assistance they have provided in helping to organize the workshop in Waterloo and the production and assembly of this volume. We are also especially grateful for the financial support provided by the International Development Centre, the Centre for International Governance Innovation, and Carleton University. Without the generous support of these institutions, this book would not have been possible.

Message from Canada's Foreign Affairs Minister

THE HONOURABLE JOHN BAIRD

I am very pleased to contribute to this edition of *Canada Among Nations*. In the coming pages, you will read a number of thought-provoking articles that neatly lay out the past and the present of Canada's bilateral relationship with Mexico. This collection not only challenges us to be innovative as we build on the future of this relationship but offers a number of ideas on how we might do so.

Several authors note our two countries' shared commitment to promoting and protecting freedom, democracy, the rule of law, and respect for human rights. These commitments were reiterated and, I believe, strengthened during meetings I had with my Mexican counterpart in Mexico City in August 2011. I am quite confident that productive discussions will continue in the months and years ahead.

The last twenty of our two countries' more than sixty-five years of diplomatic relations have been transformative. Trade is but one aspect of our rich and growing relationship. This strengthening of ties has not happened by accident. The many steps that led to advances in the Canada-Mexico relationship reflect the vital economic, security, and social interests that we share. They are the platform from which we can take our relationship to a new level.

Abbreviations

ABD	Asian Development Bank
ACCBP	Anti-Crime Capacity Building Program
ALADI	Asociación Latinoamericana de Integración
AMEXCID	Agencia Mexicana de Cooperación Internacional para Desarrollo
APEC	Asia-Pacific Economic Cooperation
APFC	Asia Pacific Foundation of Canada
ASEAN	Association of Southeast Asian Nations
BRICS	Brazil, Russia, India, China, and South Africa
CAFTA/DR	Dominican Republic-Central America-United States Free Trade Agreement
CAN	Comunidad Andina
CARIBCAN	Caribbean-Canada Trade Agreement
CARICOM	The Caribbean Community
CCS	carbon capture and sequestration
CELAC	Comunidad de Estados Latinamericanos y Caribeños
CFE	Comisión Federal de Electricidad
CIDA	Canadian International Development Agency
CIDAC	Centro de Investigación para el Desarrollo, Asociación Civil
CIDE	Centro de Investigación y Docencia Económicas
CIFSRF	Canadian International Food Security Research Fund
CISEN	Centro de Investigación y Seguridad Nacional
CMP	Canada-Mexico Partnership
COMEXI	Consejo Mexicano de Asuntos Internacionales

CONACYT	Consejo Nacional de Ciencia y Tecnología
CONAGO	Conferencia Nacional de Gobernadores
COP	Conference of Parties
CRE	Comisión Reguladora de Energía
CSR	corporate social responsibility
CTCBP	Counter Terrorism Capacity Building Program
CUFTA	Canada-United States Free Trade Agreement
DOE	Department of Energy
EAPC	Euro-Atlantic Partnership Council
EBRD	European Bank for Reconstruction and Development
EGADE	Escuela di Graduados en Administración y Dirreción de Empresas
EIA	Energy Information Administration
ELAP	Emerging Leaders in the Americas Program
ENAP	École nationale d'administration publique
EPA	Environmental Protection Agency
FDI	Foreign Direct Investment
FERC	Federal Energy Regulatory Commission
FOCAL	Canadian Foundation for the Americas
FORDECYT	Fondo Institucional de Fomento Regional para el Desarrollo Cientifico, Tecnológico y de Inovación
FTAA	Free Trade Area of the Americas
FTAAP	Free Trade Area of the Asia Pacific
FTC	Free-Trade Commission
FUNSALUD	Fundación Mexicana para la Salud
IDB	Inter-American Development Bank
IDEA	Institute for Democracy and Electoral Assistance
IDRC	International Development Research Centre
IEA	International Energy Agency
IFE	Instituto Federal Electoral
INAP	Instituto Nacional de Administración Pública
INSP	Insituto Nacional de Salud Publica
JMC	Joint Ministerial Commission
LAFTA	Latin American Free Trade Agreement
MERCOSUR	Mercado Común del Sur
MINUSTAH	United Nations Stabilization Mission in Haiti
NAEO	North American Energy Outlook
NAEWG	North American Energy Working Group
NAFTA	North America Free Trade Agreement
NALS	North American Leaders' Summit
NAPAPI	North American Plan for Avian and Pandemic Influenza
NASCO	North American Super Corridor

NEB	National Energy Board
NEMA	National Electrical Manufacturers Association
NERC	North American Electric Reliability Corporation
NGO	non-governmental organization
NORAD	North American Aerospace Defense Command
NWMO	Nuclear Waste Management Organization
OAS	Organization of American States
OECD	Organization for Economic Co-operation and Development
OEI	Organización de Estados Iberoamericanos para la Educación, la Ciencia y la Cultura
OPEC	Organization of Petroleum Exporting Countries
OSCE	Organization for Security and Cooperation in Europe
PAN	Partido de Acción Nacional
PRI	Partido Revolucionario Institucional
RCMP	Royal Canadian Mounted Police
REDD	Reducing Emissions from Deforestation and Forest Degradation in Developing Countries
SAWP	Seasonal Agricultural Workers Program
SECI	Southeast European Cooperative Initiative
SELA	Sistema Economico Latinamericano y del Caribe
SENER	Secretaría de Energía de México
SICA	Sistema de la Integración Centroamericana
SPP	Security and Prosperity Partnership
SRE	Secretaría de Relaciones Exteriores
TPP	Transpacific Partnership
UNASUR	Unión de Naciones Suramericanas
UNSC	UN Security Council
WCI	Western Climate Initiative
WIPO	World Intellectual Property Organization

Canada Among Nations, 2011–2012

PART ONE

Introduction

Viva Canada y México

THE HONOURABLE BILL GRAHAM AND
SENATOR AMBASSADOR ROSARIO GREEN

As Mexican and Canadian nationals who share a common understanding and mutual respect for each other's country, we welcome this thoughtful and thought-provoking collection. The timing could not be better. North America is at a crossroads. The combined challenges of regional integration, national self-determination, and globalization have created a nexus of contending forces that are pulling our nations in multiple directions. Without a strong understanding of these forces, sound strategies to deal with them, and able leadership, we risk succumbing to the dangers they present and missing the opportunities they create. Canada and Mexico have much in common in the high-stakes game playing out in our countries, our region, and our world. As citizens of Canada and Mexico with long and varied experience working with and in each other's country, we welcome the opportunity to more fully examine and discuss these important issues.

B. GRAHAM: Like most Canadians, I first came to know Mexico as a tourist. Early in my life, I travelled to Mexico with my parents and I would subsequently take my own children there to introduce them to the extraordinarily rich culture and history of Mexico. Since then, I have come to know the modern Mexico of business, the Mexico in which reliable partners, productive enterprises, and modern infrastructure serve as both a market and a logical entry point for Canadians seeking business opportunities in the Americas. My political career has also provided me with numerous opportunities to engage with Mexico and Mexicans. As a parliamentarian, chair of the Standing Committee on

Foreign Affairs and International Trade, and the first elected chair of the Inter-Parliamentary Forum of the Americas, and, subsequently, Foreign Minister and Defence Minister, I witnessed many instances in which Canadian and Mexican interests were mutually reinforcing. Based on my experience with colleagues in Mexico from all walks of life, I have concluded that our common values and interests make our two countries natural partners.

R. GREEN: Unlike most Mexicans, my first visit to Canada had nothing to do with tourism or personal enjoyment but rather with a tough job. In 1990, as the Executive Secretary of the recently created National Commission for Human Rights (1990), I travelled around the world to introduce the commission and to make it clear that Mexico had decided to comply fully with national and international human rights legislation. These travels brought me to Canada, a vast and wonderful country with a profound vocation in favour of human rights, and included stops in Ottawa, Montreal, Toronto, and Vancouver. When I later became the Foreign Minister of Mexico, I visited Canada on more than one occasion, both as minister and accompanying President Zedillo. Later, while I served as an Assistant Secretary General at the United Nations, I returned several times to Montreal where my daughter Daniela had decided to attend senior high school. I realized a few days into my first visit to Canada that our two countries shared an important link: we are both multicultural, multiethnic, and multilingual.

In the last two decades, we have witnessed a remarkable strengthening of ties between Canada and Mexico. The growth of national, and continental, connections has benefited both our nations. Today, however, we are convinced that Canada and Mexico are at a critical juncture in their relationship and that our political leaders need to take fresh steps in forging the next stage in our relations.

As is well known, the signing of the North American Free Trade Agreement (NAFTA) served as a catalyst for a steady growth in ties between Canada and Mexico. NAFTA facilitated a rapid growth in trade and investment and the integration of our supply chains on a continental level, making both countries more competitive. Of equal, if not greater, importance has been the growth of a web of other connections creating a quiet but de facto integration.

Our deep interconnection affects our societies at all levels and goes far beyond a mere trade agreement. Our federal governments have successfully co-operated on a variety of issues over the last two decades, including the environment, health, crime, and governance, and on such multilateral initiatives as the Landmine Ban Treaty and the International

Criminal Court. In important areas such as the issues of indigenous groups and the importance accorded by our parliaments to political stability, human rights, and democratic practices, our governments have common concerns. This federal engagement, though important, encompasses only a small part of the integration between our countries. States, provinces, and even municipalities have begun working together across borders through agreements promoting further trade, cultural, and technological co-operation. Our business sectors have taken advantage of NAFTA's investment clauses leading to the growth of continental production chains that seize on our national complementarities and make North American industry more competitive in global markets. Our citizens are engaging with each other in large numbers, with Canada the third largest receiver of Mexican tourists and over one and a half million Canadians visiting Mexico in 2010 for tourism, business, and study.

Much of the growth in our relationship has occurred with limited direction from our federal governments, a form of benign neglect. While relations have expanded and deepened across many sectors, they have not benefited from any significant degree of strategic vision or leadership. This bottom-up development has achieved significant results, but it has not been optimal. If we are to realize the full potential of the Canada-Mexico relationship, our federal governments will need to take a more active role and provide greater direction, while working in collaboration with subnational governments, business, and civil society.

The development of this relationship is vitally important to both countries and we should not discount it as a mere side-show to NAFTA. We live in an age where innovations in communication and transportation technologies have made physical distance of diminishing importance. What were once national issues are now continental or even global and we must approach them accordingly. Our countries gain advantages from this situation, since we can now profit from each other's comparative advantages through the construction of continental production chains and through the sharing of expertise. On the negative side, this shrinking of distance allows criminal and terrorist networks, environmental hazards, and pandemics to stretch across borders. This current reality of integration and blurring borders is neither an inherently good or bad development, but it presents challenges that require our governments to accept that "co-operative continentalism" is the only long-term solution to our common problems. As we found during the HINI pandemic, many problems cannot be confined to just one country, and they are best addressed through the concerted efforts of multiple stakeholders. Mexico and Canada, being neighbours in North America, lose out globally if they do not work together on concerns that are felt at home yet transnational in scope.

The relevance of the Canada-Mexico relationship is only increased by our shared neighbour, the United States. Some Canadians have argued that the nation should distance itself from Mexico and trilateralism in order to focus more fully on its relationship with the United States. This, in our view, would be short-sighted and could undermine our long-term competitive position. Of course, both our nations benefit from their strong relationship with the United States since we gain advantages, domestically and in our broader global relations, through the privileged position we occupy with our powerful neighbour. However, we are not reaching optimal conditions if we allow our relations with the United States to obstruct our ability to maximize our bilateral relationship. For Canadians, engaging Mexico means a more effective supply chain, more affordable and productive labour, and market access to a Mexican middle class that is larger than the entire Canadian population. Those arguing to exclude Mexico have the cost-benefit analysis terribly wrong; our bilateral relationship has significant value for its own sake.

There is ample reason to support increased bilateral co-operation, but this type of collaboration must be put in the context of our broader trilateral environment. We accept that some issues may be addressed only through bilateral channels for historical, legal, or domestic reasons. However, that still leaves a number of areas where Canada and Mexico have common or similar positions, where we should and could be working together at a trilateral level. The "thickening" of the US border and restrictions on trade, although for different reasons on the northern and southern borders, reflects a more insular and security-conscious United States. Whatever the reasons, this trade obstruction has significant impacts on both the Canadian and Mexican economies. Additionally, the lack of a common trade framework and strongly coordinated efforts by Canada and Mexico on issues such as trucking and softwood lumber provides the US with greater scope to take unilateral measures that protect its immediate interests and exacerbate our asymmetries. As these economic issues play out, drug traffickers in Canada and Mexico make vast fortunes exporting into the United States while guns come back across the border and onto the streets of our cities. Our continent needs a coordinated climate change strategy and, with Washington hesitant to move strongly on the issue, Mexico and Canada could show real leadership. The United States is a great ally to both Canada and Mexico, but asymmetry stemming from its overwhelming size and power, combined with a political system that favours special interests, puts the two smaller nations at a disadvantage when engaging unilaterally.

Despite our shared North American challenges, trilateral co-operation at the national level has stalled and even retreated in recent years. In truth, it was never robust. The efforts of Jorge Castañeda, Mexico's secretary of Foreign Affairs (2000–2003) and Bill Graham, Canada's minister of Foreign Affairs (2002–2003), to engage Colin Powell in trilateral discussions met with indifference in the face of more urgently perceived business. Additionally, while in Article 2001 NAFTA provides for a "Commission" consisting of relevant ministers meeting to supervise the agreement, a permanently active institutional structure has never developed. In fact, important initiatives like the Mid-Continental Trade Corridor have largely been the result of the work of concerned states, municipalities, and private actors. North America has great potential, with a combined Gross Domestic Product (GDP), according to 2010 World Bank figures, $5 trillion greater than that of the Eurozone and $6 trillion greater than the BRIC (Brazil, Russia, India, China) economies, and a continental age demographic that is the envy of most major economies. If we are to take advantage of these strengths, however, our national leadership must develop stronger trilateral institutions that recognize our shared interest in the future success of North America.

National leadership is required in two areas: to provide the framework within which the more organic social and business integration can flourish and to provide direction to ensure that North America develops in the most effective, productive, and just fashion possible. The collapse of the Security and Prosperity Partnership and the failure to hold a North American Leaders Summit in 2010 are indications of a trend away from continental co-operation. Increasingly, Canada, Mexico, and the United States are falling back to what Robert Pastor calls the "dual bilateralism" of North America, where each smaller nation engages with the United States individually. Not only can this leave the third nation in the proverbial wilderness, but it strengthens the hand of the United States and encourages it to act unilaterally. Co-operative continental approaches to our shared problems and opportunities, on the other hand, benefit all three nations and the retreat from trilateralism should thus be a concern to the citizens of all NAFTA partners.

While our governments appear to be drifting apart, changes in the global economy are making a strong and united continental union increasingly important. New powers are rising, reducing the relative economic significance of traditional powers like the United States. Asian giants such as China and India are exerting increasing influence on the global economy. At the same time, Brazil is emerging as a major power broker in Latin America. Much of the world is moving toward further, rather than lesser, regional integration, whether in Europe, South America, or Southeast Asia. Within our own hemisphere there are renewed efforts by the leading Pacific Rim economies, including Mexico, to forge a new trade alliance to foster trade with Asia. Canada's silence and absence from these discussions is as telling as it is troubling and certainly not consistent with the present government's much welcomed focus on the Americas.

Canada is renewing efforts to engage with emerging markets, but needs to do so from a position of strength. Mexico can and should be a natural ally in this engagement. Yet Canada's difficulties in fully engaging with Mexico hamper this co-operation and do not bode well for Canada's ability to successfully engage with other emerging markets with whom it has far less in common and to whom it is far less connected. For Mexico, a fragmented and disunited North America does little to help it be more competitive and to meet the challenges of the changing global order.

The publication of this volume of *Canada Among Nations* – an examination of the Canada-Mexico relationship and of the ways in which we can improve our relations – is therefore timely. Building on the efforts of the government-run Canada-Mexico Partnership and the Canada-Mexico Joint Action Plan, as well as the independent work of the Canada-Mexico Initiative led by FOCAL (The Canadian Foundation for the Americas) and COMEXI (The Mexican Council on Foreign Relations), this volume strengthens the case for enhancing our bilateral relationship and proposes how we can do so. Canada and Mexico complement one another in numerous ways and it is vital that we learn to use these complementarities to strengthen our countries and our continent as a whole. We should seek to build on our trilateral relations but also on the "third bilateral" relationship. Thomas d'Aquino once stated, "three can talk, two can do." Although he was referring to Canadian co-operation with the United States, the same can be said for greater co-operation between Canada and Mexico. This "third bilateral" contains great possibilities; it presents an opportunity which Canada and Mexico must not miss.

In this edition of *Canada Among Nations*, Mexican, Canadian, and American authors address some of the key opportunities and issues calling for greater collaboration and engagement between Canada and Mexico. We would like to lend our voice to encouraging these directions.

Our countries have made major gains in economic co-operation since the signing of NAFTA, but there remains room for much more. Bilateral trade has increased rapidly since 1994, making us each other's third largest trade partners, yet this trade remains a small fraction of either country's trade with the United States. In order to facilitate greater trade, we need to increase bilateral investment and create stronger bi- and trilateral production chains, including energy and transportation infrastructure. Joint productive initiatives could profit from the opportunities provided by larger regional and continental markets.

Likewise, both countries could achieve long-term benefits if we expanded and promoted academic exchange programs, including training opportunities for students and personnel, particularly in the area of energy. We must also actively facilitate the legitimate movement of people between our countries, including tourists, business people, and students, if we are to expand the relationship. We need to review, improve, and expand the highly successful Seasonal Agricultural Workers Program, which is a positive model of how we can facilitate the short-term movement of people to address labour shortages in one country while providing important skills and employment, without the "brain drain," for the other. In order to fully understand this relationship, we need better ways to collect statistics so that we have solid empirical information on the depth and nature of Canada-Mexico relations.

We have made exceptional improvements in the quality and depth of our political engagement, but we can do more. Unlike the European Union, the North American project, in a number of respects, is developing from the ground up, through the day-to-day contacts of tourists, students, and business people, and through provinces, states, and municipalities working together on issues of mutual concern. We need to support this co-operation and enhance it through promoting greater engagement between our citizens. We need to find ways to rationalize the system of subnational contacts so as to encourage the greatest growth of these ties.

Finally, we need to make a greater effort to work together in the multilateral arena. Canada and Mexico have many common ideals, including respect for human rights, democracy, and the rule of law, and these should translate into common approaches in regional, hemispheric, and global forums. The evolution of this relationship from the ground up demonstrates our commonalities; the next stage will require greater leadership from our governments if we are to continue to build on our successes.

Canada and Mexico share an economic bloc, a continent, a system of values, and deep ties at the state and provincial levels. There are thus multiple areas in which enhanced co-operation can be of value to both our nations. At home we have opportunities to work together on protecting our citizens through security and health initiatives. We can work together to ensure that our continental energy and transportation networks are ready for the challenges of the twenty-first century, which means integration, co-operation, and environmental sustainability. Our two countries share the great challenge of reducing their greenhouse gas emissions, and the transition to a low carbon economy offers the opportunity to work on achieving both energy security and the sustainable development of North America. We can use our common values and institutional linkages to promote democracy, trade, and good governance both within the region and on a global scale. Perhaps most importantly, we can use a strong and vibrant Canada–Mexico relationship as a model for collaboration in the region and to reduce the attraction for the United States of more unilateral pathways.

The challenges of the twenty-first century can seem daunting, but with them come many new opportunities. Through enhancing our partnership and strengthening Canada-Mexico relations, we better prepare ourselves to meet these challenges. There are many possibilities for co-ordination, reciprocal aid, and joint planning. It is our hope that this volume will serve to inform academics, government officials, and the public at large of the deep relations that have developed between our nations and that it will inspire all of us to continue building these bridges to promote a brighter future for ourselves, our families, and our great nations.

The Canada–Mexico Relationship: Looking Back and Ahead

OLGA ABIZAID AND GRAEME DOUGLAS

Over the last two decades, the Canada-Mexico relationship has consistently increased in importance for both nations. Mexico has become one of Canada's most important international partners and has entered the ranks of our "strategic allies."

In the economic and political spheres, there has been remarkable growth in our interconnections. Political ties between ministries and departments at all levels of government have increased over these years, especially on economic and trade issues, while exchanges between public officials and legislators have become progressively more formalized. Multiple people-to-people contacts are facilitating a rapprochement between societies, be it through flows of tourists, academics, researchers, students, and artists, through expanding diasporas in both countries, or through civil society initiatives. The Canada-Mexico relationship also goes beyond bilateral and North American issues and includes partnerships in multilateral and regional forums as well as in the Americas. This constellation of points of contact makes the bilateral relationship strong and dynamic, and yet inaudible.

In fact, so many things go well with the relationship that our countries often take it for granted. It seems that Mexico gets significant coverage only when the news is bad – the dramatic rise in organized crime or the Canada-Mexico visa issue – which thrusts an unpleasant image of Mexico into the popular consciousness in Canada. The old journalism adage that "if it bleeds it leads" rules here and promotes an environment where stories about increasing trade or new state-provincial agreements rarely make it into the Canadian press.

We thus see two dimensions of the Canada-Mexico relationship; a glass half full and a glass half empty.

The glass is half full in that much is occurring and going well with the relationship, especially for the private sector and the states and provinces. The glass is half empty in that seventeen years after the North American Free Trade Agreement (NAFTA) brought both countries into closer contact and provided many opportunities for joint endeavours continentally, regionally, and globally, we have seen relatively little materialize.

AN ECONOMIC RELATION AT THE HEART
OF NORTH AMERICAN AFFAIRS

Without question, the establishment of NAFTA brought renewed energy into the Canada-Mexico relationship. With a six-fold growth in bilateral trade in goods between 1993 and the first semester of 2010 and the multiplication of Canadian companies in Mexico (2,600 as of 2010) that cater to the domestic and the US markets, it is evident that the economic relationship has thrived in unexpected ways.

Bilateral trade between the two countries has grown at higher rates than Canada-US or Mexico-US trade – over 12.5 percent yearly, according to Mexico's Secretariat of Economy. Thus, despite both countries' focus on the US, the Canada-Mexico trade relationship has flourished. Mexico was Canada's third largest trade partner in 2010, according to Statistics Canada, with CA$27.1 billion in total bilateral merchandise trade, following the United States (CA$501.6 billion) and China (CA$57.7 billion). This was the first year that trade with Mexico exceeded trade with the United Kingdom (CA$27 billion). By the end of the second quarter of 2011, bilateral merchandise trade had increased by an additional CA$1.5 billion, continuing the growth trend.[1]

Trade with Mexico also displayed a relative degree of resiliency during the financial crisis, indicating the strength of the two nations' economic ties. Although 2009 witnessed a decline of over 10 percent in bilateral trade between Canada and Mexico from 2008 levels, trade with the United States and the United Kingdom suffered much larger declines of 24.2 percent and 16.1 percent, respectively.

Unfortunately, even when considering the remarkable pace at which the Canada-Mexico economic relationship has grown in the seventeen years since NAFTA entered into force, much of its potential remains untapped. Though Canada has become the fourth largest source of foreign direct investment (FDI) for Mexico, with US$9.185 billion accumulated as of 2010,[2] it is not one of the ten preferred destinations for Canadian investment. Mexican investments in Canada were CA$253 million in 2009, trailing well behind the Mexican private sector's US$2.2

billion investment in the United States and the nearly US$36 billion of investments they have made in Latin America. This lack of deeper investment exchanges is significant since it may be slowing progress in the establishment of integrated production chains, a goal that both countries have pledged to advance. To remedy the situation, the Department of Foreign Affairs and International Trade (DFAIT) has included Mexico in its FDI Strategy.

Now that the elimination of tariffs planned for in NAFTA has been achieved, both countries agree that to get additional benefits out of the agreement, they must dismantle bottlenecks at border crossings, ease regional rules of origin, and harmonize regulations. They also agree that North American economic competitiveness must be maintained and increased, and understand that this goal needs to be achieved while meeting the United States's security concerns. Unfortunately, Canada and Mexico have differing visions for the future of North American integration in a number of other respects. While Mexico has pushed for more trilateralism and integration based on a model similar to that of the European Union, Canada has preferred to promote bilateral engagements between itself and its North American neighbours. This type of engagement reflects a Canadian propensity for encouraging the so-called "special relationship" with the United States.

In summary, since the entry into force of NAFTA the Canada-Mexico economic relationship has grown to unforeseen levels, even though both countries have focused predominantly on their trade relationship with the United States. However, the potential of the relationship will remain untapped until more action is taken to deepen economic linkages and develop integrated chains of production, which will translate into more commercial and investment exchanges. Of course, developments – or the lack thereof – in the trilateral North American competitiveness agenda will also affect the dynamics of the bilateral relationship.

EXPERIENCES IN GOVERNANCE AND STRENGTHENING OF DEMOCRATIC INSTITUTIONS

Political changes in Mexico paved the way for greater convergence with Canada in the field of governance, which has helped to solidify the relationship further. Canada was an important ally for Mexico during its democratic transition, providing ongoing support, encouragement, and technical assistance. The gradual convergence in the governance structures and socio-political values of Canada, Mexico, and the United States has served to benefit and strengthen North American co-operation.

Bilateral efforts on governance and institution-building have included formal and informal exchanges on many issues, among them access to information and privacy laws, federalism, indigenous affairs, transparency and accountability, human rights, modernization of the civil service, e-government, judicial reform, and more recently, public security. Ministerial exchanges have also been successful in dealing with specific issues, such as economic policy, labour, infrastructure, foreign policy, and health – notably the bilateral co-operation on the HINI crisis in the spring of 2009 which was swift and key to slowing the spread of the pandemic.

More recently, annual inter-parliamentary meetings have acquired greater relevance in advancing the shared political agenda. During these meetings, legislators from both countries have had the opportunity to discuss important bilateral and trilateral issues.

Perhaps the most emblematic example of co-operation between the two countries is the two-decade collaboration of Elections Canada and Mexico's Federal Electoral Institute (IFE). At the outset, Elections Canada became actively engaged in assisting in the organization of transparent elections in Mexico and in strengthening the capacity of IFE. Today, IFE has a strong reputation and is itself providing electoral assistance in countries such as Haiti and Iraq. Further, continuous interaction between Elections Canada and IFE has served to improve both countries' electoral systems, addressing issues including media access during elections and public versus private funding. These institutions also work together closely within international organizations on matters related to electoral assistance.

Economic and political relations are not limited to federal ministries. Following the lead of Quebec, which established a representation office in Mexico in the 1980s, the government of Alberta and, more recently, the government of Ontario have opened similar offices in Mexico to promote their interests. Whereas the work of Alberta and Ontario has focused mainly on economic issues, Quebec has also put in place numerous cultural, research, and educational exchanges. Recently, Alberta and the State of Veracruz agreed to strengthen their ties. Similar agreements exist between Quebec and Nuevo León, Ontario and the State of México, as well as Alberta and Jalisco. In March 2009, the Attorneys General from British Columbia and the state of Baja California signed a statement of intent on the need to work collaboratively to prevent criminal activities, including human and arms trafficking, money laundering, and internet crimes against children. There are also a number of agreements between cities to promote exchanges on municipal matters, such as those between Edmonton and Guadalajara, Gatineau and Querétaro, and Calgary and Zapopan. Moreover, there is room for even greater action, as cities assume a larger role on issues of international resonance (e.g., environmental policies). In signing these partnerships, the objectives of provinces and cities may converge with those of the federal governments, but there is as yet no concerted effort to coordinate between the different levels of government.

Decentralization has been useful for dealing with new issues in a technical manner, and for progressively incorporating a multitude of themes and stakeholders into the relationship's political agenda. Insofar as there is mutual interest in working together, this agenda will continue to grow. However, these numerous linkages at all levels of government make it difficult for people to know what is happening in the relationship in other areas; hence, many opportunities to build on previous successes and to bring lessons learned to the international level have been overlooked.

SECURITY: THE EMERGING AGENDA

During the post-Second World War period and throughout the era of the Cold War, security was not an issue in which Canada and Mexico shared many, if any, common areas of interest. However, following the attacks on the United States on 11 September 2001, the concept of the security of North America moved dramatically and suddenly from a focus on threats posed by traditional state actors to asymmetrical threats from non-state actors. The American reaction to the terrorist threat has been unprecedented in strength and has forced a drastic redefinition of the security of North America to which Canada and to some degree Mexico has had to respond. With the rise of organized crime, drug trafficking, and violence in Mexico, another set of asymmetrical threats has emerged along the US border. This has forced a second drastic redefinition of the security of North America by the United States to focus on a different set of asymmetric threats from a different set of non-state actors. While Mexico bears the brunt of these security concerns, Canada is not immune to their impact.

Responding to the two different aspects of the new definition of the security of North America has pushed Mexico and Canada further apart. On terrorism, the United States does not consider Mexico to be a source of concern. On the other hand, segments of the American media still portray Canada, incorrectly, as the entry point for the September 11 hijackers. Mexico has no desire to become associated with Canada's terrorism "problem" and Canada has even less desire to become involved in Mexico's crime "problem." Though both countries can commiserate on mistreatment by the American government and defamation by the American media, a common front has not and likely will not emerge.

What movement we have seen on co-operation between Mexico and Canada on the new security issues in North America has, therefore, largely come from pressure by the United States. The clearest example is the slowly growing assistance from Canada to aid Mexico in the fight against the drug cartels. At this stage, security co-operation has centred on fostering dialogue, exchanging information, and building trust, but it is likely to expand in the future, as illustrated in the Joint Plan of Action for 2010–2012.

Of particular relevance was the creation of a multi-track process within the previous Canada-Mexico Joint Action Plan for 2007–2008 to promote dialogue on security, defence, and public safety in order to address issues such as organized crime and irregular migration. This process encompasses all bilateral initiatives related to security, including the annual government-wide security policy consultation coordinated by DFAIT and Mexico's Ministry of Foreign Relations (SRE); the bilateral working group on security led by the Canadian Ministry of Public Safety and the Mexican Centre for Investigation and National Security (CISEN); and the political-military talks during which Canada and Mexico discuss civilian-military relations and peace support operations.

The other impetus for co-operation has come from Mexico as part of a broader strategy to engage countries other than the United States in its conflict with the drug cartels. At the request of Mexico, visits and exchanges with Mexican counterparts by personnel from the ministries of Public Safety, Justice, National Defence, and the Royal Canadian Mounted Police (RCMP) are increasing. For example, a delegation of Mexican judges visited Canada in 2010 to learn about the Canadian justice system. Canada also participated in training programs to strengthen the capabilities of Mexico's Federal Preventive Police alongside other countries including Colombia, France, and the US. In 2009, Spanish-speaking officers from the RCMP went to Mexico to train federal police recruits and medium-level officers, and later Mexican management-level officers attended a seminar on managerial and leadership skills in Canada.

The creation of the Anti-Crime Capacity Building Program (ACCBP) for the Americas announced by Prime Minister Harper in August 2009 on the margins of the North American Leaders Summit could be a centrepiece to enhance bilateral co-operation on security-related matters. This program seeks to enhance the capacity of the countries of the region to cope with crime – particularly illicit drugs, arms trafficking, corruption, human trafficking, and money laundering – and to strengthen security systems and crime prevention. Canada earmarked nearly CA$4 million of the ACCBP's total CA$15 million annual budget for Mexico in 2010. Canada is working closely to assist Mexico in implementing its judicial reform program, approved in 2008, which will establish a new adversarial and oral criminal justice system. Canada will assist in training Mexican judges on oral trials (CA$1.6 million), provide support for national-state licensing and educational systems for lawyers to make the transition to oral trials (CA$1.2 million), and provide assistance for the harmonization of criminal legislation and the strengthening of prosecution service (CA$1.1 million). Anti-crime co-operation with Mexico in the western hemisphere is also expected to grow as pledged by both countries under the Joint Plan of Action for 2010–2012.

Although security co-operation is relatively new within the relationship, it is evolving in a positive way. The most important obstacle to building trust and developing new projects in this area lies in the scarce resources available.

A PARTNER IN THE WORLD: FOREIGN POLICY

Exchanges, and at times convergence, on foreign policy are not new to the Canada-Mexico relationship. Even before NAFTA, both countries found common ground in the United Nations (UN) and in support of the efforts of the Contadora peace process in Central America. However, a deeper rapprochement between the two countries occurred with changes in Mexico in the 1990s. Yet, the limits of this co-operation have become evident.

In recent years, there has been an increased interest in enhancing co-operation on foreign policy. For instance, on the international stage, Canada and Mexico have called for a ban on anti-personnel landmines and for the creation of the International Criminal Court and are now pushing for reform of the UN system and international financial institutions. They also collaborate in other forums such as the G20, the Asia-Pacific Economic Co-operation (APEC), the Summits of the Americas, and the Organization of American States (OAS), where they are jointly pressing for reform. Both countries are strong opponents of rising protectionism worldwide and have unilaterally reduced their trade tariffs.

Canada and Mexico have also pledged to collaborate with the US on hemispheric issues. While tangible examples of that commitment remain to be seen, the 2009 political crisis in Honduras indicated that Canada and Mexico were indeed willing to exchange views and information both at the bilateral and trilateral levels.

Despite the potential for co-operation, there have been notable cases where it has not materialized. For instance, Canada and Mexico have wavered when dealing with an inward-looking US. They exchanged information and consulted with each other immediately after candidate Barack Obama expressed a desire to reopen NAFTA during the 2008 presidential race. Yet, when the United States later implemented the "Buy American" clause to cope with the economic recession and reserved projects benefiting from the stimulus package for American firms, both Canada and Mexico decided to handle the issue bilaterally with the United States.

Mexico's decision to host the second Latin America and Caribbean Summit in 2010, a heads of state meeting initiated by Brazil that excludes Canada and the United States, and its agreement not to invite Canada to the Arc of the Pacific meeting it hosted that same year have raised questions regarding the importance that Mexico places on its relationship with Canada.

The continuation of foreign policy exchanges and their promotion will be key if both countries are to bridge differences and promote co-operative and coordinated actions in North America. Canada and Mexico should work to make their foreign policy strategies more complementary within North America, multilateral organizations, and the western hemisphere, particularly when it comes to Central America and the Caribbean. Haiti's January 2010 earthquake and the challenges faced by the international community to coordinate relief efforts present important lessons for the Canada-Mexico relationship, highlighting the need to strengthen communication between the different ministries and agencies dealing with emergency situations.

THE RELATIONSHIP:
A SNAPSHOT OF PEOPLE-TO-PEOPLE EXCHANGES

People-to-people exchanges show the intensity of the interconnections between Canadians and Mexicans. While the movement of people facilitates relationships and fosters greater understanding, it can, however, also be a source of friction.

During the past decade, a problematic issue has emerged with the dramatic increase in the number of Mexicans requesting refugee status in Canada. Between 2005 and 2008, these numbers grew from approximately 3,400 to over 9,500. Mexico was then the single largest source of refugee claimants in Canada but also had one of the lowest rates of acceptance. The rising number of refugee claimants was a growing irritant for both countries and culminated with Canada's decision to impose visa requirements on Mexican travellers in July 2009. Refugee claims from Mexico declined to approximately 7,600 by the end of 2009 and are no longer a significant issue. The Canadian government has since implemented a number of measures to mitigate some of the negative impacts following the visa imposition. These include the establishment of visa application centres, the creation of the Business Express Program and, more recently, the waiving of the medical examination requirement for long-term stays. However, Canada can solve the underlying problem only through a revision of the refugee system, which has yet to occur in any meaningful way.

People-to-people contacts between our countries remain strong, with over one and a half million Canadians visiting Mexico in 2010 and an increasing number of retirees making Mexico their home. Flows in the opposite direction are no less significant, but have suffered a sharp decline following the imposition of the visa requirements. By the end of 2010, Mexican overnight tourist visits to Canada totalled 120,499, less than half of the 250,000 visitors registered in 2007 and 2008.

In addition to tourist visits, approximately 23,000 Mexican temporary workers entered Canada in 2008 – 17,000 under the Seasonal Agricultural Workers Program and the remainder under the umbrella of Canada's Foreign Workers Program – to work in the agriculture, construction, hospitality, and energy sectors. Canada issued approximately 9,000 visas to students from Mexico who wished to study in our high schools, universities, graduate schools, and language programs in 2010 and there are over 400 academic exchange agreements between universities in Canada and Mexico. Canada also offers scholarships for Mexican students through Canada's Emerging Leaders in the Americas Program, which offers short study tours to expose young leaders from the region to Canadian education models and expertise in the areas of security, democratic governance, and prosperity. Canada's commitment to fostering cultural exchanges with Mexico was further bolstered by the signing and entry into force of a Youth Mobility Programme under the International Experience Canada (IEC) initiative in January 2011. Mexican youths demonstrated their growing interest in Canada, as the quota of 250 Mexican citizens was reached by June 2011.

Temporary flows of people are important, but more attention should also be devoted to those who decide to relocate permanently. There are almost 6000 Canadians living in Mexico, while estimates put the Mexican community in Canada at over 50,000, forming one of the largest diaspora groups from a Latin American country in Canada.

In large part, Mexican immigrants are highly skilled professionals contributing to Canada's competitiveness and innovativeness; notably, many of them work in the high-technology sector. Prominent Mexicans work in Canadian government, firms, universities, and research institutes. These roles are significant, but more research is needed to better assess the contribution that both the Mexican and Canadian diasporas make in their country of adoption and the role they could play in strengthening the bilateral relationship.

MECHANISMS TO HANDLE
THE BILATERAL RELATIONSHIP

The bilateral relationship between Canada and Mexico is conceptually structured around the principles of convergence and complementarity. This structure allows for great flexibility in the determination of objectives over time within the economic, political, and social spheres, including the calibration and pace of discussions and the delimitation of regional settings for co-operation. It is also a reflection of Canada and Mexico's choice of a very institutional framework that relies on personal ties between leaders and legislators and ad hoc exchanges between technical experts from different ministries and departments.

Despite its generally informal organization, the changing focuses of their bilateral agreements reflect the evolving nature of the Canada-Mexico relationship. In the *Declaration of Objectives of the Mexico-Canada Relationship* of 1996, there was a clear focus on the economic agenda, while the 2001 *Mexico and Canada: Friends, Partners and Neighbours* focused more on bilateral political co-operation, especially in the areas of consolidation of democracy and promotion of good governance practices, though the economic agenda remained important. Finally, security, labour mobility, environment, and co-operation in the Americas were identified as priorities in the relationship in the *Joint Action Plan of 2007–2008*, in addition to existing areas of co-operation.

The *2010–2012 Joint Action Plan* marked an important step forward: it defined mutual priority areas and added a number of more concrete proposals to move forward with the bilateral relationship. It proposed four areas for joint action: fostering competitive and sustainable economies; ensuring citizens' safety through co-operation on addressing illegal activity and criminal networks, health concerns, and emergency preparedness; encouraging people-to-people contacts, including facilitating the legal and secure movement of individuals and promotion of labour market complementarities; and, finally, projecting their partnership both globally and regionally – particularly in Central America – on issues including security and humanitarian relief.

One of the most important innovations for handling the bilateral relationship is the Canada-Mexico Partnership (CMP), created in 2004, which provides a space to address issues that could help redress asymmetries between Canada and Mexico. It currently encompasses seven working groups that bring together public and private stakeholders with a focus on trade, investment, and innovation; agri-business; labour mobility; energy; human capital; housing; and forestry and environment. The CMP identifies practical initiatives to promote exchanges between stakeholders from the two countries, thereby strengthening the bilateral relationship. The annual CMP meeting convenes all working groups to take stock of developments and results and to set new priorities.

Overall, strengthening the bilateral relationship presents challenges related, ironically, to the features that initially contributed to its development. If the high degree of flexibility and decentralization of the relationship has allowed for pragmatic exchanges between stakeholders without having to maintain an elaborate institutional structure, that decentralization now entails important shortcomings. Indeed, the relationship is so atomized between different sectors or government technical groups that it is difficult to understand it in its totality. Atomization has also impacted the nature of the projects put in place, especially considering that ministries' limited resources have jeopardized the sustainability of some projects undertaken by the Canadian ministries.

The development of a clear, overarching framework linking all bilateral interactions remains one of the main challenges for Canada. This framework would help "make the case" for stronger engagement with Mexico and justify devoting more resources to the relationship while attracting greater attention from media, analysts, and policy-makers. Further thinking is required to take full advantage of growing exchanges between parliamentarians and existing mechanisms that convene a variety of stakeholders, including the CMP.

CONCLUSIONS

Since 1994, the Canada-Mexico relationship has grown remarkably and organically, with limited leadership from the public sector. The substantial increase in bilateral trade and investment has greatly expanded economic interdependence between our countries. This economic interconnection strengthens the competitiveness of Canadian and Mexican industry and brings prosperity to citizens of both countries. Critically, the growing connections between Mexico and Canada go beyond the economy and bypass national governments to include subnational governments, non-governmental organizations, and individuals. The depth and expanse of these networks demonstrates the strength and dynamism of Canada-Mexico relations. This is in marked contrast with Europe, where integration has been a top-down political process.

However, at some point strengthening relations will require greater political leadership. The full potential of the relationship will remain untapped until more attention is devoted to the depth and diversity of issues addressed within the bilateral agenda. There needs to be a better understanding of how the dynamics of this bilateral relationship play a role in the future of North American integration and in the achievement of key Canadian foreign policy goals.

It is important to reflect further on existing mechanisms to handle the Canada-Mexico relationship in order to make the most of exchanges between legislators, governments at all levels, and other stakeholders. This will help determine how to redress existing challenges and boost co-operation.

Canada-Mexico co-operation, whether domestic, continental, or global, makes each nation stronger and offers numerous realized and potential advantages. Both countries have already benefited enormously from improved relations; the challenge now is to take the initiative to make the many possibilities inherent in the Canada-Mexico relationship a reality.

NOTES

1 http://cansim2.statcan.gc.ca/cgi-win/cnsmcgi.pgm
2 http://embamex.sre.gob.mx/canada_eng/index.php?option=com_content&view=article&id=2119:substantial-growth-of-canadian-business-investment-in-mexico&catid=230:february-2011&Itemid=38

PART TWO

The Bilateral Relationship

The Evolution of Government Relations

JULIÁN VENTURA AND JON ALLEN

By any measure, Mexico and Canada enjoy a thriving relationship. Prime Minister Stephen Harper underlined its significance on the occasion of President Felipe Calderón's address to parliament on 27 May 2010 when he said that, while no relationship or partnership is perfect, "on the fundamental, timeless principles that underpin free societies and successful economies, Canada and Mexico are as one." President Calderón, for his part, stated that "we are partner countries, neighbours, but above all we are friends."

Through more than sixty years of diplomatic relations, the two countries have developed a mature relationship that today encompasses a wide range of bilateral, trilateral, regional, and global issues. We operate as neighbours in North America and as strategic partners in the Americas and beyond.

This chapter chronicles major government initiatives through three different periods: pre-North American Free Trade Agreement (NAFTA), the 1990s with NAFTA in place, and the twenty-first century. The chapter's primary focus is the relationship as it stands today taking into account opportunities we have and challenges we face. The Canadian and Mexican governments' joint efforts over the years have focused on economic development, security, institutional co-operation, people-to-people contacts, and co-operation on the international stage.

FROM 1944 TO THE 1990S

Although NAFTA was a landmark moment in the history of Mexico-Canada relations, propelling our economies and political relationship forward to unprecedented levels of co-operation and partnership, the two countries enjoyed solid relations before its entry into force.

Formal diplomatic relations between Canada and Mexico were established in 1944. In the ensuing quarter century, relations were focused primarily on formal political dialogue and an incipient economic relationship. In 1958, for example, Mexican president Adolfo López Mateos visited Ottawa and Prime Minister John Diefenbaker reciprocated with a visit to Mexico the following year. These high-level visits resulted in agreements extending most-favoured-nation status to each other and established aviation linkages.

With trade expanding in the 1970s and 1980s, the relationship became more multifaceted and structured. The number of high-level diplomatic visits began to increase, culminating, notably, with President Luis Echeverría's state visit to Canada in 1970 and Prime Minister Pierre Elliot Trudeau's state visits to Mexico in 1976 and 1982.

Given the growing importance of the relationship, Mexico and Canada launched two mechanisms reserved for special partners during this period. The first was the Joint Ministerial Commission (JMC), created in 1968. The JMC brought together ministers and senior officials from both countries under the leadership of each country's foreign affairs minister. The JMC enabled both countries, at the highest level of government, to discuss issues of mutual interest on a regular basis, determine strategic objectives, and sign bilateral agreements. By 1990, ten Canadian and Mexican government departments or agencies had signed eighteen agreements covering, among other things, agriculture, transport, justice (transfer of offenders), postal services, consular affairs, and communications. Inter-Parliamentary Meetings (IPMS), the second mechanism established during this period, provide an opportunity for Mexican and Canadian parliamentarians to discuss and advance key bilateral interests. IPMS have been a regular feature of the relationship since they were introduced in 1975.

Also in 1975, Mexico was included in Canada's Seasonal Agricultural Workers Program (SAWP). Launched in 1966, SAWP has become one of the longest-standing and most successful labour mobility programs in North America. As originally conceived, the program allowed for the organized entry of foreign workers to meet the needs of Canadian agricultural producers during peak harvesting and planting periods. Authorities from both countries co-operate to run the program, in close coordination with the employers, all the while safeguarding the labour rights of the employees. Some 17,000 Mexican seasonal workers now come to Canada each year.

Early in their relationship, Canada and Mexico also found common ground on various regional global and multilateral issues, including the decision, in 1959, to maintain diplomatic relations with Cuba and, in the early 1980s, collaborating in an effort to advance peace in Central America, notably in El Salvador and Nicaragua. The two countries also co-operated on global issues of common interest such as the Nuclear Non-Proliferation Treaty (1970) and the Law of the Sea Convention (1982).

THE 1990S AND NAFTA

Mexico-Canada bilateral relations significantly expanded and intensified during the 1990s, as did the two countries' coordination and partnership in international affairs.

In 1992, the North American Free Trade Agreement was signed by President George H.W. Bush, President Carlos Salinas de Gortari, and Prime Minister Brian Mulroney. NAFTA, which came into effect in 1994, is a comprehensive trade agreement aimed at eliminating most tariff and non-tariff barriers and fostering greater trade among North American countries. Side agreements on labour and environment were also signed.

Pursuant to the NAFTA, Canada and Mexico, in conjunction with the United States, meet annually under the Free-Trade Commission (FTC), the central "institution" of the NAFTA, which consists of ministerial-level representatives from the three member countries. It supervises the implementation and further elaboration of the agreement and helps to resolve disputes arising from its interpretation. It also oversees the work of the NAFTA committees, working groups, and other subsidiary bodies.

Mexico and Canada recognized the benefits that would come from closer regional economic ties and saw great potential in their relationship. They also shared a strategic interest in maintaining preferential access to the United States market. NAFTA was the catalyst for the spectacular increase in North American trade and investment. At the same time, it had profound bilateral implications, propelling the Canada-Mexico partnership forward in response to the political and social implications of a dramatically deeper trade and investment relationship.

The Joint Ministerial Commission (JMC) reached its high-water mark during this period, when the number of departments and agencies involved in the relationship more than doubled (from ten to twenty-five) to establish new areas of co-operation such as education, health, elections, tourism, human rights and indigenous affairs, environment, and labour. The total number of bilateral agreements quadrupled from eighteen to eighty-two, reflecting the increasing depth and breadth of the relationship.

One example of this new heightened relationship was the technical co-operation agreement between Elections Canada and the Mexican Federal Electoral Institute (1996). The co-operation had its roots in the early 1990s, when both agencies initiated consultations and exchanges on the administration of elections, including joint research and comparative analysis of the two countries' electoral systems. Today, Mexican and Canadian electoral authorities have well-earned international reputations and continue to look for opportunities to work together to provide training and advice to electoral bodies in emerging democracies.

Co-operation on electoral matters marked the beginning of a very productive series of institutional co-operation initiatives that covered, among other areas, privacy and access to information, an on-line training program for civil servants, federalism, and more recently, judicial reform and police training. The list of issues addressed includes those upon which democratic governance is based, a reflection of fundamental values shared by both societies.

By the end of the 1990s, however, the JMC had become a victim of its own success: the elaborate architecture of agreements between various departments and agencies it had fostered was firmly in place, and leaders, ministers, and senior officials now had numerous occasions to meet bilaterally or on the margins of multilateral meetings. As a result, the JMC ceased to meet after some thirty years of activity.

As a result of joining the Organization of American States in 1990, Canada opened up new avenues of hemispheric co-operation with Mexico. In the mid-1990s, for example, Canada and Mexico, building on previous collaboration aimed at promoting peace in Central America, engaged in support of the Guatemala Peace Accords and the UN mission established to verify their implementation. On the global scene, both countries worked as close partners on the creation of the Arrangement on Model Forests (1993) and on the Convention on the Prohibition of the Use, Stockpiling, Production, and Transfer of Anti-Personnel Mines and on Their Destruction (Ottawa Convention), which entered into force in 1999.

FROM 2000 TO TODAY

Mexico-Canada bilateral relations have become even more extensive and more productive over the last decade. Canadian and Mexican leaders, ministers, and senior officials hold frequent bilateral meetings, including in the framework of trilateral, hemispheric, and multilateral meetings. Foreign Affairs Minister John Baird's visit to Mexico in August 2011, early in his mandate, is testament to the importance the government of Canada attaches to its relationship with Mexico. Annual parliamentary meetings still constitute a dynamic element of our relationship, covering all major aspects of our bilateral and global agendas, and complement other government-to-government ties.

Key developments in the bilateral relationship have included the creation of innovative mechanisms such as the Canada-Mexico Partnership in 2004 and the launch of several security initiatives, for example, the Canada-Mexico Political-Military Talks in 2006. There have also been significant trilateral initiatives involving Mexico, Canada, and the United States, chief among them the Security and Prosperity Partnership of North America and the North American Leaders Summit process. Furthermore, the Canada-Mexico relationship has been advanced through rapidly expanding government contacts and activities at the provincial/state and municipal levels.

The action-oriented practical focus on the relationship was further strengthened under Prime Minister Harper and President Calderón's leadership with the adoption of the Joint Action Plans of 2007–09 and 2010–12 and the creation of specialized working groups and consultation mechanisms. All these initiatives have imbued the relationship with a strong whole-of-government approach, of which there are few parallels in the international system, and which provide a solid platform for enhanced bilateral contacts.

The Canada-Mexico Partnership

The relationship between Mexico and Canada has been strengthened by the creation, in 2004, of the Canada-Mexico Partnership (CMP) to give a larger role to other levels of government and to the private sector. The CMP brings together representatives from the public (federal and state/provincial) and private sectors to further co-operate on topics relevant to our competitiveness, such as bilateral trade, investment, public-private sector partnerships, business-to-business links, good governance practices, education, institutional reforms, and citizen-focused government.

The CMP currently comprises seven working groups: agri-business; energy; environment and forestry; housing and community development; human capital; labour mobility; and trade, investment and innovation. These working groups engage throughout the year and meet jointly for the annual CMP meeting, where they build on initiatives developed during the year and benefit from contacts and synergies with the greater CMP community.

An Elaborate Trilateral Agenda

Mexico and Canada share an elaborate trilateral agenda with the United States that reinforces our bilateral relationship. Over the last decade, this agenda has expanded to address new challenges to our common security and prosperity.

North American leaders initiated their annual summits in 2005. Mindful that security and prosperity are mutually dependent and complementary, they launched the Security and Prosperity Partnership of North America (SPP). The SPP provided a technical umbrella mechanism for extensive and ongoing bilateral and trilateral co-operation.

On the security front, the SPP placed a strong emphasis on anti-terrorism initiatives (travellers, cargo, aviation and maritime co-operation, law enforcement, and bio-protection). The SPP also addressed other threats to security, such as food safety and emergency management and preparedness, with the latter leading to the establishment of the North American Plan for Avian and Pandemic Influenza (NAPAPI). An updated version of this plan is currently being finalized by the three governments.

Thanks to the NAPAPI framework that facilitated coordination and co-operation in the event of a health crisis, the three countries were able to respond in an efficient, transparent, and responsible way to the H1N1 pandemic in 2009. The Public Health Agency of Canada's National Microbiology Laboratory in Winnipeg worked closely with Mexican health authorities on sample testing during the pandemic. The coordinated response was a clear example of the effectiveness of a regional approach to human security and underscored the need to advance the principle of shared responsibility.

On the prosperity front, trilateral initiatives have focused on improving North American competitiveness in light of the emergence of new economic players and a rapidly changing global economy. To this end, particular emphasis has been placed on the manufacture and movement of goods, overcoming regulatory impediments, financial services, transportation, and agriculture.

With tariffs largely eliminated, the NAFTA work plan has turned its focus to reducing unnecessary regulatory differences. Other areas of work include updating NAFTA rules of origin to reflect current sourcing and production patterns, collaboration on environment and labour issues, and supporting small- and medium-sized enterprises.

Trilateral co-operation continues under the framework of the North American Leaders' Summit, with a special emphasis on North American competitiveness, the environment and clean energy, North American security, and citizens' safety. In recent years, the North American security agenda has included strengthening co-operation to address the threat to the continent posed by transnational criminal organizations in the region, including Central America.

Subnational Government Initiatives

Subnational governments of both countries have also developed extensive linkages. Quebec opened a government office in Mexico City in 1980, the first province to do so. In 2002, Alberta opened an office in the Canadian Embassy in Mexico, followed by Ontario in 2007. These provinces, as well as Manitoba and British Columbia, have developed links with Mexican states such as Nuevo León, Jalisco, Campeche, the Federal District, Baja California, and Veracruz, and have signed numerous co-operation agreements to cover areas such as trade, agriculture, forestry, and environmental management. Cities from both countries are also promoting exchanges on municipal matters.

A STRONG GOVERNMENTAL PARTNERSHIP FOR A BETTER FUTURE
In May 2010, the governments of Canada and Mexico issued a Joint Action Plan for 2010–2012, which affirmed four bilateral priorities centred on fostering competitive and sustainable economies, protecting our citizens, enhancing people-to-people contacts, and projecting our partnership globally and regionally. These priorities, which build on those contained in a 2007 Joint Action Plan, are more relevant than ever in a world shaken by economic turmoil and facing increasingly complex regional and global challenges.

FOSTERING COMPETITIVE AND SUSTAINABLE ECONOMIES
Since the launch of NAFTA in 1994, the success of the Mexico-Canada commercial relationship has been spectacular: bilateral merchandise trade has grown by 500 percent since 1994 and two-way trade reached $27 billion in 2010.[1] Canada and Mexico are each other's third-largest merchandise trading partners. Mexico is Canada's third-largest source of imports, with merchandise imports totalling $22 billion in 2010,[2] an increase of 33.7 percent over 2009. Mexico is Canada's fifth-largest export destination.[3]

Most significantly, the economic partnership has also evolved from an export-based economic relationship to one based on integrated supply chains, providing a solid strategic foundation for both bilateral and North American economic competitiveness. The value of Canadian investment in Mexico was over 4.5 billion in 2010,[4] much of it in the mining, automotive, and aerospace sectors. Mexico ranks as the eighth-largest destination of Canadian direct investment in the Americas. Canada is Mexico's fourth-largest source of foreign direct investment.[5] There are some 2,500 Canadian companies with a physical presence in Mexico, ranging from the very large, such as Bombardier and Research in Motion, to medium-sized enterprises. In Mexico's mining sector, 75 percent of foreign direct investment is Canadian, with some 200 Canadian mining companies exploring or producing in Mexico, including approximately 40 mines in operation (i.e., advanced development or extraction stage) under Canadian ownership.

Several working groups of the Canada-Mexico Partnership are examining means to further enhance our economic competiveness.

- The Trade, Investment, and Innovation Working Group is a mix of public and private sector participants looking for ways to increase competitiveness in both countries, enhance bilateral trade of goods and services and two-way investment, and seek viable areas to promote bilateral innovation collaboration. Key areas of focus include the extractive sector, manufacturing technologies (automotive and aerospace), information technologies, investments, and clean energy.
- The Agribusiness Working Group is examining ways to enhance bilateral agricultural trade by promoting the trade potential of agribusiness in both countries, identifying market access opportunities, and providing technical co-operation that strengthens public and private institutions that foster agribusiness.
- The Working Group on Housing and Community Development, for its part, is looking to enhance quality of life by making housing and communities more sustainable and affordable. Numerous training sessions and exchanges have already taken place in the areas of housing finance, technology innovation, and sustainable community planning. A recent success story involves the collaboration with the Energy Working Group that resulted in the launching of "net zero housing" demonstration projects at the 2010 United Nations Climate Change Conference in Cancun.
- The Energy Working Group enhances co-operation and technical strategic alliances through its two technical committees, one on oil and gas and the other on electricity. Provincial involvement has strengthened the working group, as Alberta officials and companies working with key Mexican stakeholders are creating new strategic alliances and business opportunities. By exchanging information on the new regulatory regime that Mexico is implementing for the exploration and production of oil and gas, the working group is promoting new mutually beneficial trade and investment opportunities. The working group is also interested in offshore oil, including a focus on the requirements for strict safety measures.

Mexico and Canada also work closely on a bilateral basis to address environmental issues and advance positive action on climate change. A great deal of our current co-operation is the result of the CMP's Environment and Forestry Working Group and, more specifically, the Environment Subgroup, which has led to progress in the development and implementation of activities including the monitoring, reporting, and verification of greenhouse gas and greenhouse gas inventories, reductions in methane emissions in key industrial sectors (oil and gas, landfill and agriculture), and the development of zero-energy housing.

For its part, the Forestry Subgroup is focusing, inter alia, on climate change as it relates to forests, illegal wildlife trafficking, environmental services, and scientific and training issues related to forestry production and conservation. This initiative reinforces ongoing collaboration on the possibility of a legally binding international instrument on sustainable forest management, and in trilateral and multilateral forums.

Canada and Mexico also collaborate closely on environmental issues on a trilateral basis with the United States, notably under the North American Forestry Commission as well as the Agreement on Environmental Cooperation and the commission that it established.

At the 2010 UN Climate Change Conference, hosted and chaired by Mexico, both countries joined international partners in adopting the Cancun Agreements, a set of decisions that together represent a significant step forward in establishing the type of global climate-change regime necessary to achieve real environmental results. The Cancun Agreements illustrate what can be accomplished with the collective will of the community of states, and acknowledge the global reality that all states need to take action now if we are to succeed in effectively addressing climate change. Mexico and Canada share the view that the balanced package of outcomes achieved at Cancun represents a significant step forward in international climate change negotiations. Mexico and Canada will continue to engage constructively in international negotiations on climate change with our international partners.

Protecting Our Citizens

Security co-operation is rapidly becoming a key feature of Canada and Mexico's bilateral relationship today, as part of a strong bilateral commitment to address transnational threats. A Consultation Mechanism on New and Traditional Security Issues and a Mexico-Canada Security Working Group were established in 2007 to complement the Canada-Mexico Political-Military Talks. Other institutional contacts on security issues of mutual concern include those between Public Safety Canada and Mexico's Centre for Investigation and National Security (CISEN) and Secretariat for Public Safety.

The Security Consultations, an umbrella mechanism regrouping departments and agencies involved in the broad field of security, are at the centre of our co-operation. Held annually, the Security Consultations enable the departments and agencies to share information on their activities with a view to promoting coherence and identifying new areas for potential collaboration. This mechanism is complemented by various working groups that aim to enhance co-operation in law-enforcement, border administration, emergency management, and critical infrastructure protection.

In 2008 Mexico undertook far-reaching and ambitious reforms of its judicial system and police forces. Canada's Anti-Crime Capacity Building

Program (ACCBP), created in 2009, is the main channel of co-operation for supporting this effort to enhance capacity-building against transnational organized crime. Thus far, Canada has committed over $4.1 million in direct bilateral projects with Mexico

To date, the Royal Canadian Mounted Police has provided law enforcement training to 1500 Mexican federal investigative police officers, 250 mid-level federal police officers, and 45 federal police commanders. In terms of judicial reform, the ACCBP contributed to the harmonization of criminal procedures between jurisdictions, professionalization of prosecutors and defence counsels, and training of judges. In 2010–11, over 400 Mexican judicial officials participated in 18 activities organized by the Canadian Department of Justice. In other priority areas of corrections and crime prevention, Canadian and Mexican partners are strengthening co-operation through visits and seminars and jointly preparing specific proposals.

Among other programs, Canada's Counter Terrorism Capacity Building Program (CTCBP) supports bilateral and regional projects in the areas of border and transportation security, critical infrastructure protection, and bioterrorism response. Through the Global Partnership Program, a G8-led initiative, Canada, the United States, and Mexico are working together to convert a Mexican research reactor from highly enriched uranium to low-enriched uranium fuel, as an expression of their firm commitment to global nuclear security.

Defence relations are centred on two initiatives: the Military Training and Cooperation Program (MTCP) and the Canada-Mexico Political Military Talks. Since 2004, Canada has offered training opportunities to Mexico under the MTCP. The political-military talks are co-chaired by each country's respective foreign and defence ministries and advance dialogue and co-operation on foreign policy, defence, and security matters. In May 2011, the countries held the first military-level staff talks between Canada Command and the Mexican secretariats of National Defence and the Navy to provide a framework for advancing direct military-to-military collaboration.

Recently, Canada and Mexico have shown an interest in advancing trilateral defence co-operation through initiatives such as the North American Maritime Security Initiative, creating the first trilateral mechanism for military co-operation and participation in the US-led Joint Interagency Task Force to counter drug trafficking in the region's maritime and air space

Building on the close collaboration we forged during the A (H1N1) crisis, Mexico and Canada's bilateral partnership on influenza pandemics and other emerging infectious diseases, emergency preparedness, and surveillance is serving our citizens well. Canada and Mexico are committed to a trilateral approach to North American health security and continue to work closely with other international partners through the Global Health Security Initiative. We also work bilaterally and trilaterally to review and strengthen health emergency protocols of conduct for North American authorities and promote joint training on rapid response to health emergencies arising from natural disasters. Finally, we work with international partners to strengthen health security partnerships, in particular with regard to the detection and prevention of infectious-disease outbreaks.

Enhancing People-to-People Contacts

Each year, more than 1.5 million Canadians and 160,000 Mexicans visit each others' countries. Mexico and Canada recognize the importance of fostering people-to-people contacts, since citizens are the foundation of our rich and sustainable bilateral relationship. Both countries are pursuing initiatives that encourage greater exchanges between their citizens, whether for tourism, work, or study.

The number of workers participating in the Seasonal Agricultural Workers Program has increased steadily over the years, from 264 in 1975 to approximately 17,000 in 2010. The SAWP is an important labour mobility program that benefits Canadian farmers, who have access to much-needed agricultural labour, and Mexican workers, who have access to a legal, safe, and well-organized temporary worker program.

The CMP's Labour Mobility Working Group is a key mechanism for developing this important aspect of our bilateral relationship. Co-chaired by Human Resources and Skills Development Canada, Citizenship and Immigration Canada, the Mexican Ministry of Foreign Affairs, and the Mexican Secretariat of Labour and Social Welfare, the working group is exploring opportunities to manage the movement of temporary workers from Mexico to Canada in a mutually beneficial, orderly, and legal manner, while sharing information pertaining to the protection of workers and recognition of their skills and foreign credentials.

In 2009, a pilot project in the tourism/hospitality and construction sectors was launched to facilitate the organized temporary migration of Mexican workers outside of agricultural sectors. The pilot project involved the governments of Mexico, Canada, and selected provinces and was implemented mainly in Alberta and British Columbia, with the first Mexican workers arriving in Alberta in September 2009. An evaluation of the pilot was completed in June 2011, and its results served to further shape Canada and Mexico's collaborative work in the area of labour mobility with an ongoing mechanism now in place to manage the participation of Mexican workers in all sectors of Canada's labour market according to employer demand.

CONSULAR CO-OPERATION

Mexico is the second most popular tourist destination for Canadians after the United States, with some 1.5 million Canadians travelling to Mexico each year, a number that is growing by over 15 percent annually despite the global economic downturn. A significant number of Canadians, especially retirees, have purchased property in Mexico and spend extended periods of time in the country. The Mexican government has supported the growth of economic activities such as health and home-care in order to better accommodate them. Today, some 75,000 Canadians are thought to reside in Mexico either full- or part-time.[6] Canada also receives a significant number of Mexican visitors each year, including businesspeople, students, and temporary workers in agriculture and other sectors.

While travel to either Mexico or Canada is usually a positive experience, as the growing number of visitors indicates, emergencies and complications can occur. To assist citizens of both countries facing difficulties while travelling, the two governments created Consular Rapid Response Mechanisms in both capitals to respond quickly to respective complex consular cases and deepen overall consular co-operation.

The governments will reinforce their efforts to promote a comprehensive view that goes beyond consular protection issues and that better reflects the importance of the bilateral relationship to the well-being of all Mexicans and Canadians.

VISAS

In July 2009, Canada introduced a visa requirement for Mexican nationals in response to the increasing number of refugee claims from Mexico. To facilitate legitimate travel, Canada has implemented several initiatives to streamline the visa process. These initiatives include simplified paperwork, the establishment of three visa application centres in Mexico, a new visa office in Mexico City with increased capacity, and a Business Express Program targeted at qualified Mexican businesses and their employees.

As a consequence of the visa requirement, Canada and Mexico have begun working more closely on broader migration issues common to both countries. To this end, Citizenship and Immigration Canada and Mexico's Secretariats of Government and Foreign Relations created a high-level working group to address such migration issues as biometrics, document integrity, and irregular migration. Since many of the unfounded refugee claims appear to have involved unscrupulous migration consultants, the group identified action against such illegal and unethical practices as a priority.

ACADEMIC AND YOUTH MOBILITY

Through the CMP's Human Capital Working Group, both governments are promoting enhanced co-operation between Mexican and

Canadian universities and colleges that already have signed some 250 co-operation and exchange agreements.

Mobility programs, such as scholarships and exchanges, exist at the federal, provincial, and institutional levels. The latest addition to these programs is the Emerging Leaders in the Americas Program (ELAP), launched in 2010. ELAP provides Mexican college, undergraduate, and graduate students with the opportunity to pursue short-term studies or research in Canada.

Through Canada's Understanding Canada Program, Mexican institutions of higher learning and academics have access to various grants to promote linkages with their Canadian counterparts. Programs and centres devoted to Canadian Studies have been established in a number of Mexican universities, and the Mexican Association of Canadian Studies (Asociación Mexicana de Estudios sobre Canadá), founded nearly twenty years ago, enjoys a membership of nearly four hundred academics.

In addition to academic ties, a Memorandum of Understanding on Youth Mobility was signed in 2010 which simplifies the administrative process for Canadian and Mexican youth to travel and work in each other's country for up to one year.

Projecting Our Partnership Globally and Regionally

The fourth priority of our bilateral agenda is projecting our partnership globally and regionally by working constructively and by deepening our strategic collaboration to address security, prosperity, democracy, human rights, and good governance priorities in the region and beyond. On these issues, consultations and dialogue occur through the Mexico-Canada Consultations on Multilateral Issues, the Trilateral Consultations on Human Rights with the United States, and through informal discussions among senior officials. Through these, we are better able to forge convergent positions, formulate shared initiatives, and agree on mutual support on issues arising at regional and global governance forums.

Canada and Mexico share common values and a belief in multilateralism. Over the last decade, our foreign policy convergence has led to consultation and co-operation on major issues of interest within a wide range of multilateral organizations, including the United Nations, the G20, the Organization of American States (OAS), the Summit of the Americas, the Asia-Pacific Economic Cooperation forum (APEC) and the Organization for Economic Co-operation and Development (OECD). While working together on the substantive agendas of these organizations, we also strive to strengthen the organizations with a view to improving international governance.

At the UN, we worked closely on the creation of the International Criminal Court (2002) and the UN Human Rights Council (2006). We share similar views on Security Council reform, non-proliferation of weapons of mass destruction, humanitarian assistance, and disaster relief. Both countries support the promotion of sustainable democracy worldwide through political initiatives such as the International Institute for Democracy and Electoral Assistance (International IDEA).

We are both members of the Group of Friends for Haiti and we participated in the two international conferences that were convened in response to the earthquake. We both contributed to the relief efforts in Haiti, bringing together regional partners in support of a common hemispheric neighbour.

Mexico and Canada also share similar views on the world economy. At the G20, for instance, we have worked together in support of open markets and reform of the architecture underpinning the global financial system.

In the hemisphere, Latin America and the Caribbean are priority regions for both countries and we work together with our regional partners to promote democratic governance, prosperity, equality, and security through the Summit of the Americas process and the OAS. We are working with our Latin American and Caribbean partners on disaster risk reduction in Central America and the Caribbean. Both our countries are involved in a broad dialogue between international partners and the Central American countries on security in Central America. We have demonstrated commitment to ongoing efforts to strengthen institutions in that neighbouring region, including within the framework adopted by the Central American Integration System (CAIS).

As the second- and third-largest donors, respectively, of the Organization of American States, Canada and Mexico view the OAS as the principal multilateral organization in the Americas and as a key venue for co-operation with hemispheric partners. Mexico and Canada are working together and with others to broaden the application and implementation of the Inter-American Democratic Charter, strengthen inter-American human-rights institutions, advance our co-operation on security issues, and reform OAS finances.

CHALLENGES AND OPPORTUNITIES

Over the years, Mexico and Canada have developed a solid and mature relationship based on intense political engagement, substantial and growing economic relations, and a shared outlook on many of the most important regional and global challenges. Our strong bilateral framework for dialogue and co-operation, increased contact between all levels of government, and dynamic civil society interaction, whether through tourism, business, educational exchanges, or other people-to-people contacts, provide Canada and Mexico with the necessary tools to continue forging deeper, mutually beneficial ties.

The transformation of the relationship from both the bilateral and North American perspectives is undeniable. Yet, as both governments recognize, much more can be done to achieve its full potential from a long-term perspective. The strategic dimension of the bilateral relationship can be further strengthened. Success will come from guaranteeing that the broad and flexible co-operation mechanisms that have been developed over time continue to respond effectively to the challenges that we will face in the coming years at the national, bilateral, and North American level. Most importantly, however, we realize that we must ensure the convergence of various initiatives. The many actors involved in the relationship constitute its driving force, to which governments can provide a unified discourse and a sense of direction.

A. The North American agenda: NAFTA – now in its eighteenth year – has contributed significantly to increase trade and foreign direct investment in North America and continues to serves as a cornerstone of economic co-operation. It has made all three partners more competitive and allowed businesses to better realize their potential by operating in a larger, more integrated market. Under the direction of the ministerial-level Free Trade Commission, the parties continue to explore and address trade opportunities and issues, working to develop new and creative ways to increase trade and competitiveness within a dynamic global trading environment. Bilateral and trilateral approaches are necessary to reflect the current political and economic climate, as well as the individual interests and concerns of each country.

Both Mexico and Canada have developed bilateral initiatives with the United States on issues such as regulatory co-operation and harmonization, border security, trade facilitation, customs co-operation, and trusted traveller programs. Although often presented as a rejection of the trilateral approach, the fact is that these initiatives are complementary and can converge from a medium- and long-term perspective. A key challenge will be to extend the success of co-operation against pandemics to other components of the agenda.

Strong trilateral dialogue and co-operation centred on political dialogue, competitiveness, trade facilitation, and security should continue to be a priority for Mexico and Canada. The North American Leaders' Summits process provides an important opportunity to renew political will and give new momentum to the trilateral dimension of the relationship. The key challenge is to work together to enhance North American competitiveness in the international economy and to build a stronger North American "voice" on regional and global issues in which we have a common outlook.

B. Toward greater labour mobility: In the context of our efforts to enhance competitiveness, the success of the Seasonal Agricultural Worker

Program is a powerful indicator of the significant opportunity that exists to take better advantage of the complementary nature of our demographics and labour markets. The completion of the successful labour mobility pilot projects that were established in key sectors of the Canadian economy have set the stage for an expansion of labour mobility for the long term in all sectors of the Canadian labour market according to demand by employers; this will mutually reinforce our economic development and competitiveness.

c. Taking advantage of educational opportunities: Educational, academic, and scientific exchanges represent some of the most transformational elements of people-to-people contacts. The dynamism and range of co-operation in this area can be fostered by both governments through greater facilitation of visas, enhanced institutional agreements, and scholarship programs. The recent establishment of the Mexican Agency for International Cooperation for Development can give new impetus to scientific and technical co-operation, both bilaterally and toward third countries in which Canada and Mexico have shared interests.

d. An enhanced security agenda: Mexico and Canada face common challenges as they address the transnational dimensions of organized crime from their respective national contexts. Through its bilateral co-operation program with Mexico, Canada's support of judicial and police reform is having a significant positive impact in two key areas of Mexico's capacity-building efforts. This experience, together with closer contacts and information sharing on security and defence issues, will enable both governments to consolidate and expand their co-operation. At the same time, Canada and Mexico's complementary diplomatic presence and interests in Central America and the Caribbean are providing a solid platform for regional co-operation with other key partners, including the United States, which can be consolidated and expanded.

e. Changing perceptions: Both countries face a challenge in promoting positive perceptions that reflect the direct importance of the bilateral relationship to both societies. Our governments will continue to work together with the private sector, academics, and the media to better project a more comprehensive and forward-looking vision.

Our nations are respected, responsible players in the international arena and they play a leadership role on many issues. They are fully integrated into the world economy and exemplify the benefits of free trade, open markets, and responsible public finances. Our strategic partnership can include renewed joint action on regional and global issues.

a. A stronger partnership in the Americas: The strategic impact of Canada's engagement in the Americas cannot be underestimated. Mexico and

Canada have demonstrated over the years how much can be achieved by working together both within and beyond the Inter-American System. As the Americas face new and traditional challenges, both countries can be a powerful voice on behalf of human rights, democracy, and civil society participation.

B. An enhanced Pacific Rim approach: As APEC members and key players in trans-Pacific trade with significant bilateral political and economic relationships in Northeast, Southeast, and South Asia, Mexico and Canada can strengthen the Pacific Rim dimension of their exchanges through an enhanced bilateral dialogue on Asia-Pacific issues related to free trade and economic co-operation, among other issues.

C. Strengthened co-operation on the global agenda: Through their inclusive approach to addressing global challenges, whether in the United Nations, the G20, OAS, or other fora, Canada and Mexico can expand their footprint in shaping the international agenda. The impact of Canada's decision to support the candidature of the governor of Mexico's Central Bank to the position of Managing Director of the International Monetary Fund sends a strong message in this regard.

This chapter, and indeed this book, are an invitation to reflect on our links and to think creatively about the path ahead. Our common interests and challenges are clear. Our perceptions on many issues are closer than ever. There is much we can do as federal governments, in partnership with the increasing number of stakeholders in the relationship. The limits of what we can do together will be set by the limits of our imagination.

NOTES

1   Statistics Canada
2   Office of the Chief Economist, Foreign Affairs and International Trade Canada, http://www.international.gc.ca/economist-economiste/assets/pdfs/PFACT_Annual_Merchandise_Trade_by_Country-Eng.pdf
3   Mexican official statistics valued total imports from Canada in 2010 at $8.6 billion, an increase of 17.8 percent over 2009.
4   Office of the Chief Economist, Foreign Affairs and International Trade Canada, op cit.
5   Mexico's Secretariat of the Economy, http://www.economia.gob.mx/swb/work/models/economia/Resource/2825/1/images/IED_Mexico_pais_1999–2011.xls
6   Mexico is also home to a large community of Mennonites of Canadian origin who have flourished in the Province of Chihuahua since settling there in the 1920s.

A Business Perspective

CARLOS E. REPRESAS
AND OSCAR VERA

INTRODUCTION

Since NAFTA's implementation in 1994, the economic relationship between Mexico and Canada has substantially increased in terms of trade and investment, as well as in other areas such as tourism.

Bilateral trade has grown at an average rate of 12.5 percent per year, reaching US$30 billion in 2010, and each country is the third largest trading partner of the other. In fact, Canada's trade with Mexico exceeds that with the rest of Latin America combined.

The accumulated Canadian investment in Mexico is close to US$10.5 billion, making Canada the fourth largest foreign investor in Mexico, and there are more than 2,400 registered companies with Canadian capital operating in Mexico.

In 2010, almost 1.6 million Canadian tourists visited Mexico and some 50,000 have become semi-permanent residents with some form of property in the country. Prior to the introduction of the visa requirement by the Canadian government in 2009, approximately 250,000 Mexicans visited Canada each year.

Despite these positive developments, in our view the Canada-Mexico trade and investment relationship remains well below its potential; as naturally complementary economies and, most important, as partners for successfully competing in the global economy, they can achieve much more.

SUCCESSFUL COMPLEMENTATION

The reasons for establishing business operations in Mexico are diverse; they include being part of the North American production chain, taking advantage of lower production costs, benefiting from Mexico's network of free trade agreements with different countries and regions, and becoming a production base for supplying North America's market.

These factors account for the significant success of Canadian multinationals operating in Mexico – Bombardier (Aerospace and Transportation), Research in Motion (RIM), Bombardier Recreational Products (BRP), Goldcorp, Magna, and Scotia Bank, among others.

However, there are still relatively few joint ventures among Canadian and Mexican businesses and the presence of Canadian small- and medium-sized companies (SME) in Mexico is relatively sparse. On the other hand, Mexican companies have almost no presence in Canada, not only because of Canada's relatively small market size compared with the United States, and the fewer cost advantages relative to Mexico, but mainly because of the lack of information, political drive, and strategic vision in both countries.

THE NEED FOR A STRATEGIC VISION

The importance of each country's bilateral relationship with the United States has led to "benign neglect" of their own bilateral relationship. Through a combination of short-term political, social, and international issues and concerns in the three countries, North America's competitiveness has been relegated to a lower place on the agenda. As a consequence, today there exist three bilateral relationships that overshadow North America's integration and put at risk its long-term competitiveness.

A competitive North America requires deeper integration of the three economies, particularly under the current global trend toward increased regionalization.

Canada and Mexico are naturally complementary, but this reality has not been fully exploited either within NAFTA or in the global marketplace where it could enhance both countries' international competitiveness vis-à-vis other trading blocs and countries. Canada has a vast natural resource base and state-of-the-art technology in different sectors, but is losing manufacturing competitiveness mainly because of high labour costs and increasing labour shortages. On the other hand, Mexico has an ample supply of labour at competitive costs and its geographical position allows companies to access very competitive logistics both within the NAFTA region and in relation to the rest of the world.

Additionally, Mexico's currency stability under a free-floating and capital controls-free exchange regime provides significant advantages for companies that have business models based on the American dollar.

Bombardier's decision to establish aerospace manufacturing facilities in Mexico provides an excellent example of complementarity and the development of a production partnership between the two economies. A Bombardier internal study in 2003–2004 concluded that, "compared with other locations with equivalent labour costs, Mexico had clear advantages that tilted the scales in its favour: time zone, geographic and cultural proximity, bilingualism, communications system, the proactive engagement of federal and municipal authorities and the trade agreements signed by the Mexican government, not only in North America, but also with Europe."

Of the two largest Latin American economies, Mexico is most naturally complementary (further to NAFTA) with Canada in terms of economic structure, geographical location, technology, and natural and labour resources. The complementarities between Canada and Brazil, for example, are far fewer and several of their most important economic sectors like agriculture, mining, aerospace, and manufacturing, actually compete with each other.

Due to its network of seventeen free trade agreements with forty-nine countries, Mexico also offers an important opportunity for Canadian companies as an entry to most of Latin America, the European Union, Japan, and other countries.

SCOPE FOR INCREASED CO-OPERATION

The economies of Canada and Mexico are about the same size and thus should be attractive to small- and medium-size local companies from both countries, even in the American market. The rising importance of the Hispanic market in the United States, already the largest minority group (overwhelmingly of Mexican origin) with a population of 50 million, opens a whole new area of opportunity for Canadian-Mexican business co-operation.

Canadian investment in Mexico has been primarily through wholly-owned subsidiaries, although Canadian SMEs have an adequate scale and technology for setting up joint ventures with Mexican companies. So far, they have had little presence in Mexico for a variety of reasons, among them the lack of specific policies to promote these associations.

Success stories like Bombardier's show the potential for developing whole new sectors in Mexico beyond exclusively low-cost manufacturing operations, for training skilled labour, and for competitively entering into a global supply chain. They also show Mexican workers' high adaptability and the geographical and logistical advantages of manufacturing in Mexico.

To illustrate the potential of a successful manufacturing partnership from a company's perspective, we asked Laurent Beaudoin, Chairman and former CEO of Bombardier Inc. to provide a brief description of the company's development in Mexico. This contribution is presented in the annex to this paper.

Perhaps more important from a Canadian perspective is the fact that this production partnership would also benefit Canada's domestic consumers and workers, as their companies become more competitive and expand in the world marketplace. Production integration in North America is a not a negative or zero-sum game but a positive one for both countries.

However, given the concerns of unions, mostly in Canada, with the impact of such integration on jobs, we believe it is critical that business organizations, government agencies, and academics in both countries work together to demonstrate, based on empirical evidence, that the increased production partnership between Canada and Mexico has a positive impact on the standard of living of both Canadian and Mexican workers.

There are several areas with good potential for complementation between the two economies:

- energy (technology and services)
- mining
- agricultural production
- tourism services
- financial services
- manufacturing in general
- white collar outsourcing (accounting, IT, engineering, call centres)
- logistic activities
- clean energy and environmental technologies

Further, there are two areas that have so far received little attention and that could lead to increased complementation. The first is the establishing in Mexico of engineering and design centres for various industries with highly skilled local professionals at comparatively low costs vis-à-vis Canada and the United States. The second involves the use of the research and development (R&D) capabilities within Mexican institutions of higher-education by Canadian companies, whether these companies are or are not established in Mexico. There is a vast network of academic research centres in Mexico (most of them under-used, unfortunately), such as the National University, the Polytechnic Institute, and the Monterrey Technology Institute, as well as the National Health Institutes network, which provide research capabilities at very competitive costs. Similarly,

Canada's array of fiscal incentives for R&D, together with the availability of highly qualified professionals, could be attractive for Mexican companies in some sectors (e.g., mining). Even in the auto sector, where there is competition for investment between Canada and Mexico, there is scope for greater co-operation among auto-parts suppliers from both countries in manufacturing, training, and design.

Thus, rather than looking at each other solely as trading partners, Canada and Mexico should look at each other as "production partners" in the North American and global supply chains.

There is also room for greater co-operation between the two countries' business sectors in international forums such as Asia-Pacific Economic Co-operation (APEC), the G20, and the Organization for Economic Co-operation and Development (OECD), where both countries are members. Up to now, there has not been a common platform/approach to tackle issues of mutual interest in these forums. There is no common strategy between governments or among business organizations/leaders from both countries to increase economic co-operation or to promote common objectives in international forums.

AN AGENDA FOR CANADA'S AND MEXICO'S BUSINESS SECTORS

The economic relationship between Canada and Mexico will continue to grow simply because of the strong economic rationale. However, it is imperative to relaunch the relationship based on a long-term strategic vision for the two countries and for North America's competitiveness in the global economy.

To achieve this objective, Canada's and Mexico's business sectors, with the support from their academic sectors, should take the initiative to put back the benefits from, and the need for, a significantly stronger partnership on their countries' political and public opinion agendas. This also calls for an explicit "media strategy" in order to increase public support and understanding.

But even if building political and social support takes time, there are a number of "micro" initiatives that could be taken in a step-by-step approach and that will contribute to a stronger bilateral relationship until such support is achieved. Among these, we propose the following:

- harmonization of basic regulations and standards in different sectors
- a convergence in their economic competition policies
- educational and technical equivalencies and certification
- preferential educational fees
- binational public funding for joint ventures and research projects

- immediate elimination of visa requirements and any limitation on intra-company labour mobility and student exchanges

Also, Canadian and Mexican business sectors should actively lobby their governments for an agreement on rules of origin accumulation in order to fully exploit each country's free trade agreements and their economic complementation.

With a clear and committed vision on the part of Canada's and Mexico's business and academic sectors, these countries could realize a much deeper economic relationship.

However, in order to achieve this, Canada and Mexico must first *define their common ambition* within North America. Rather than continuing to give priority to bilateral relations with the United States, a Mexican-Canadian understanding (governments, business sectors, academics, unions, and the general public) on key issues could be achieved and would help to bring the United States on board. Canada and Mexico must understand that, although far more complicated than a bilateral relationship, in the long term a North American trilateral relationship will be far stronger in the global economy than the three separate bilateral relationships.

This "common future approach" will move North America's economic integration forward into what might be called "North America 3.0." The ultimate goal of both countries should be a North American Common Market, with the establishment of a Customs Union as an intermediate step.

In the end, further integration will make North America an increasingly competitive and successful region and allow for sustained improvement in the standards of living of its workers and society in general.

ANNEX
BOMBARDIER INC. DEVELOPMENT IN MEXICO[1]

Transportation

Bombardier started to show interest in Mexico toward the end of the 1970s, when the company was broadening its North American market for passenger rail products. The company wanted to extend its reach in the Latin American market, in a sector dominated by French manufacturers.

In 1981, the Mexican government awarded Bombardier the contract to build 180 subway cars for Mexico City. The cars were for a rubber-tired subway, the same technology used by Bombardier in 1974 for the Montreal métro. Mexico City's subway car order was, at the time, the largest export order for mass transit equipment ever won by a Canadian or American manufacturer.

In May 1992, Bombardier acquired the assets of Constructora Nacional de Carros de Ferrocarril S.A., known as Concarril (now Bombardier Transportation). Created in 1954 by the government of Mexico, Concarril produced a wide range of vehicles, including rubber-tired and steel-wheeled subway cars, light rail vehicles, passenger coaches, and freight cars.

At the time, Bombardier's CEO, Laurent Beaudoin, stated, "The acquisition of Concarril puts us in a favourable position to seize new opportunities and take up new challenges not only in Mexico but in the southern United States as well. It is in line with the free trade negotiations currently being carried out among Canada, the United States and Mexico. In addition, this Mexican base will enable us to better meet the growing transit equipment needs of the Latin American countries."

In July 1993, Bombardier-Concarril concluded its first large-scale contract for transportation equipment in Mexico, to rebuild and overhaul 234 rubber-tired subway cars in Mexico City.

In March 1998, Bombardier-Concarril marked the assembly of its first locomotive built in Mexico for GM's Electro-Motive Division. Two months later, it created a joint venture with The Greenbrier Companies to build freight cars at its manufacturing site.

As a new century unfolded, in October 2002 in Mexico City, Bombardier signed its biggest contract in North America with the Spanish firm CAF. With a value of CA$508 million, this contract, awarded by Mexico City's transportation authority, involved the manufacture of cars and bogies for the subway network in Mexico's capital, the bulk of which would be built at Bombardier's installations in Ciudad Sahagún in Mexico.

Aerospace

Bolstered by its success in rail transportation, when Bombardier was looking for a new site that would boost its competitiveness in the aerospace sector, it naturally took a closer look at Mexico.

An internal study showed that compared with other locations with equivalent labour costs, Mexico had clear advantages that tilted the scales in its favour: time zone, geographic and cultural proximity, bilingualism, communications system, the proactive engagement of government and municipal authorities, and the trade agreements signed by the Mexican government not only in North America but also in Europe.

In May 2006, Bombardier Aerospace relocated a small portion of its production to Querétaro, north of Mexico City. A team of fifteen set up shop in a temporary plant to manufacture electrical wiring harnesses.

In order to train a specialized workforce, in 2007 the governments of Mexico and the state of Querétaro officially launched the National Aeronautic University of Querétaro (UNAQ) with support from the École des métiers de l'aérospatiale de Montréal. Bombardier is committed to building an intensive training program.

On 8 February 2008, Bombardier inaugurated its world-class installations for the sub-assembly and manufacture of aerospace components in Querétaro, a $250 million investment. The Canadian manufacturer was the first to set up shop in the Querétaro aerospace cluster; its site would host the assembly of electrical harnesses and the manufacture of the rear fuselage for Global Express jets, in addition to manufacturing the structure of the Learjet 85 and assembling the harnesses for its upcoming medium-range CSeries aircraft.

By January 2011, 1,400 people were employed at the manufacturing centre in Querétaro, a figure that is expected to grow to 2,000 with the production launch of the new Learjet 85 business jet. Looking to the future, the company decided to add an aerospace engineering centre to its existing production centres. This initiative will allow Bombardier to not only support its current installations but also promote its future expansion into new operations.

In conclusion, Bombardier looks back favourably on its experience in Mexico since 1981. Staffs in both the transportation and aerospace sectors have shown a remarkable capacity for learning and great productivity. The site's level of competitiveness matches that of the company's best plants around the world.

Bombardier's development in Mexico is expected to grow at a sustained pace. In addition to serving the local market, Bombardier Transportation's installations in Sahagún are doing ever more sub-assembly work on products for shipment to North American plants, much like the aerospace plants in Querétaro. Buoyed by its strengths and the next generation of engineers that is currently in training, Bombardier believes that Mexico has become a key development partner for its North American operations.

NOTE

1 Remarks by Laurent Beaudoin, Chairman and former CEO of Bombardier Inc.

Doing Business in Mexico:
Some Success Stories

REDLINE, SCOTIABANK, PALLISER FURNITURE, LINAMAR, GOLDCORP, APOTEX

REDLINE: BRIDGING THE DIGITAL GAP

Redline Communications is a technology leader in designing and manufacturing standards-based wireless broadband access solutions. The company's award-winning products provide unmatched high capacity and capabilities with proven performance, reliability, and security to carriers, service providers, and enterprises worldwide. Redline is a principal member of the WiMAX Forum™, a nonprofit organization that promotes a standard universal protocol for broadband internet access.

Redline has over 20,000 installations in seventy-five countries across six continents through a global distribution network of over eighty partners. Its headquarters are in Markham, Ontario, Canada, with engineering and design centres in Romania and sales offices worldwide.

Redline has deployed a trial project in the Mexican state of Tabasco and is aiming to become a partner and supplier for e-Mexico. E-Mexico is a large-scale federal government project aimed at providing all of Mexico with public internet connectivity and other electronic services.

Redline, which has done business in Mexico since 2003, has been awarded contracts from the state governments of Chiapas, Nuevo León, Puebla, and Yucatan, among others, to supply WiMAX technology for municipal, rural, and school emergency response systems, and other government connectivity programs. Redline's work with Mexico's federal and state governments places it at the forefront of Mexico's emerging broadband market and positions it as a partner in Mexico's economic development.

SCOTIABANK:
SUPPORTING BUSINESS IN LATIN AMERICA

Scotiabank Inverlat is one of Mexico's leading financial groups with more than 500 branches and 1,000 ATMs. With 6 percent of market share, Scotiabank is Mexico's seventh largest bank. Scotiabank consistently ranks high in customer satisfaction, providing excellent banking services and a strong commitment to corporate social responsibility.

Scotiabank has been operating in Mexico since it established a representative office in 1967 and it now employs more than 7,000 people. While other Canadian banks have established representative offices in Mexico, only Scotiabank has made the move to retail banking.

At a time when many local banks were failing, Scotiabank decided to make Mexico the focus of its international strategy in the Americas through the gradual acquisition of the Mexican financial institution Grupo Financiero Inverlat (GFI).

Following the financial and economic crisis in Mexico in 1994, the banking industry collapsed under skyrocketing interest rates and unprecedented credit defaults. In 1996, the government's bank restructuring unit approved Scotiabank's bid to acquire 10 percent of GFI shares, an amount that was increased to 55 percent in 2000. The government retained ownership of 36 percent and a small number of shareholders owned the rest. In 2001, GFI officially changed its name to Scotiabank Inverlat. And in 2003–2004, Scotiabank, along with the remaining private shareholders, acquired the remaining government shares.

Scotiabank used its international banking experience to its advantage in Mexico and supported the burgeoning Canadian business clientele (now the fourth largest foreign direct investor in Mexico). Scotiabank also developed a strong local clientele by providing access to home mortgages and automobile loans at a time when most Mexican banks were still wary of providing credit. Many in Mexico have credited Scotiabank with assisting in the development of Mexico's strong middle class.

Scotiabank's location in Mexico has proven strategic in assisting its long-term expansion into the hemisphere, where it is now located in thirty-five countries (22 percent of its profits last year came from international banking). Its early presence and growth in Mexico has positioned it to become a key financial player in Mexico and in the hemisphere where it is playing a central role in supporting economic growth and Canadian business.

PALLISER FURNITURE: "MADE IN NORTH AMERICA"

Palliser Furniture Upholstery Ltd. illustrates the advantages to be gained by using NAFTA and the North American supply chain to improve quality, pricing, and competitiveness in supplying consumers in Canada, the US, and Mexico. With plants in Winnipeg, Manitoba and Saltillo, Mexico, Palliser has succeeded in meeting the growing demand for high-quality North American furniture. It has taken full advantage of NAFTA and, by supplying customers from production centres in both the north and south of the continent, has reduced its environmental footprint while ensuring just-in-time delivery and cost-efficient service.

Palliser is Canada's second largest furniture maker and manufacturer. It began its operations in northern Mexico in 1998 with a plant in Saltillo, Coahuila, which was the first stage of a larger North American strategy. The success of this production facility led to subsequent operations in Matamoros in the state of Tamaulipas.

Palliser had originally considered expanding to China but chose Mexico for several reasons. The first was location: Mexico's proximity to the US market reduced both freight and storage costs. The second was industrial skill: the area of Saltillo had qualified textile workers available, particularly skilled leather stitchers, who are in high demand. The third was labour: while wages were lower in China, this was compensated by higher productivity in Mexico. Finally, Mexico's foreign direct investment regulations made it easier for Palliser to set up its own company without the need to enter into a more complicated joint venture.

Palliser has a strong reputation as a good employer and corporate citizen. Its corporate ethic promotes a workplace culture of respect for the integrity and dignity of employees, the environment, and the local community in which it operates. Palliser emphasizes workplace education and training, including English as a second language, health and safety, computer skills, and leadership training.

LINAMAR: GLOBAL SUPPLY CHAINS AND THE AUTOMOTIVE SECTOR

In 2010 Linamar was ranked twenty-ninth among original equipment manufacturers (OEMs) in North America and seventy-fourth globally. Linamar designs and manufactures precision metallic components and systems for the automotive, energy, and mobile industrial markets. The company operates in Canada, the US, Mexico, Asia Pacific, and Europe.

Linamar Corporation was among the first companies to understand the concept of global supply chains. To get closer to its customers, it relocated some of its auto manufacturing facilities to Mexico before NAFTA was even concluded. Linamar made its first investments in Mexico just prior to NAFTA's entry into force in 1994, negotiating a five-year contract with Volkswagen in Mexico to manufacture parts for two of its models.

This was the beginning of a business strategy that leverages the complementarities of the Canadian and Mexican markets. This approach has been highly successful for Linamar, which expects to manufacture and supply parts for the sale of up to 13 million vehicles in North America from its location in Mexico.

Geography has worked to Linamar's advantage. Following the devastating impact of the economic and financial crisis of 2009, the automotive industry throughout North America was forced to readjust to a new reality. Mexico used the opportunity to consolidate its position in North America as a competitive automotive manufacturer. Linamar's location in Mexico became a strategic asset, providing it with a real cost advantage in producing components like transmissions for the Mexican auto industry. Location, location, location!

Linamar's Mexico operations have since expanded and the company now has four plants in the states of Nuevo León, Coahuila, and Durango. Linamar's Mexico plants supply local car manufacturers who sell to markets in both Mexico and the southern US. Linamar's location provides a competitive advantage given its proximity to the market.

Linamar understands that the global business model is the new reality, and as automotive manufacturers from Nissan to GM to Ford Motor Company expand their Mexican facilities, Linamar is strategically situated and prepared to supply this increased demand.

GOLDCORP:
MINING FOR SUCCESS IN
A SOCIALLY RESPONSIBLE MANNER

Mining is a controversial subject in any country. Goldcorp, however, has broken the mould in becoming an efficient, sustainable, and socially responsible producer. Over a short period, Canadian Goldcorp has grown from a strong intermediate player to one of the top gold producers in the world. Its expansion into Mexico forms part of its larger strategic plan to invest in important, low-risk countries. Goldcorp was the largest foreign investor in Mexico in 2010 and its number one gold producer.

The company began its business relationship with Mexico nine years ago when it took control of Minas de San Luis (Luismin). Starting with a production of 50,000 ounces of gold per year, Goldcorp now produces 650,000 ounces annually. The company plans to increase production to 1 million ounces per year – 55 percent of Mexico's total gold production.

Goldcorp employs 6,000 people in Mexico and its operating assets include El Sauzal, Los Filos, San Dimas (Tayoltita), and Peñasquito gold/silver mines. Goldcorp has invested around US$1.5 billion in Peñasquito, Mexico's largest open pit mine.

To reach its production goals, Goldcorp has developed a solid pipeline of projects. The company is currently working on two major mining operations – the second stage of the Peñasquito mine and the recently acquired Camino Rojo mine – and is investing around US$60 million annually to extend existing mine production and to explore new reserves.

Goldcorp attributes a large part of its success to its strong commitment to environmental protection and corporate social responsibility (CSR). Often seen as the "poster child" for CSR in mining, Goldcorp prides itself on three important CSR pillars in its business model: people – "everything we do begins with our people"; safety – "safe enough for our families"; and robust engagement with all their stakeholders, as the foundation of constructive, creative, and sustainable development. Goldcorp seeks to respond to negative perceptions of the mining industry by devoting time and resources to protecting the environment and the human rights of its employees and the residents of the communities in which it operates. Goldcorp also contributes to the economic development of these communities and is guided by international standards and best practices.

APOTEX: GOING LOCAL A GOOD PRESCRIPTION

Apotex, the largest Canadian-owned pharmaceutical company, is an example of how the combination of research, development, manufacturing, distribution, and a strategic view to the future and beyond one's borders can lead to a highly successful company.

Apotex was founded in 1974, starting with two employees and one product. Today, the company works in 115 countries and has more than 6,800 employees. Apotex is a global leader in generic medicines and produces more than 300 products. The company dedicates a considerable amount of money to research and development and employs more than 2,000 scientists worldwide.

Apotex established its first operations outside Canada in Mexico when it purchased the Mexican manufacturer Protein in 1996. Since then, Apotex Mexico has developed partnerships with the public and private sectors in Mexico to sell generic medicines. Mexico has also become a gateway for Apotex to sell its medicines to thirteen countries in Central and South America.

Today, Apotex has about 600 employees in Mexico with a research and development centre that has created fifty-three new products. Apotex Mexico owns three production plants in two major Mexican cities and has a large central office in Mexico City.

Generic pharmaceuticals are increasingly important in Mexico as an alternative to high-cost medicines in difficult economic times. The Mexican pharmaceutical market holds huge potential for Apotex and other generic drug manufacturers. Currently, generic drugs represent only 6 to 7 percent of total pharmaceutical sales in Mexico. However, when Apotex first entered the Mexican market, there was no regulatory framework for commercializing and selling generics; a generic drug market has emerged and evolved since the passage of Mexico's 1998 law on generics.

In 2011 Apotex celebrated fifteen years in the Mexican market and announced the addition of sixteen new products to its generic line. The company is making further investments in Mexico, building a new manufacturing plant and distribution centre, and purchasing additional machinery. Apotex's decision to enter the Mexican market has paid dividends several times over: it has allowed Apotex to expand, has given it access not just to the Mexican market of 100 million but potentially to the huge Latin and South American market, and has helped bring affordable pharmaceuticals to Mexico's consumers.

A Partnership Approach
to Development and
Global Challenges

JENNIFER JEFFS[1]

INTRODUCTION

The World Intellectual Property Organization in Geneva (WIPO), a specialized agency of the United Nations, was established to develop an international intellectual property system to stimulate innovation and contribute to economic development. The organization has defined climate change, health, and food security as the three major global challenges to human survival and has recently set up a section to look specifically at work being done globally in these areas. The urgent and global nature of these issues demands collaborative efforts and the leveraging of limited resources. Less developed countries will suffer disproportionately from challenges related to climate change, health, and food security, and their suffering will have an effect on richer nations. Thus, in addition to the ethical imperatives of addressing inequalities, partnerships between rich and poor nations make good practical sense. Collaborations between countries at disparate levels of development that share a continent make particularly good sense, since they share regional, as well as global, concerns. By addressing global issues in partnership, Canada and Mexico could serve as an example to the rest of the world.

With their shared NAFTA and G20 identities, their shared regional and global challenges, and their shared powerful neighbour, Canada and Mexico have a strong rationale for a bilateral partnership that leverages national research resources to create collaborative research agendas. Canada-Mexico research programs could produce useful technology while attracting attention and, potentially, additional funding from the

United States. A Canada-Mexico research agenda could appeal to the major Canadian research councils, the National Research Council (NRC), the *Natural Sciences and Engineering Research Council* (NSERC), and the *Social Sciences and Humanities Research Council* (SSHRC), which encourage international partnerships. While the United States is likely to be preoccupied with domestic concerns for some time to come, Canada and Mexico should work to make their collaboration sufficiently important, visible, and relevant to attract the attention and resources of the US. Rather than continuing to differentiate itself from Mexico in order to capture US attention, Canada should shift its strategy to attract US attention by working *with* Mexico, not only on issues of regional security and crime but also on global problems.[2]

AN INNOVATIVE DEVELOPMENT AGENDA:
RESEARCH COLLABORATION

This chapter calls for an approach to certain issues – North American development asymmetries and the lack of significant development funding for Mexico from its NAFTA partners – that differs from but complements Isabel Studer's chapter in this volume. While Dr Studer stresses the need for research on the Canada-Mexico commercial relationship, I suggest that research communities in Canada and Mexico could work together on major global challenges. Collaborative national research programs on climate and energy, health, and food security would lead to contributions of knowledge and intellectual property relevant to major global issues. With strong research outputs and appropriate intellectual property frameworks to manage them, a knowledge creation and accumulation partnership agenda on specific international problems between a wealthy small country and an emerging large economy carries a powerful message of legitimacy. And from a development and prosperity perspective, the production of research that leads to management strategies for global problems holds out immense wealth-creation opportunities.

It is increasingly apparent and acknowledged that almost all – if not all – major global challenges will affect developing countries disproportionately more, and sooner, than they will affect wealthy and industrialized nations, at least in the near term.[3] But it is also increasingly clear that developed nations cannot be complacent when it comes to these challenges. In a regional grouping – North America – that involves integrated production structures on such a large scale, the costs of these challenges to Mexico will negatively affect North American prosperity overall. Canada must help Mexico combat the negative effects of major global challenges. Such a contribution would benefit Mexico, Canada, and nations worldwide. Given the development imperatives and integrated production structures described in Isabel Studer's chapter, the potential of a Canada-Mexico partnership is unique.

A smaller wealthy country working with a populous emerging economy to tackle global challenges by galvanizing their complementary demographic and geographic resources would be a compelling example for others. Recognizing the development asymmetries in North America, Canada needs to work with its southernmost NAFTA partner, with which it also has an asymmetrical bilateral relationship, to develop research agendas that convene, engage, and develop emerging knowledge in specific areas of common interest. Once the two countries produce value-adding research and, even more importantly, the resulting intellectual property in the forms of patents and licensing agreements, they will attract the attention of – and conceivably funding from – their powerful and wealthy neighbour-in-the-middle. Rather than continuing its habit of trying to capture US attention by differentiating itself from Mexico, Canada needs to shift its strategy to attracting US attention by *working with* Mexico, not only on issues of security and crime but also on issues that pose challenges to global survival.

North America's global influence will be strengthened if the research communities of Canada and Mexico are engaged to combine the experience and capacity of two countries at different stages of development and with very different national profiles. Such initiatives would demonstrate that Canadian investment – not only direct financial aid but active joint ventures in less-developed countries – results in long-term mutual benefit exceeding that of mere subsidy, particularly when the participating countries share a continent.

INNOVATION AND JOBS

While all three NAFTA countries have their own particular domestic concerns, whether they pertain to political and governance challenges, crime and drugs, or economic upheaval, all these concerns involve and have implications for jobs and employment. A productively employed population provides the bedrock of stability, both political and economic, for any nation. While everyone understands the importance of jobs, people tend to be slower to make the connection between jobs and research – a connection fundamental to the evolving paradigms for global issues that will generate employment in the future. The drivers of the global economy are starting to shift. Most of us do not understand how this evolution is happening, how fast it will happen, or where it will lead; but we need to understand that future jobs will be found in areas and in industries that do not yet exist, and that research on specific global issues is critical to innovative approaches to those issues and to the development of new technologies, economies, knowledge formation, methods of production, and management techniques. These innovations, and the ways we harness and integrate them, will be critical to the future of the planet. Starkly put, from the perspective of future prosperity, the global challenges that we face could hold within them the greatest wealth-creation opportunities in the history of humankind. There could not be a better opportunity for Canada and Mexico to work together on those challenges through jointly funded and executed research agendas involving well-defined partnerships between the research institutions of the two countries.

ALTERNATIVE ENERGY SOURCES AND CLIMATE CHANGE

Both Canada and Mexico suffer from disproportionate dependence on their national oil industries for their energy needs and their Gross National Product (GNP). The oil industry provides extraordinarily rich fodder for research on clean extraction technologies and is an excellent example of an area where universities and industry can work together to create intellectual property related to issues of mutual concern. Canada recently created an intellectual property sharing consortium among oil companies operating in the Canadian oil sands for developing clean and environmentally friendly extraction technologies.[4] It would be in the best interests of Canada and Mexico to co-operate in the energy area for many reasons. The post-Copenhagen Accord era represents a major challenge to these two countries: both have committed themselves to reducing greenhouse gas emissions, yet both national economies depend disproportionately on the production and export of hydrocarbons as their main income. This contradiction presents a good opportunity for Canada and Mexico to work together to comply with current low-carbon energy policies while maintaining their roles as leading energy suppliers. The main areas on which they can work together include the implementation of energy-efficient policies and the development of renewable energies through political and technical dialogues (while the relationships around oil and gas still play the most important role) both at federal and provincial/state levels.

Bilateral interaction to date has taken place mostly between Canadian provinces and the Mexican federal government or with the state-owned oil company, Pemex. For example, in 2007, Alberta's and Mexico's energy ministries signed a co-operation agreement which includes the sharing of best practices on regulations of hydrocarbon exploration, development of energy efficiency, and promotion of technical co-operation.[5]

RENEWABLE ENERGIES

A focal report tells us that Canada has a small installed generation capacity in wind, solid biomass, and photovoltaic energy.[6] Mexico has a similar profile with an even smaller percentage of wind generation but greater installed capacity in biomass and geothermal energy. Both countries could further develop their renewable energy capacities. With the exception of hydro and ocean energy, provincial governments have jurisdiction over renewable resources in Canada. Notably, Mexico could launch a program of co-operation in wind power generation with Alberta, Ontario, Quebec, and Manitoba.[7] Canada, meanwhile, should pay attention to, and invest funds and research into, existing companies and projects developing innovative energy technologies in Mexico. One such company, Canromex, has adopted biogas-to-energy development projects in Chihuahua, Quintana Roo, Atizapan, and San Luis Potosi, and it continues to secure new projects in the State of Mexico with its partner company, Green Point Energy.[8]

CLIMATE CHANGE AND ENVIRONMENT

Mexico's specific interest in preserving and enhancing sustainable ecosystems stems from the fact that it is one of the most biodiverse countries in the world. As with any country, Mexico's resilience to the effects of climate change depends on co-operation with its regional neighbours. After the Conference of the Parties (COP) 16 in, Canada and Mexico agreed to further implement bilateral Cancún initiatives to fight climate change.[9] These include mitigation of methane emissions at oil facilities, energy efficiency, and anaerobic treatment of residuals in the pork industry in Yucatan. So far, the most important outcome of this dialogue is the implementation of a joint model to measure greenhouse gas emissions.[10] The 2011 initiative, under the Canada-Mexico Partnership, proposes implementing the Canadian model of carbon emissions detection and capture in Mexico. This model also helps prevent soil contamination, fires, and other environmental dangers. To implement this model, Canadian experts organized a workshop for Mexican environmental authorities in March 2011. The Canadian government should not ignore these precedents for Canadian-Mexican environmental research projects. By sharing and co-producing models for addressing climate change, Canadian and Mexican research communities can demonstrate to the rest of the world that climate change research is most productive when collaborative, since countries with vastly different climates share environmental problems that may have common solutions.

GLOBAL HEALTH

There are equally good precedents and many more opportunities for Canadian-Mexican collaboration on research relating to global health concerns. Mexican health professionals are often trained abroad and have strong connections with Europe and the United States. New research initiatives could take advantage of programs already in place, particularly those of the International Development Research Centre (IDRC), which identifies health care as Mexico's priority research area. FUNSALUD, a non-profit Mexican research centre, is leading IDRC-supported research on health financing, equity, and poverty in Argentina, Brazil, Chile, Colombia, Costa Rica, Mexico, and Peru. Research teams are assessing and quantifying household spending on health and household impoverishment under a variety of national health care models. They aim to identify the policy lessons learned from several recent health financing models, such as Mexico's Seguro Popular for the uninsured. In particular, the project analyses the impact of out-of-pocket health care expenditures on household poverty. The Teasdale-Corti Global Health Research Partnership Program was developed by the four founding partners of the Global Health Research Initiative, including IDRC, to investigate Mexico's childhood obesity epidemic.

Canada and Mexico have already worked together on H1N1 – Canada loaned five million doses of the H1N1 vaccine to Mexico when the pandemic first broke in 2009 – but most Canadian-Mexican initiatives in matters of global health have been independent from these countries' governments. In December 2009, the National Research Council Institute for Biological Sciences hosted a vaccine workshop to strengthen the dialogue between key Canadian government officials, stakeholders, and researchers in the health and vaccine sectors and their Mexican counterparts. The Mexico-Canada Joint Health Research Program in Tuberculosis was established in 2004 to promote co-operation between universities and research organizations of both countries.[11] Policymakers and managers in Mexico need research results and scientific evidence in order to make decisions about ways to improve health systems. With IDRC support, the National Institute of Public Health (INSP) in Mexico has partnered with the Canadian Health Services Research Foundation to select and adapt innovative approaches to bridge the research-to-policy gap. These programs demonstrate the potential for greater collaboration between Canada and Mexico should such programs be integrated under a larger bilateral mandate.

According to the Canada-Mexico Joint Action Plan 2010–2012, both countries will work together on topics of health and emergency response with a focus on protocols of conduct during health emergencies and natural disasters, including bilateral and trilateral communication frameworks for pandemics and infectious disease outbreaks.[12] The IDRC-funded health research in Mexico in areas of childhood obesity and health financing should concern Mexico's more developed neighbours, which are burdened by these health care issues as well. The United Kingdom has identified maternal health as one such issue and has funded research that demonstrates the effectiveness of advocacy in reducing maternal mortality in Mexico.[13] This research points to affordable solutions to a problem that affects underdeveloped countries worldwide. Canada should follow the UK's example, in collaboration with Mexican health care researchers, who are experienced in navigating Mexico's different levels of government. By identifying public health research areas as shared priorities with Mexico, Canada could integrate disparate research initiatives with the larger goal of reforming both countries' health care systems to provide innovative models to the United States and the world.

FOOD SECURITY

Lack of food security is a growing global threat that necessitates investment in agricultural research. The rising price of corn has created a food crisis in Mexico and contributes to poverty and political unrest. Canada should work with Mexico to stabilize these prices. In addition to researching climate change – a principle cause of the food crisis – Canada and Mexico could collaborate in introducing convenient, accessible, healthy, and sustainable products. Canada learned a hard lesson when an innovative Canadian company created the process by which canola is made from rapeseed before it was sold to the United States.[14] Now western Canadian farmers pay licensing fees to a US company to make canola in Canada. The next canola could be a development that would benefit Mexico and Canada alike. For example, Canadian researchers have developed the use of barley as a supplement for the corn that is traditionally used for basic products like the Mexican tortilla. Barley is a mainstay in Saskatchewan agriculture used more often in animal feed and for malting and rarely produced for human consumption, though its high levels of beta-glucan help to lower cholesterol and control blood sugar. Barley is not only a healthier alternative to traditional corn products but also a more economically stable one. Mexico could benefit greatly from such Canadian innovations through collaboration on research into food-biotechnology and its integration into the market.

The food sector is research and development-intensive; trial and research are necessary before introducing to the market any product intended to ease food access difficulties. There are already programs in place that would facilitate collaboration in this sector. Canada could organize research with Mexico through the Canadian International Food Security Research Fund (CIFSRF), which is a joint program of the IDRC and the Canadian International Development Agency (CIDA) that funds partnerships between research organizations in Canada and in the developing world.[15] Monterrey, a high-tech research city in Mexico, held a food biotechnology workshop in 2008 with exclusively Canadian and Mexican participants and in 2010 hosted the International Biotechnology Summit.[16] These workshops were designed to bring together Canadian and Mexican systems biologists to enhance existing bilateral collaboration and promote new alliances. With more encouragement from Canadian research institutions and universities, these kinds of initiatives could take place more frequently and productively under a bilateral mandate.

CONCLUDING REMARKS

To date there have been enough Mexican and Canadian-Mexican research initiatives in the areas of climate change and energy, global health, and food security to demonstrate the potential of such collaborations to make significant contributions to knowledge. These contributions to knowledge would be profitable both in their practical applications to global problems and in their value as intellectual property. Canada has already shown a commitment to research co-operation with other nations. The Canada-India scientific and technological co-operation agreement promotes research into alternate energy and sustainable environmental technologies, biotechnology, health, and disaster management, but it does so through seminars, conferences, symposia, and workshops rather than long-term projects. The 2008 Canada-Brazil Framework Agreement for Cooperation on Science, Technology and Innovation provides a better model, promoting greater collaboration in research and development between Brazil and Canada in the areas of agriculture, biotechnology, nanotechnology, and renewable energy development, among others. Canada and Mexico should come to a similar agreement, one that is ambitious and broad in scope and that involves common objectives that can be benchmarked. This bilateral agreement would address global concerns while benefiting the co-dependent North American economies, results that would further legitimize Canada's and Mexico's future endeavours.

NOTES

1 The author is grateful for the research and editing assistance provided by Lorena Gutierrez and Naomi Joseph.

2 I recently argued that Canada needs to support the US and hemispheric efforts to increase security in the region. See Jennifer Jeffs, "Get off the sidelines, Canada. Join Ameripol," *Globe and Mail*, 1 March 2010.

3 See Paul Collier, *The Bottom Billion: Why the Poorest Countries are Failing and What Can Be Done about It* (Oxford: Oxford University Press, 2007); Thomas Pogge, *World Poverty and Human Rights: Cosmopolitan Responsibilities and Reforms*, 2nd ed. (Cambridge: Polity Press, 2008).

4 Nathan Vanderklippe, "Oil companies finalize pact to share tailings research," *Globe and Mail*, 13 December 2010, accessed 26 July 2011, http://www.theglobeandmail.com/globe-investor/oil-companies-finalize-pact-to-share-tailings-research/article1835655/.

5 "Declaration on Cooperation in the Field of Energy Between the Ministry of Energy of the Province of Alberta, Canada and the Secretariat of Energy of the United Mexican States," Ministry of Energy, Mexico Federal Government. Accessed 26 July 2011, http://www.energia.gob.mx/webSener/res/473/DECLARATION%20ALBERTA.pdf.

6 "The Canada-Mexico Relationship: A Backgrounder," Canadian Foundation for the Americas (FOCAL), accessed 26 July 2011, http://www.focal.ca/images/stories/Canada-Mexico_FOCAL_Backgrounder_October%202010_e_sm.pdf.

7 See "In search of relevance for Canadian-Mexican energy relations," Lourdes Melgar, FOCAL, accessed 26 July 2011, http://focal.ca/images/stories/pdfs/CMI_Melgar_In_Search_of_Relevance_for_Canadian-Mexican_Energy_Relations_March_2011.pdf.

8 "Canromex: History," Canromex, accessed 26 July 2011, http://www.canromex.com/History.html.

9 "Com. 65/11 - Fomentan México y Canadá lazos de entendimiento en cambio climático," Sala de Prensa On-line de la Semarnat, accessed 26 July 2011, http://saladeprensa.semarnat.gob.mx/index.php?option=com_content&view=article&id=3025:fomentan-mexico-y-canada-lazos-de-entendimiento-en-cambio-climatico&catid=50:comunicados&Itemid=110.

10 Augustín del Castillo, "México contará con un sistema de medición de gases de efecto invernadero," Milenio, 17 March 2011, accessed 26 July 2011, http://www.milenio.com/cdb/doc/noticias2011/7124535617041c8e5402057a53154c55.

11 "Mexico-Canada Joint Health Research Program in Tuberculosis," Canadian Institute of Health Research, accessed 26 July 2011, http://www.cihr-irsc.gc.ca/e/28621.html.

12 "Canada-Mexico Join Action Plan, 2010–2012," CanadaInternational.gc.ca, accessed 26 July 2011, http://www.canadainternational.gc.ca/mexico-mexique/assets/pdfs/Mexico-JAP.pdf.

13 "Advocacy Reduces Maternal Mortality in Mexico," Research for Dialogue, Department for International Development, accessed 26 July 2011,http://research.dfid.gov.uk/r4dconsult/2010/03/01/advocacy- reduces-maternal-mortality-in-mexico/

14 The Canadian company Cargill sold Canola – then called Low-Erucic-Acid
    Rapeseed – oil seed and processing to US farmers.
15 "Canadian International Food Security Research Fund," International
    Development Research Centre, accessed 26 July 2011,http://www.idrc.ca/EN/
    Programs/Agriculture_and_the _Environment/Canadian_International_Food_
    Security_Research_Fund/Pages/default.aspx.
16 "Systems Biology and the New Frontiers of Food Biotechnology, Workshop –
    20–22 October, 2008, Monterrey, Mexico," The Centre for Nonlinear
    Dynamics in Physiology and Medicine, accessed 26 July 2011, http://www.cnd.
    mcgill.ca/Monterrey/program.html.

A Joint Research Agenda

ISABEL STUDER

Academic research on Canada-Mexico relations is as under-developed as the bilateral relations between these two countries. Existing studies tend to be descriptive and very few have explored areas that could foster a more strategic view of the interactions between these countries. While the perception of the Canada-Mexico relationship as a dynamic and a strategic one prevails in government circles, it is clear that such a relationship has become largely irrelevant in the foreign policy of each of these countries. Since 9/11 and the subsequent crisis of North American integration as a political project, many analysts have delved into how to give the Canada-Mexico relationship greater strategic weight. Their suggestions have ranged from institutionalizing the multiplicity of contacts that have developed since the early 1990s; establishing a reduced number of relevant projects and priorities; separating the Canada-Mexico relationship from the trilateral, North American framework; and avoiding the encapsulation of such a relationship in North America by putting more emphasis on foreign policy initiatives, either in multilateral or regional forums, particularly in Latin America.[1] None of these proposals have prospered or led to the creation of a true partnership (let alone a strategic one) with a community of purpose. A strategic vision for the Canada-Mexico relationship requires a focus on strengthening the North American agenda and addressing regional asymmetries. Developing such a vision requires a sound and creative research agenda that shows where the interests of these two countries converge and where there are opportunities for collaboration. This chapter broadly identifies a number of areas where the complementarities and strengths of the two countries can constitute the basic elements of their strategic partnership.[2]

A STRATEGIC VISION

That the bilateral relationship between Canada and Mexico has become marginalized in their foreign policies does not mean that it has not grown in the last fifteen years, or that it has no potential. Bilateral contacts have multiplied and economic exchanges have taken root. Rather, Canada and Mexico have forgone the opportunity provided by the North American Free Trade Agreement (NAFTA) to develop a sound trilateral agenda that could serve their individual and joint interests, in particular those related to the promotion of a competitive, prosperous, and secure North America. After all, the smallest bilateral relationship in North America can become relevant to each country only if it addresses the issues that matter most to them, i.e., regional problems that require collective action with their common neighbour. Instead, Canada and Mexico have gone to the opposite extreme, abandoning every effort to strengthen the trilateral agenda, thus rendering their bilateral relationship marginal to their core interests. Despite government rhetoric, the lack of a common purpose to serve their joint and individual interests through a North American agenda has resulted in a succession of empty bilateral initiatives that have produced little or no concrete results.

While a few analysts have identified Canada's preference for a dual-bilateralism approach as one of the elements resulting in the demise of a sound trilateral agenda,[3] it is rather the reluctance of both Canada and the United States to address existing asymmetries in North America that explains the failure of the "optimistic experiment" called NAFTA.[4] Although 40 million Mexicans live in poverty, Mexico is not entitled to receive official development assistance and the Canadian International Development Agency does not have a bilateral program with Mexico. Even so, in 2007–2008, Spain alone offered over four times more development assistance to Mexico than did Canada – $24 million compared with $6 million – whereas the United States provided $93 million in the same years. Canada has a direct interest in assisting Mexico to address its "development" challenges, whether in the fight against transnational crime, the alleviation of poverty and inequality, or the development of democratic governance. "The last thing Canada needs is a failed experiment in liberal democratic capitalism on the doorstep of our most important strategic partner. If the US is already distracted by Mexico to the detriment of Canada, Mexico beset by political and economic disorder will only make matters worse."[5]

In fact, some of the most successful programs that Canada has developed in Mexico are those related to building capacity in the area of democratic governance. Mexico's Access to Information Act of 2003 was modelled after Canada's Access to Information Act, among other national models; the strong relationship between Elections Canada and the Mexican Federal Electoral Institute allowed for sharing of best practices between the two institutions; and the Canadian Program @Campus Mexico, in collaboration with the Mexican Secretaria de la Función Pública, sought to professionalize Mexican career civil servants through online training courses, discussion forums, a digital library, etc.

There are also opportunities for Canada and Mexico to work together in fostering their common interests in North America. A research agenda that is developed on the basis of these strategic interests could help support a sound agenda (bilateral and trilateral) for co-operation between the two countries.

ECONOMIC EXCHANGES

Economic exchanges between Canada and Mexico were almost non-existent before NAFTA, but they exploded after the agreement was signed. And this fact is the point of departure of virtually any analysis of the Canada-Mexico relationship. By virtue of geography and the size of the US economy, the Canada-Mexico economic relationship will always be small when compared with the other two North American bilateral relationships: Canada-Mexico trade represents about 7 percent of US-Mexico trade and 5 percent of US-Canada trade; US Foreign Direct Investment (FDI) in Mexico is over twenty times the investment coming from Canada and the latter tends to be smaller than that of countries like the Netherlands and Spain. Often excluded from trade analyses is the existence of transnational systems of production in North America, which account for a significant part of total bilateral Canada-Mexico trade and are associated with significant costs reduction and efficiency-gains. Autos and electronics jointly represent about 65 percent of Mexican exports to Canada and 35 percent of Canadian exports to Mexico. In contrast, oil, gas, meat, and grains represent a higher proportion of Canadian exports to Mexico than manufacturing goods, which may explain Canada's lack of interest in including the auto industry competitive issues in the bilateral agenda with Mexico. Nonetheless, with a major crisis in the US auto industry and the extent of integration of the industry in North America, the lack of both sustained efforts to coordinate the policies of the three countries to strengthen the industry's competitiveness and analyses to enhance the competitiveness of one of the region's most important industries is surprising. While the Canada Mexico Partnership Trade and Investment Working Group has included actions on manufacturing technologies in the automotive and aerospace industries, they are very preliminary and pale in comparison with the Canada-US initiatives that include providing funds for the restructuring of Chrysler and General Motors, harmonizing safety and environmental standards with the US, and investing in border infrastructure to reduce transaction costs for the industry.[6]

The emergence of global value chains of production offers significant opportunities to re-energize NAFTA through strategies that address this new reality. The stakes for maintaining access to the US market for both Canada and Mexico are high as they face the twin challenges of thickening of the US border and competing with US imports of Chinese goods and products. Canada and Mexico could benefit from aggressively energizing regional value chains of supply by advancing the implementation of the Regulatory Cooperation Framework that was adopted at the 2007 Security and Prosperity Partnership (SPP) summit. This framework already identifies the regulations, standards, and other non-tariff barriers in key industries (automotive, electronics, transportation, and information and communications). More systematic, sector-based research is needed to identify opportunities to use regional value chains to compete globally.

Canada has a direct interest in strengthening NAFTA for another reason which is often taken for granted, i.e., the certainty that the agreement provides to Canadian investors in Mexico. A number of large Fortune 500 firms such as Royal Bank of Canada, Bank of Nova Scotia, Manulife Financial, Sunlife Financial, Power Corp of Canada, Magna International, Alcan, and Bombardier operate in Mexico, although the large majority of the 2,500 Canadian firms established in the country are small and medium-sized. In recent years, Canadian investments in the mining sector have increased substantially. Because workers' safety and environmental concerns run high in this economic sector, the Competitiveness and Technology Working Group of the Canada-Mexico Partnership has, not surprisingly, placed strong emphasis on social corporate responsibility, including the goals for the Mining Task Force to develop sustainable mining projects, to share best practices, and to develop a toolkit for social corporate responsibility. More can be done through the North American Commission for Labor Cooperation which has undertaken at least one co-operative project in the area of occupational safety and health in the mining sector. The North American Commission for Environmental Cooperation could also undertake studies, and offer seminars and workshops, to identify best practices and make recommendations to develop "green" mining projects. There is also room for Canada and Mexico to develop stronger mechanisms to strengthen bilateral and trilateral co-operation in this very important economic field.

ENERGY AND CLIMATE CHANGE

Energy and climate change are becoming central in determining the future economic prosperity and competitiveness of nations, and represent a huge potential for co-operation between Canada and Mexico. The two countries are the most important oil suppliers to the United States, and their resources have been critical to their neighbour's long-term energy security. However, US public opinion is demanding independence from foreign energy sources and greater availability of cleaner energy sources, thus posing challenges but also opportunities for regional co-operation. Oil production has peaked in Mexico and the country is on the road to becoming a net importer of hydrocarbons. Both the natural gas fields being developed in the United States and the tar sands in Alberta represent possibilities, although expensive ones, for new energy capacity. As with the coal deposits that abound in the United States and particularly the Gulf of Mexico's oil resources, these "new" sources of fossil energy represent significant environmental challenges for North America. Co-operation opportunities are also emerging through technology transfer, as carbon-capture and storage technologies aim at reducing emissions in the oil sands in Canada and substantial low-cost reductions emerge from energy-efficiency actions in the oil and gas sector in Mexico. [7]

For Canada and the United States the cost of reducing emissions will be high, but a co-operative approach that includes Mexico will help minimize mitigation costs, alleviate concerns about the possible negative competitive effects of reducing greenhouse gas emissions, and even strengthen the North American competitive position in the world economy. Both the high levels of energy interdependence and the existence of an institutional context of North American co-operation – the Commission for Environmental Cooperation and the North American Development Bank – could build the foundations for regional/transnational renewable energy markets and a climate emissions trading system to help cope with an unstable energy outlook.

The electricity trade, although not significant at the North American aggregate level, is significant between Canada and the United States. Demand for electricity on the Mexico-US border is projected to grow, and in the United States, states, particularly California, are increasingly adopting Renewable Portfolio Standards. Therefore, regional co-operation could be developed in the harmonization of policies within North America to deploy appropriate technologies and to establish cross-border grid interconnections of non-CO_2 emitting sources of electricity. The three countries have adopted efforts to "align" their energy efficiency standards as an objective in their climate change and clean energy co-operation agenda, although so far the results have been limited. [8]

MIGRATION, DEMOGRAPHICS, AND LABOUR MOBILITY

Because of a combination of factors, including population aging and the transition toward a knowledge-based economy, immigration has become central for Canada's future economic growth, population, and labour force. The growth of Canada's labour force will slow over the next ten years as a consequence of the expected slowdown in population growth combined with a declining rate of labour force participation as aging baby boomers begin to retire. In Canada as in the United States, immigrants are a significant source of labour supply, representing about one fifth of new job seekers, and their participation in the labour force is expected to grow. Each year Canada receives about a quarter of a million permanent immigrants – half of whom are economic and business immigrants – and over 100,000 temporary foreign workers, a majority of whom are now highly skilled workers.[9]

So far, most Canada-Mexico efforts have focused on facilitating the "orderly, legal, and secure movement" of citizens across borders, instead of an "interest-based" approach that could exploit existing labour market complementarities as a means to strengthen the future competitiveness of North America. To be sure the number of Mexicans in Canada is a small fraction of those going to the United States, but Mexicans have become the largest immigrant group of Latin American origin. Mexico is also the second most important source of temporary foreign workers to Canada with 20,900 workers in 2008, exceeded only by the United States with 31,399.[10] A large majority of Mexicans (close to 15,500 in 2009) enter Canada as temporary workers for up to eight months (five on average), through the Seasonal Agricultural Workers Program (SAWP), a program that has existed since 1974 and has contributed to the survival of the horticultural and tobacco farms in Ontario and Quebec through the constant flow of cheap labour.[11] Many studies highlight the program's virtues as a best-practice model for how migration can work in an orderly and legal way for the benefit of workers and farmers. Nevertheless, the SAWP is fairly small. Also, few have paid attention to the difficulties in ensuring the enforcement of rights for temporary workers in Canada; immigration policy is a shared responsibility between the provinces and the federal government, whereas labour policy is in the hands of provincial governments. Bilateral efforts to expand the program to other areas – construction, hospitality, and finance – would have to consider these institutional concerns.[12]

An incipient trend that also needs to be better documented is the growing number of Canadians who are choosing Mexico as a second residence. Many Canadians who spend a few months in the country to seek refuge from the cold weather enter Mexico with tourist visas. According to some studies, Mexico has a huge potential as a location for retirees from Canada and the United States who are in search of a "second home." Considering the demographic dynamics of the two countries and the geographic proximity, it is not implausible to expect that an increasing number of Canadians will choose Mexico as a place to retire.

HUMAN CAPITAL

The transition toward a knowledge-based economy has fostered the demand for highly skill workers. Over the 2006–2015 period, more than two-thirds of all new jobs in Canada are expected to be in occupations requiring postsecondary education (university and college) or in management. In contrast to the United States, where immigrant workers are concentrated at the extremes of the education ladder, immigrants in Canada tend to have skill levels that enable them to contribute quickly to labour market development and thus tend to be as educated as the Canadian-born population. Canada's immigration points system, in which skill has been the key component since the 1990s, was designed to attract immigrants who were more likely to succeed in the Canadian labour market.

Whereas US and Canadian businesses could once assume that they would be able to recruit high-skilled or well-educated immigrants to fill critical occupations either from the ranks of US and Canadian colleges and universities or directly from overseas, the expanding economies of China, Korea, and India are retaining and attracting back many of their nationals. Foreign students have thus become an important source of skilled labour for Canada and, since many of the integration issues faced by other immigrants are resolved through the Canadian education process, students are viewed as high-potential permanent immigrants. Starting in 2005, Canada introduced a number of measures to facilitate the immigration of foreign students and to allow them to gain some Canadian off-campus work experience. Despite concerns that it may lead to a "brain drain" of Mexican talent, Canada and Mexico recently signed a Youth Mobility Agreement through which young people can travel and work for up to a year in the other country.

In spite of the demographic dynamics that are complementary in North America, current overall skills and educational levels in Mexico suggest that the country does not have sufficient numbers of competent workers to capture the potential offshore investments that would ensue from the labour situation that its two neighbours will face with aging populations. Mexico has been increasing its investment in education and is undertaking a variety of reforms to improve quality, but educational opportunity remains poorly distributed with many obstacles to continuation beyond primary education for poor and rural students. Compared with other manufacturing countries, Mexico faces relatively high production costs and a workforce with relatively low-level skills.[13]

Hundreds of university and research exchange programs between Canada and Mexico now exist, but the number of Mexican students in Canada is still relatively low, reaching in 2001 the historical high of over

5,000 but dropping to about half that number thereafter, and it is well below numbers for India, Saudi Arabia, China, and Korea. Also, many more Mexicans prefer to study in other countries. Only 5 percent of Mexican citizens enrolled in universities abroad study in Canada compared with 51 percent who attend US universities and 14 percent in universities in Spain.[14] Something similar happens with scholarships for students and academic exchanges. According to Consejo Nacional de Ciencia y Tecnología (CONACYT), in 2009 this institution provided 104 new scholarships to Mexican students to undertake graduate studies in Canada, while three and four times this number were awarded for study in countries such as Spain and the United States.[15] In 2009, Mexican researchers received only three out of 196 grants given under the Understanding Canada Program, whereas countries such as France, China, and Argentina received between thirteen and nineteen grants.[16] In sum, the potential for co-operation and for developing programs that invest in human capital are significant and beneficial to all parties involved, but the list of projects developed by the Canada-Mexico Partnership Human Capital group is small and largely irrelevant.[17]

SECURITY

Mexico clearly has insufficient resources to fight its war against drug trafficking, which has become a critical challenge for the security of Mexico, the US-Mexico border region, and the stability of North America as a whole.[18] The country needs international help, which has come, so far, mainly from the United States through the Mérida Initiative ($1.4 billion) and some European countries. Canada's co-operation projects with Mexico on intelligence, defence, and assistance programs involving the Royal Canadian Mounted Police and different Mexican police forces are incipient and could be substantially expanded.

CONCLUDING REMARKS

In their bilateral relationship, Canada and Mexico have so far missed the opportunity to develop a partnership that adopts a strong North American agenda and thus to work together to tackle regional problems and grasp global opportunities. The lack of a common purpose has made it difficult for the two countries to take advantage of the rapid expansion of bilateral contacts in the last fifteen years and to focus those efforts into making the Canada-Mexico relationship relevant for each country and for the region. The lack of a strategic partnership has also allowed small problems to acquire a larger dimension than desired, led to unilateral decisions that have been unnecessarily harmful for both countries, and revealed that the formal commitment to developing a strategic partnership has no real substance.

Canada and Mexico could help develop win-win strategies for North America. They could act to strengthen regionally integrated industries that are already part of global value chains and to secure investment and trade flows; undertake projects ensuring a competitive workforce for North America, investments in human capital, and promotion of the rights of labour immigrants; adopt a coordinated approach to the twin areas of energy security and climate change; and create a common framework for addressing security challenges. Common action in these areas has great potential for making the Canada-Mexico relationship relevant to each country's strategic interests, i.e., maintaining sustained access to the US market and enhancing the competitiveness of the North American region. Canada could also be more active in helping its southern neighbour to build capacity in areas where progress in North American competitiveness and security is impeded. In doing so, Canada could be serving regional interests as much as its own and could facilitate US engagement in positive solutions to deal with the North American asymmetry conundrum.

NOTES

1   Olga Abizaid Bucio, "The Canada-Mexico relationship: The unfinished highway" (FOCAL 2004), http://www.focal.ca/pdf/Mexico-Canada_ Abizaid-FOCAL_Canada-Mexico%20Relationship%20Unfinished%20 Highway_October%202004_FPP-04-8.pdf and Andrew F. Cooper, "Thinking outside the Box in the Canada-Mexico Relations: The Long Road from Convenience to Commitment," in *Big Picture Realities: Canada and Mexico at the Crossroads*, ed. D. Drache (Waterloo, ON: Wilfrid Laurier University Press, 2008): 237–51.

2   This essay presents a summary of Isabel Studer, "Mexico and the Forgotten Partnership – Is It Better to Forget (or Learn to Love) Trilateralism?" in *Forgotten Partnership - 25 Years On*, ed. Greg Anderson and Christopher Sands (Washington, DC: Cambria Press, 2011).

3   Robert Pastor, "The Third Side of the North American Triangle: Canada-Mexico Relations." *The North American Dialogue Series -CEDAN* 14 (2010): 1–20. Armand Peschard-Sverdrup, "The Canada-Mexico Relationship: A view from Inside the Beltway," *FOCAL Point. Focus on Canada-México* 9, no. 4 (2010): 5–7, http://www.focal.ca/pdf/focalpoint_may2010.pdf. Raul Benítez, "Mexico-Canada: Building North America's Security Framework," *FOCAL Point. Focus on Canada-México* 9, no. 3 (2010): 11–13, http://www. focal.ca/pdf/focalpoint_may2010.pdf.

4 Carol Wise and Isabel Studer, *Requiem or Revival? The Promise of
   North American Integration* (Washington, DC: Brookings Institution
   Press, 2006).

5 Greenspon, in Canadian International Council, *Open Canada: A Global
   Positioning Strategy for a Networked Age* (Ottawa 2010), 52, http://www.
   onlinecic.org/opencanada.

6 Government of Canada, "Government Response to the Second Report
   of the Standing Committee on Industry, Science and Technology: A Study of
   the Crisis in the Automotive Sector in Canada" (Ottawa, 2009).

7 See Isabel Studer, "Supply and Demand for a North American Climate
   Regime," in *Designing Integration: Regional Governance on Climate Change
   in North America*, ed. Neil Craik, Isabel Studer, and Deborah VanNijnatten
   (to be published by University of Toronto Press).

8 Security and Prosperity Partnership of North America,(2007) *Montebello,
   Joint Statement, Prime Minister Harper, President Bush and President
   Calderón, North American Leader's Summit*, 2007, http://www.spp.gov/pdf/
   leaders_statement_2007_english.pdf.

9 Citizenship and Immigration Canada, *Facts and figures: Immigration
   overview, permanent and temporary residents* (Ottawa, 2008), http://www.cic.
   gc.ca/english/resources/statistics/facts2008/index.asp.

10 Ibid., 57.

11 Austina J. Reed, "Canada's Experience with Managed Migration: The Strategic
   Use of Temporary Foreign Worker Programs" *International Journal* (Spring
   2008): 479.

12 Studer, "Mexico and the Forgotten Partnership."

13 Stephanie Guichard, *The Education Challenge in Mexico: Delivering Good
   Quality Education for All*. OECD Economic Department Working Paper
   No. 447, (September 2005), 4, http://www.oecd-ilibrary.org/
   economics/the-education-challenge-in-mexico_047122723082.

14 OECD, *Education at a Glance: 2009 Indicators*, http://www.oecd.
   org/document/24/0,3343,en_2649_39263238_43586328_1_1_1_1,00.
   html#4.

15 Consejo Nacional de Ciencia y Tecnologia, Sistema Integrado de Información
   sobre Investigación Científica y Tecnológica (SIICYT), "Capítulo IV" (México,
   2010), 314, http://www.siicyt.gob.mx/siicyt/indicadores/SeriesEstadisticas.
   do?id_capitulo=004&id_subcapitulo=012.

16 International Council for Canadian Studies, (2009)*Annual Report* 2008–2009
   (Canada, March 2009), 24, http://www.iccs-ciec.ca/pdf/reports_
   and_summaries/completeannualrep-0809.pdf.

17 See Studer, "Mexico and the Forgotten Partnership."

18 For a thorough discussion of the opportunities in the security area, see
   R. Morden, "Hemispheric Security: The Canada-Mexico Conundrum"
   in this volume.

Beyond Margaritas and Mariachis

MARINA JIMÉNEZ

Canadians pride themselves on being more worldly than their insular American cousins. And yet, on the subject of Mexico, they are grossly ignorant. The country is invariably viewed as alien and wantonly violent – the volcano, ever poised to rain destruction.

Yes, Mexico has become embroiled in a global drug war – fuelled largely by the demands of consumers in the US and Canada. However, that violence is limited to a very few locations in the country, largely along the border with the US, and the incidence of violence is far less than in Brazil, though this country is portrayed much more favourably by the Canadian media.

Mexico, the world's thirteenth largest economy, should not be dismissed as a violent backwater and a place for cheap vacations. It has much more to offer than margaritas and mariachis.

With an expanding middle class, a 4 percent growth rate and a democratic government, Mexico is an increasingly important player in the global economy. It manufactures everything from RIM BlackBerries to Bombardier aircraft and is a mecca of world-class film, art, and cuisine. In the last fifteen years, its democracy has matured, poverty has declined, and incomes have generally risen.

And yet, with no permanent Canadian correspondents in Latin America, the media's framing of the continent, and of Mexico, remains limited. Journalists are parachuted in to write about elections or the military initiative President Felipe Calderón has launched against the drug cartels and the associated violence.

This in turn narrows public knowledge and the discourse about the country's present and future. "The Canadian media have only two ways of dealing with Mexico: either as a cultural curiosity, or a lost cause – sombreros, or machine guns," says Agustin Barrios, the director of the Canada-Mexico Initiative for the Mexican Council on Foreign Relations. "There are many other stories. We are the 13th largest economy in the world, we are the BRIC of Latin America."[1]

A 2010 public opinion survey conducted by Leger Marketing found that 39 percent of Canadians have a favourable impression of Mexico, while 47 percent view the country unfavourably. In contrast, 61 percent have a favourable impression of Brazil, and just 17 percent view it unfavourably. Coincidentally, media coverage of Mexico was more negative than of Brazil: of the 23,000 stories about Mexico which ran in major Canadian newspapers last year, only one fifth were favourable. There were half as many stories published about Brazil, but nearly one third were favourable.

"Mexican culture doesn't always resonate with Canadians," notes John Stackhouse, the *Globe and Mail*'s editor-in-chief. "There is the pervasive association of Mexico with a cheap beach vacation. There is also no domestic constituency, unlike with India. The unspoken challenge is, how is Canada affected by Mexico's rise and fall?"[2]

The 1980s and 1990s were a different era; most major Canadian news organizations had correspondents based in the region, covering Central America's dramatic and bloody revolutions, Mexico's transition to democracy, and the signing of the North American Free Trade Agreement in 1994. These were captivating stories, filled with tension and conflict.

Today, however, the region is calmer, and interest has faded. Media outlets are distracted by the war on terror, the Arab spring, and the rise of China and India. There is a lack of interest in covering the full complexity of Mexico's political, economic, and cultural developments. Only Connie Watson, with the Canadian Broadcasting Corporation (CBC), works as a full-time Canadian correspondent in Latin America, until recently based in Mexico.

Of course, there are many other sources of information, including the *Economist*, under Americas editor Michael Reid, the *New York Times*, *Washington Post*, *Los Angeles Times*, and British newspapers such as the *Guardian*. But it helps to have national media organizations that cover their own hemisphere. "There is no doubt that Mexico punches below its weight in our consciousness. The fact that it is foreign, and yet not overseas, and is a distinct culture, yet not as exotic as India or China, creates a certain complacency," says Stephen Northfield, the *Globe and Mail*'s former foreign editor. "The slow building of governance and institutions, civil rights and free speech, these are not big stories compared to the exciting democratic transformations of the 1980s and 1990s."[3]

And yet, in spite of the many challenges, there is no stopping Mexico's rise. It is moving ahead with institutional reforms and strengthening its democracy. It has a large and dynamic middle class. It weathered the 2008 global recession well, a testament to the inherent strength of its banking system. And it will, with time, prevail over its complex security challenges.

As Michael Reid wrote in his book *Forgotten Continent*, the efforts of countries such as Mexico, Brazil, and Chile to build fairer and more prosperous societies make the region one of the world's most vigorous laboratories for capitalist democracies.

As Mexico rises in importance on the world stage, there are signs that the journalistic paradigm is about to shift as well.

Mexico is Canada's largest trading partner in the Americas, and third largest overall, with $27 billion in two-way trade last year. There are 2,500 Canadian companies operating in Mexico in industries including banking, aerospace, manufacturing, and technology. The tail assembly for the Global Express aircraft of Bombardier is made in Mexico, shipped to Montreal for assembly, and within eight days is joined to a fuselage. Last year, 1.5 million Canadians visited Mexico. The expatriate community numbers 75,000.

"There has been a huge explosion in the economies of Latin America, and we have not been paying close enough attention to the growing importance and success of Mexico and Brazil," notes Mr Northfield. "In the same way that China surprised us with its growth four years ago, there will be that moment soon in Latin America. We will recognize how deep our ties are, and our interests and the business audience will demand more coverage, and the political class will become more engaged."[4]

Not only is there tremendous potential for growth in coverage from mainstream media – newspapers and broadcasters – but the plethora of social media provide fresh ways to communicate information, build bridges, and present new narratives.

The *Globe and Mail* is considering reopening its Latin American bureau in 2012, based in either Mexico or Brazil. This reflects an increasing appetite among readers for more business, political, and economic news, and the paper's willingness to broaden the prevailing discourse on Mexico. The *Toronto Star* has no plans to reopen its bureau in Mexico City, which closed a few years ago, but has committed to broadening coverage through sending correspondents on a regular basis to the region. "There is so much more to Mexico than the drug cartels and a cheap beach vacation," says Michael Cooke, editor-in-chief of *The Toronto Star*. "There are stories of hope and progress, of optimism and innovation. It's the job of Canadian journalists to find these stories."[5]

The CBC's Latin American bureau will open in Brazil this fall, with a mandate to travel to other parts of the region, including Mexico. "Mexicans have a real sense of who they are. I want to continue telling the stories of the country's dynamism, as well as of the fragility of its democracy and strengthening of its institutions," notes Ms Watson.[6]

The presence of 40 million Latinos, many of them young Mexicans, in the US, is also profound for Canada. They are re-shaping the political, economic, and cultural landscape, as the US undergoes a dramatic demographic transformation.

Of course, Canada's relationship with and understanding of Mexico has always been influenced by the presence of their large and powerful shared neighbour. Ottawa has over the years regarded Mexico as the unwelcome partner in the trio and as a threat to Canada's so-called special relationship with Washington.

But this too is changing. With the US increasingly preoccupied with both Mexico's challenges and its opportunities, a close partnership with Mexico has the added benefit of giving Canada extra clout in Washington.

With a majority in parliament, the Conservative government can now act more decisively on its Americas initiative and work to enhance the region's democracy, security, and prosperity. While an internal review found that the 2007 strategy lacked focus and funding, the government has pledged to strengthen these efforts, under newly appointed minister for the Americas, Diane Ablonczy.

Understanding a country as diverse as Mexico is not easy, especially in a time of intense pressure on media organizations to cut costs and adapt to new and rapidly changing technologies.

Mexico's icons, idioms, and idiosyncrasies are complex. Its identity is in many ways defined by its history as a country that bears the scars of both Spanish and American colonization. Strands from the country's long and bloody past are woven into its identity, from the richness of the pre-Colombian civilization and culture, to the consolidation of the Aztec empire, the arrival of the Europeans, and the 1910 revolution. Mexicans often view themselves as victims of this turbulent past; as Octavio Paz, one of Mexico's greatest writers, wrote in *Labyrinth of Solitude*, "We are taught from childhood to accept defeat with dignity."

As a federation, there is also great regional diversity, from the wealthy north and cities such as Monterrey, to Chiapas in the south, to the vibrancy of el DF (the Federal District), one of the world's great capitals, with 20 million inhabitants. Jorge Castañeda, an author, academic, and Mexico's former foreign minister, talks about his country's identity in the just released book *Manana Forever*. He describes how certain traits shape public attitudes and self-perception, including a focus on the individual, a desire to avoid conflict, the role of ritual in society, the country's

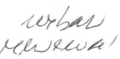

mestizo (Spanish and Indian) heritage, the potent lure of El Norte, and a resentment of outside intervention.

Mexicans have a sense of irony best captured in the character of Cantinflas, a 1940s comedian who played an impoverished simpleton fighting for justice. The character prompted the invention of the verb *cantinflear*, meaning to speak rapidly without saying anything of meaning. Mexicans are also devoted fans of telenovelas, soap operas, and Lucha Libre wrestling (few Canadians know that el Vampiro Canadiense, played by a Canadian named Ian Richard Hodgkinson, is an iconic Lucha Libre wrestler).

Mexicans of all social classes venerate the Virgin of Guadalupe, and value their own rich artistic tradition, including the pyramids of Chichen Itza and the country's 30,000 active archeological sites, as well as their film-makers, artists, and public intellectuals such as Carlos Fuentes. Carlos Slim, the world's richest man who made his fortune in the telecom industry, just opened a museum, Museo Soumaya, to display his vast private art collection. Eugenio Lopez, heir to the Grupo Jumex food processing empire, is following suit, with a contemporary art museum nearby. The trio of outstanding Mexican filmmakers – Alfonso Cuaron, Guillermo del Toro, and Alejandro Gonzales Inarritu – have garnered global acclaim through their films.

The Mexican tourism industry is trying to market the country's rich cultural heritage through its "The Mexico you thought you knew" campaign, promoting colonial cities such as Puebla and Oaxaca, as well as the capital itself. Once known mainly for its smog, express kidnappings, and eternal traffic, Mexico City is undergoing significant urban renewal. It has become a destination in itself, thanks to better security, a vibrant art and restaurant scene, and a glut of contemporary galleries in refurbished historical areas such as Condesa and Roma.

Communicating the richness and diversity of this culture to Canadians is difficult. Most Canadians don't regard el DF as one of the world's great capitals. However, the social media, including blogs, Twitter, and Facebook, provide a good place to communicate new messages. Recently, for example, photographs of Mexico City's landmark monuments and panoramas taken by an American helicopter pilot went viral, as thousands of people downloaded the gorgeous images.

Less hierarchical and more innovative, social media also appeal more to youth. While Canada has 16 million Facebook users, Mexico has 18 million, a number that is growing at the rate of 300,000 per month. There is cyber-NAFTA potential here, although admittedly language may still be a barrier.

Another way to change the framework is through people-to-people exchanges. Already, Mexico is Canada's second most popular tourist destination, after the US. In spite of the negative coverage about the drug

wars, the number of Canadian visitors to Mexico has been steadily growing, with a 20 percent increase last year. Though most of the 1.5 million
annual Canadian visitors go to the beach, many also take a quick trip to
the pyramids.

As well, 75,000 Canadian expatriates live in Mexico, and more than
50,000 Mexicans live in Canada, mostly skilled professionals who
entered through the immigration points program. They could use social
media to provide context and to broaden the narrative, so that when a
drug beheading does occur, there is a better understanding of its larger
meaning. If someone is shot in the border city of Tijuana, there is no
reason to believe crime will increase in Cancún, some 3,200 km away, in
a state with a crime rate lower than many American cities.

Mexico, of course, is nowhere near the most crime-ridden country in
Latin America. The crime associated with the drug cartels is still mostly
confined to border cities such as Tijuana and Ciudad de Juarez. Last
year, 70 percent of the homicides linked to organized crime took place
in just three percent of municipalities. Mexico's rate of violent deaths
per 100,000 people is lower than those of Brazil, Colombia at the height
of its drug wars, and Central America. Only twelve Canadians died in
Mexico last year, including those who died of natural causes – though
every consular case attracts undue attention.

And what of Canada's image in Mexico?

Since 2006, Canada has been the most popular country in Mexico,
according to a yearly poll conducted by the Centro de Investigación y
Docencia Economicas (CIDE). This generally positive view temporarily
soured in 2009, when Ottawa imposed a visa for Mexican visitors following a dramatic increase in the number of Mexicans claiming asylum in Canada. The visa imposition was a psychological blow, and
created bureaucratic obstacles for Mexicans who had to produce everything from mortgage documents to marriage certificates to obtain a visi-
tor's visa.

Notwithstanding this setback, Mexicans still tend to view Canada as
an orderly and civilized society which is tolerant of minorities. Many
regard Canadians as "los gringos buenos." There is still a lack of knowledge, however, about Canada's particular cultural icons, political
landscape, essential values, and characteristics. Mexicans may be
familiar with Celine Dion, Michael Bublé, Cirque du Soleil, and
Arcade Fire, but know less about Canada's aboriginals, the tensions
between English and French Canada, Canadian writers, filmmakers,
and comedians. This is due, in part, to the language barrier.

Each country could engage in soft diplomacy to alter perceptions and
foster dialogue. Literary, academic, and journalistic exchanges and cultural programs, as well as linkages between major cultural and scientific
organizations, could help accomplish these goals. Mexican and Canadian

journalists could undertake journalistic exchanges and enhance each country's understanding of the other through reportage and seminars.

On November 2011, in a collaboration between Mexico's National Institute of Anthropology and the Royal Ontario Museum (ROM), the exhibit "Maya: Secrets of their Ancient World" will come to the ROM and the Canadian Museum of Civilization in Ottawa. This exhibit of 250 artifacts, ceramics, masks, and other works will give Canadians unfiltered access to Mexico's patrimony. Two years ago, the Art Gallery of Ontario (AGO) honoured Mexican photographer Arturo Cruz, an event which also helped to broaden Mexico's image beyond mariachis and margaritas.

Social media certainly lend themselves to being a catalyst for change. They have the potential to shape a different kind of narrative on each side, a more complex and thoughtful one.

Mexico and Canada need to build on traditions that already exist, for example, sending Mexican children to summer camps in Ontario and Quebec, or to private school, although clearly this is for the elites only. Already, about 10,000 Mexican students come to study in Canadian high schools, universities, and in language programs each year. These programs could be further developed through more scholarships and better marketing. More Canadian students could consider studying Spanish or completing Third Year Study Abroad programs at Mexican universities and institutions. Establishing academic centres for North America studies is an excellent way to enhance dialogue and promote better research and a richer understanding of the bilateral relationship. This year, Simon Fraser University launched an executive Master of Business Administration for the Americas, which will partner with universities in Mexico, Brazil, and the US. Working visas for students are now available for Mexicans and Canadians to embark on working holidays in one another's countries.

Canada and Mexico need to build on these fledgling initiatives and challenge the overwhelmingly negative discourse. It is time for the media to go beyond the sombrero and the gun. Mexico is a great ally, and in the decades to come will become an even more important global player. As with all great nations, no one narrative can capture Mexico's sophistication, vibrancy, successes, and challenges.

NOTES

1 Augustin Barrios, interview by the author, May 2011.
2 John Stackhouse, interview by the author, May 2011.
3 Stephen Northfield, interview by the author, May 2011.
4 Ibid.
5 Michael Cooke, interview by the author, May 2011.
6 Connie Watson, interview by the author, May 2011.

The Enigma of Canada's Image: Neither Dudley Do-Right nor Joe Canadian

JOSÉ CARREÑO FIGUERAS

Does Canada want to be better known? For both political and economic reasons, every country wishes that its national virtues were better advertised in the world. If nothing else, a good image translates into "soft power," a tangible and desirable commodity on the world stage. In economic terms, a higher profile could mean foreign investment and tourism, especially if the country in question has, like Canada, an abundance of natural resources and magnificent landscapes.

Canada is a country with an impressive image outside its borders. Yet, if the Mexican case is typical, that popularity is due to nothing more than just being Canada.

Since 2006, Canada has been the most popular foreign country in Mexico, even after the controversy created in 2009 when the Canadian government denounced the abuse of Canada's "generous" asylum system and began requiring visas for Mexicans seeking to travel in Canada.

In Mexico, almost 82 percent of the statistical group defined as "leaders" and 68 percent of the general public consider Canada their favourite country, according to a yearly poll conducted by CIDE and published on 7 April 2011. But while the results are clearly flattering for Canada and Canadians, they pose the question, why do Mexicans like Canada?

Call it "Brand Canada." Better yet, refer to that and the "Nations Brand Index." There is no better or clearer answer. In Mexico, at least, there are no studies or polls specifically designed to identify the underlying a reason for this positive image. Internationally, it is thought that quality of life, tourist appeal, and value systems combine to create the image. But some analysts, Canadians themselves, attribute the image simply with being "nice."

They may be onto something! If Mexico is the thermometer, the positive Mexican public support for Canada does not appear to translate into knowledge or anything of particular interest.

"Countries with strong brands capture political, cultural, and economic premiums. When observers talk about Canada punching above its weight on the world stage, they're really talking about the country leveraging its political capital based on a brand," pointed out Simon Houpt in an article ("What is Canada's Brand?") published by the *Globe and Mail* on 30 June 2010.

This is helpful. But *El Universal*, the largest general daily in Mexico City, reports publishing only two news stories about Canada in the first three months of 2011. This is not a surprise: the same newspaper printed exactly the same number of news stories about Canada in an identical time period in 2010. *Milenio*, another leading daily, claims to have published "maybe four or five" stories about Canada in the first four months of 2011. The news items included the fallout of the Japanese nuclear crisis, the Canadian view of the North Atlantic Treaty Organization's (NATO) involvement in the Libyan civil war, and the federal election in early May.

Whatever the reason, the fact is that Canada is not a country that figures much in the Mexican media – or the American media for that matter. One explanation offered is that Canada and Mexico do not share a border. But geographical proximity is not a sufficient reason: distant European, Middle Eastern, and even African nations are mentioned almost daily.

And yes, in real terms Canada is an important country for Mexico, both commercially and politically. Yet, nations which are hardly known by the Mexican public find their way to the pages of the Mexican media much more often than Canada.

Then again, there is another explanation, perhaps more accurate: Canada is not a country of crises and such countries are not attractive for the news media.

A Google search in early May for news related to Canada in the Mexican press produced 119 hits in the month of April 2011. But Mexico has more than 300 daily newspapers. Even worse, some of the stories were linked either with the visits of Canadian officials or with the leader of a Mexican miner's union self-exile and search for political asylum from prosecution in Mexico.

Roberto Rock, managing editor of *El Universal*, has a simple answer: nothing happens in Canada that arouses the interest of the Mexican media. And that point provides half of the explanation of why the Mexican media do not have a presence in Canada. The other half is simple economics.

Pascal Beltrán del Rio, managing editor of another large Mexican daily, *Excélsior*, makes a similar point: "we know nothing about Canada and that may be the reason we like it." So there remains a basic and valid question: why does Canada have such a favourable image in Mexico? Is it perhaps because of Canadians themselves? Or might it be thanks to the perceived differences between the US and Canada? But again, as Rock said in an interview, it may well be because very little negative material is published about Canada.

The 2009 visa "flap" was just that, a momentary issue. The annual news items about the killing of baby seals barely create a ripple in Mexican public opinion. The stories about the separatist movement in Quebec are long forgotten. Thus, what may be considered negative news is not a factor.

So, why do Mexicans like Canada? There are no data that provide a clear answer. Even the Canadian Embassy in Mexico cannot give reasons.

But then, what is not to love about Canada? While the answer may be clear from the point of view of a Canadian, from the Mexican side it requires further explanation. Empirical research provides no clues. There is, however, "Brand Canada."

It could be, as some humorists have claimed, that the world looks at Canadians as well-mannered Americans, and Mexicans, in particular, look at them as nicer "gringos." For Mexicans, Canada appears as a pretty, quaint place, with delightful and somehow strange landscapes, where people obey the laws, make an effort to understand other cultures, and above all, are Anglo-Saxons without the imperial accent that, no matter what, taints American diplomacy, or the arrogance that some believe is part of the American character. Sometimes, it's the illusion of Canada as a civilized and law-abiding counterweight to the American behemoth.

For many people in the world, especially in Mexico, that is a huge difference. Canadian foreign policy has allowed its government to assume the role of "good cop" vis-à-vis the US "bad cop." The reputation of Canada as the "different" North American country benefited from the Canadian refusal to break relations with Cuba after the arrival of Fidel Castro in 1959, its rejection of sending troops to Vietnam, and its reluctance to take part in the invasion of Iraq in 2003 despite pressure from President George W. Bush.

And that is part of "Brand Canada." If Canadian foreign policy has contributed to the country's image in the world, this has been especially so in Mexico, pointed out Beltrán del Rio.

For Mexicans, "Brand Canada" evokes the image of a quiet, nice place to visit every now and then and, in some cases, they see it as an excellent alternative to the United States and its unpleasant ways for their children's further education. For some Mexicans, the way that other countries treat them – requiring visas that take ten days or more to chase down, making intrusive requests for personal information, immigration agents demanding to know how long you will stay, and the way those agents look at you to determine if you are planning to ask for political asylum ... oops, overstay in the country – is disagreeable if not demeaning.

Nevertheless, the truth is that Mexicans do not know Canada in spite of the fact that hundreds of thousands of Canadian snowbirds have visited Mexico through the years (almost 1.5 million in 2010) and tens of thousands Mexicans (almost 200,000 in 2010) have visited Canada or travelled there for work and study. There are growing human links, symbolized by some 70,000 Canadians of Mexican origin (Statistics Canada) but even so the Mexican idea of Canada is no clearer.

Mexicans have heard about and decidedly admire the inclusiveness, the openness, and the tolerance of Canadian society, symbolized by the way that Canada has dealt with the rights of the French-speaking minority, treated the indigenous peoples, and incorporated the growing Spanish-speaking community and Asian migrants.

But that notion is somewhat idealistic, based more on feelings than on knowledge of the whys and the hows. In many ways the Mexican view of Canada has been shaped by rosy descriptions. "Average Mexicans have kept for generations the idyllic images of Canada that were learned in primary school ... those ideas remain, uncontaminated because of the absence of static generated in the media," explains José Carreño-Carlón (no relation to the author), a teacher of public communications and public policy at the Universidad Iberoamericana. According to Mr Carreño-Carlón the situation is helped by the low profile that the media in general, and the Mexican media in particular, have granted to the Canadian political leadership and its problems after Pierre Trudeau. And Trudeau was well liked in Mexico.[1]

It is "Brand Canada."

Yet, the reality remains that even if many Mexicans point to the Canadian landscapes and culture as reasons to like Canada, only a relatively small number of Mexicans have any direct knowledge of the country and most of them would be hard pressed to remember a Canadian writer or artist.

Of course, many may remember that pop culture figures like Celine Dion, Paul Anka, Michael Bublé, and Justin Bieber are Canadian, and quite a few may be aware that William Shatner and Pamela Anderson are Canadian born, as are Mike Myers and Dan Akroyd, but if any of them had stayed in Canada, it is likely that she/he would be as unknown as other talented Canadians are (at least in Mexico but probably in the world). It is a surprise to learn, for instance, that Marshall McLuhan and John Kenneth Galbraith were Canadians.

Like his colleagues, Carlos Marín, managing editor of *Milenio*, underlined another fact: the bad news stories about Canada – if any- are few and scattered.

For example, while the killing of baby seals is reported, every year the story comes and goes and very few pay attention: Mexicans have no connection with those animals, except now and then in a circus or zoo. There are also reports about the controversial open pit mining techniques used by some Canadian companies, but beyond that, very little. Very few Mexicans are acquainted with the Canadian government or the political dynamics of the country.

There is a general awareness of the differences between English Canadians and French Canadians and the separatist movement in Quebec, but it would be difficult for most Mexicans to name historical characters or consider themselves informed about the tensions between the Atlantic and the Western provinces. "We know nothing of their style of government or their politics," pointed out Mr Beltrán del Río.

"Brand Canada," indeed.

It is Dudley Do-Right without the silliness included. It is as if Nelson Eddy in the classic film *Rose Marie* had written the script for these long-standing perceptions. And Mexicans really believe that Canadians are great, first because they are not Americans, second because they espouse freedom and peace-keeping and humanitarian relief and inclusivity and pluralism, and perhaps because of the work of Canadian NGOs or the favourable view of the Mexican seasonal workers who visit Canada every year.

It is as if the "Joe Canadian" advertisement had aired on Mexican TV. In reality however, only a few Mexicans have been aware of the Canadian character created for Molson's.

Blame it on the media, partially on the American media, but also, and in a big way, on the Canadian and the Mexican media. More on the first because, after all, Canadians and Mexicans have learned about each other in the same way and through the same lens: the lens of American eyes and interpretations.

On 19 September 1985, as a correspondent for the Mexican media, I found myself in the Canadian Broadcasting Corporation (CBC) studios in Washington trying to describe the meaning of the still incoherent images sent from Mexico City after a punishing earthquake. Years later, I found myself, all too often, exchanging with my Canadian colleagues in DC the outtakes of our countries' representatives on the NAFTA negotiations. Washington, DC is the place for information exchange between Canadians and Mexicans.

But as always, as the old Mexican joke goes, we found that the biggest obstacle between us was the United States.

There is only one Canadian journalist who has spent enough time in Mexico to be considered a real expert. Brigitte Morisette has been in Mexico for more than twenty-five years working basically for the French division of Radio Canada. But there are no English Canadian reporters in Mexico – except those who somehow have managed to be hired by American or UK companies.

And representatives of the Mexican media in Canada are virtually non-existent, unless we are talking about Alberto Rabilotta, an Argentinian-Canadian newsman who works from Montreal and occasionally writes about Mexican concerns.

According to the Canadian government, every year a few thousand Mexicans visit Canada as seasonal workers (18,010 in 2010) or students (2,925 in 2010), a number that may be increased by a few thousand temporary students attending summer courses.

In Mexico no better idea of Canada exists now than before the signing of the North American Free Trade Agreement, when Mexicans learned that Americans were not especially looking forward to having Mexico join a commercial community in North America and Canadians considered Mexico a noisy and a not exactly a welcome interloper in the "special relationship" that, despite Richard Nixon's claims, Canada believes it has with its neighbour to the south.

In March 2001, for instance, then Prime Minister Jean Chrétien presented himself in Washington to meet the recently inducted president George W. Bush, primarily to ensure the preservation of a tradition – that the first head of government to meet the new American chief executive is the prime minister of Canada. That tradition was felt to be "threatened" by the links between Bush, a former Texas governor, and Mexico. The source of the "threat" was the 2000 election of Vicente Fox, the first president in eighty years who was not from the Partido Revolucionario Institucional (PRI – Institutional Revolutionary Party) but rather from the traditional opposition National Action Party (PAN).

For Mexicans it was somewhat surprising to find out that the Canadians, ever so independent, ever so ready to present themselves as an alternative in international policy, could be so jealous of their links to the United States. Then again, perhaps Canadians are like Mexicans in the sense that our nationalism is very much based not only on who we are but on who we are not. And each country is very intent on asserting that it is not American. Joe Canadian is a character that could be very appealing for Mexicans, if we knew it, if only for the sense of pride in not being an American.

But Molson's, the Joe Canadian sponsor, went the same way as Corona, the pride of Mexican beers, sold for a big chunk of money to American brewers, Molson's to Coors, Corona to Anheuser-Busch. Yet, the Joe

Canadian message could touch a nerve in Mexico. After all, we deal with some very similar issues and the heavy presence of the same neighbour.

Beyond anything else, the question is, what to do?

Obviously, it would be desirable to have a better, bigger, and more direct exchange of information between both countries. But this would require the open intervention of our governments and a political decision, especially by the Canadian government.

It is highly unlikely that the news media in the two countries will have a sudden rush of interest in the other. In purely economic and public interest terms, it does not make sense for news organizations, either Canadian or Mexican, to exchange correspondents.

However, it would be convenient if both countries were more convinced of the strategic importance of the other. Both are neighbours to the United States and are – like it or not – part of a North American economic unit; acting together, they may have a bigger impact on that overwhelmingly powerful neighbour than each has on its own or in competition with the other, and thus both should plan for a better mutual understanding.

Does that mean that the governments should have a better public information policy? At least in the case of Canada, yes. As good as it is, and despite "Brand Canada," image alone will go only so far in the long term, especially if you want an economic partner and a political or strategic ally that should not be disappointed by reality. If nothing else, it may be desirable to have an identity that is not shaped through the views of the neighbour or seen through their lens, as nice and as pleasant as they appear to be nowadays.

The Mexican government has a responsibility of its own, certainly; it must help to educate Mexican public opinion but it also should also foster the participation of the Canadian government in building knowledge upon what is already a favourable image in Mexico.

And yes, it could be tempting to leave things alone. Why should Canada strive to be better known when it is already appreciated? It is a question begging for an answer.

But then again, and speaking from a Mexican point of view, if Dudley Do-Right can be considered among the most representative characters of your country, you may want to do something about that image.

NOTE

1 José Carreño-Carlón, interview by the author, 28 April 2011.

New Poles of Power and Influence

DAVID PARKS

The success of the North American project will depend on the degree to which Mexico and Canada can develop a bilateral relationship of significant value in the face of the two much stronger and historic cross-border relationships. The absence of a strong Mexico–Canada partnership of course supports the position of skeptics from all countries that NAFTA is and will always be nothing more than a trade arrangement, and to expect more is both unrealistic and ignorant of the continental context. It is the position of this paper that the North American project is not dead – despite a lack of strategic trilateral engagement by federal governments, academia, and civil society – and that the bilateral Canada-Mexico relationship is enhanced, and in some cases driven, by an emerging set of often unmanaged relationships between the provincial and state governments of the two federal countries. In a short space, the paper will examine aspects of the decentralization of Mexico's states, provide a brief overview of the increase in international activity between Mexican states and Canadian provinces, address the importance of this subnational diplomacy in both the bilateral and trilateral context of North America, and the challenges and opportunities faced by subnational governments of Canada and Mexico to increase subnational co-operation and develop a more profound and lasting partnership between the two countries. Finally, the paper will identify key actions that could be undertaken to strengthen and focus the institutional linkages between the Mexican states and Canadian provinces.

TWO VERY DIFFERENT FEDERATIONS

Both Canada and Mexico have federal systems of multi-tiered governance, and it is important to recognize the differences between the two countries' federal design, both as outlined in their constitutions and in the practice of intergovernmental relations. The Canadian federation is heavily decentralized, both on paper and in practice, while Mexico's states struggle to reconcile their constitutionally guaranteed autonomy with their meagre own-source revenues vis-à-vis their Canadian counterparts. Mexican states are required to consult Mexico's Exterior Relations department prior to signing agreements, while Canadian provinces only do this if the agreement in question impedes on federal jurisdiction. It should be noted that the relationships between all governments in Canada and Mexico are influenced to some degree by the presence of a third federation in North America, the United States of America. Even if many of the challenges facing the region will require trilateral co-operation, this paper submits that enhanced relationships between Canadian provinces and Mexican states will contribute to stronger bilateral – and even trilateral – relationships between the federations of North America.

A DECENTRALIZING MEXICO

Although Mexico remains a very centralized federation when compared to Canada, Mexican states have experienced a considerable degree of decentralization in the past two decades, particularly in the education and health sectors. Fiscal decentralization, however, remains incomplete, as the vast majority of state and local government revenue comes from direct federal transfers. In 1998, Ramo 33 established the orderly transfer of funds from the federal to the state and local governments, in large part to cover subnational expenditures in decentralized areas. Originally conceived to fund five expenditure areas, Ramo 33 has now expanded to cover eight areas. These funds are conditional (*aportaciones*), and the federal government maintains considerable control over the policy development of these areas. Mexican states do receive unconditional transfers from the federal government (*participaciones*) that, when combined with the aforementioned earmarked funds, can form 80 percent or more of a state's revenues. Own-source revenues continue to lag, and the current fiscal arrangements provide little incentive for a state to increase its own source revenues. Additionally, states receive unconditional transfers from the Oil Revenue Stabilization Fund, which further reduces incentive for state governments to expand their revenue base.

ECONOMIC DEVELOPMENT AND INNOVATION

In the last twenty-five years Mexico has gone from being just an oil-exporting country to becoming a major exporter of manufactured goods, including vehicles, auto parts, clothing, and electronics, to the United States and Canada. Despite this jump forward, economic growth in the 2000s lagged behind other global competitors, while the benefits of economic activity have not alleviated widespread poverty in many regions of the country. This has been attributed to a combination of several factors which include a tightly controlled access to credit, recurring foreign exchange crises, ease of conducting business in the informal sector, strong competition from other manufacturing countries, and the outmigration to the United States of unemployed and underemployed workers. While Mexico has focused on increasing its competitiveness through improved regulation, single window service delivery for business start-ups, and investments in infrastructure, it has neglected the area of innovation. Although there are important areas of domestic innovation, such as biotechnology and energy research, they form a very small part of the economy and there is a sense that the country's economy is one of branch plants: products are made in Mexico rather than created in Mexico.

While federal economic development policy rendered mixed results in the last decade, there have been many positive developments at the state level, particularly in the north of the country. These success stories are in many cases the result of co-operation between the federal and state governments, as well as the private sector. In 2011 IBM opened a Centre for Innovation in Mexico City, a strong indication that global business sees Mexico moving up the technology value chain, beyond manufacturing, toward design, development, and R&D. The states of Jalisco, Nuevo León, and Mexico, among others, now have centres for innovation and information technology to join state and federal actors together to promote science and technology development at the state level, specifically the "mixed funds" program of the National Science and Technology Council. There are several other federal innovation funds that can be accessed by state governments, including the FORDECYT (Institutional Fund for Regional Development for Science, Tech and Innovation) that provides support for clustered projects, organized around theme and geographic proximity.

States including Coahuila, Baja California, and Nuevo León have invested heavily in universities and technical schools to meet specific labour needs. This has made them doubly competitive – an educated and trained workforce for employers, as well as an education destination within Mexico. Other states have engaged in housekeeping in order to improve access to credit for infrastructure projects and make them more attractive for outside investment. Michoacán, Zacatecas, and Quintana Roo have all worked to improve financial management, including the adoption of standardized accounting practices, increased transparency tools, and professionalization of state treasury. Many states have worked to improve regulation, and have either harmonized or eliminated repetitive paperwork requirements for businesses wishing to set up in their jurisdiction.

PRESSURES TO RECENTRALIZE PUBLIC SECURITY

The last twenty years in Mexico have seen considerable decentralization of public security faculties from the federal to state and municipal governments. Historically, the state capitals did not even have their own municipal police forces; the governor would use the state police to operate in the state capital. The 1996 constitutional reform enshrined the rights of all municipalities to provide autonomous policing, and almost all state capitals now have their own police force. Drug trafficking and the presence of organized crime became more visible after 2000, at which point mayors and governors demanded more resources to combat these criminal elements. All orders of government, including the federal government under President Vicente Fox, were in general agreement that further political decentralization was warranted in order to meet these challenges.

This optimistic view of empowered local governments has been tempered somewhat by the escalating levels of drug-related violence in Mexico. President Calderón's war on organized crime, launched at the beginning of his 2006 mandate, has raised questions about the ability of municipal governments to deal with the rising threat posed to public safety by criminals. Referencing the many cases of corruption in municipal police forces, as well as the fact that local police forces are often more poorly armed than the criminals they are fighting, many of President Calderón's political allies, as well as the National Conference of Governors (CONAGO), are supportive of his attempts to reform policing in Mexico through the elimination of over 2000 municipal police forces. Although, in many cases, the municipal police would be rolled into expanded state-level security forces, critics of this recentralization point to the many cases of corruption in state and federal police forces, and also question whether state police forces could meet the security needs of local communities. This shift in the federal government's policy direction does raise questions about how Mexico's decentralization project will continue, and whether increased local government autonomy is possible in the context of the current anti-crime agenda.

SUBNATIONAL DIPLOMACY IN MEXICO AND CANADA

One area of subnational activity in Mexico that has exploded over the past decade is diplomacy. Mexican states are increasingly active on the international stage, in areas of economy and commerce but also in the political arena. Every state government has an office or, in some cases, a department tasked with managing international relations, and several states have representation offices in the United States, in areas with significant migrant populations from their jurisdictions. In 2009, twelve states and the Federal District founded the Association of International Affairs Offices of the States, an institution tasked with coordinating states' international activities, both domestically and internationally. While the Federal constitution does not prohibit subnational governments from participating in international relations, it does not permit these entities to sign treaties with other governments. For this reason, most of the "agreements" signed by Mexican states are referred to as memorandums, commitments, declarations of co-operation, etc. Additionally, all subnational governments are required to have international agreements approved by Mexico's Foreign Affairs Ministry (SRE) prior to signature, as well as to have the signed agreement registered once it has been signed.

Unlike Mexican state governments, Canadian provinces are not required to report to the Canadian government on international agreements that are signed with other subnational governments unless the agreement infringes on federal government jurisdiction. Compared with their Mexican counterparts, most provinces have not institutionalized international affairs in the government structure (Alberta, Ontario, and Quebec are the exception). In many cases, a single office manages international and domestic intergovernmental affairs, and there can be poor communication between this office and other government departments. As happens in Mexico, stories abound of signed co-operation agreements between subnational governments that are discovered after they have expired, due not to any ill will or lack of interest but rather to staff turnover or broken lines of communication. As a result, there is a movement within many provincial governments to require all departments to submit signed international co-operation agreements to the Intergovernmental Affairs departments, which are often located within the provinces' prime ministers' offices. It is hoped that such centralization of information will lead to improved implementation of the agreements.

EXISTING SUBNATIONAL TIES
BETWEEN MEXICO AND CANADA

While the government of Canada does not maintain a registry of the international commitments signed between Canadian provinces and their

Mexican counterparts, the Foreign Ministry of Mexico has documented twenty-three mutual co-operation agreements signed between 1998 and 2009. This is a conservative figure, as Mexican states historically have provided this information on a voluntary basis. Areas of co-operation are related primarily to trade, followed by agriculture, forestry, and environmental management. Mexico's registry reveals that there has been a significant increase in state-provincial engagement since 2006, led by a small number of constituent units: the provinces of Quebec, Alberta, Ontario, Manitoba, and British Columbia, and the states of Nuevo León, Jalisco, Campeche, the Federal District, and Veracruz. Many of these exchanges are thematic or sector-based; for example, Quebec has recently organized visits focusing on the aerospace industry to four states in Mexico. Additionally, there are more than 200 agreements registered between Canadian and Mexican universities, facilitating the movement of faculty and students between the two countries. Since education falls under the jurisdiction of Canada's provinces, co-operation in this field provides an important area of subnational exchange. This is demonstrated in the Alberta-Jalisco relationship, where the dynamic trade relationship is further strengthened by the movement of more than 5,000 students between the two jurisdictions over the past decade.

Public safety is one of the most important governance challenges faced by Mexico's three orders of government. Bilaterally, Canada has provided police training assistance to Mexico's federal government through the Royal Canadian Mounted Police (RCMP) college for mid-level and senior police executives from Mexico. Direct provincial-state engagement in this area is evident in British Columbia and Baja California, through the signing of a 2009 Letter of Interest to co-operate in preventing cross-border criminal activities such as weapons trafficking, money laundering, and child pornography. There are additional opportunities for Canadian provinces to support policing reform in Mexico: the debate around the recent proposals in Mexico to incorporate municipal police forces into state law enforcement bodies can certainly be informed by the experiences of Ontario and Quebec in creating amalgamated regional police forces.

In addition to bilateral co-operation, Canadian provinces and Mexican states are engaged in trilateral collaborations with their US counterparts. Given the relative maturity of subnational dialogue between US and Mexican states, Canadian provinces might be advised to push for greater involvement in regional discussions. There are successful examples of trilateral co-operation through continental associations, particularly in the policy areas of agricultural trade and climate change. For twenty years, senior federal and subnational officials from Canada, Mexico, and the United States have met on an annual basis through the Tri-National Agricultural Accord to discuss issues of both bilateral and trilateral interest that are captured in working-group action plans and informed by ad hoc meetings of technical experts. The goals set at the high-level meetings are often included in the deliberations of other national and regional gatherings. For instance, agriculture goals set at the Tri-National meetings have been brought to the agriculture working groups of the US-Mexico Border Governors Conference and the US-Canada Consultative Committee on Agriculture.

Climate change policy has presented another opportunity for regional subnational co-operation. Mexico's six northern border states, Nova Scotia, New Brunswick, and Saskatchewan hold observer status on the US state-led Western Climate Initiative (WCI), while British Columbia, Manitoba, Ontario, and Quebec enjoy full partnership. The WCI brings together independent jurisdictions working together to identify and implement policies to tackle climate change at a regional level. It has provided an unparalleled opportunity for states and provinces to lead the way in designing a de facto regional greenhouse gas reduction strategy. This is perhaps the most dramatic example of the potential impact of organized subnational co-operation, as WCI partners fill the space left by the federal governments of Canada and the United States who have yet to fully articulate their national climate change strategies.

CURRENT CHALLENGES TO SUBNATIONAL CO-OPERATION

Canadian provinces, like Mexican states, often lack the capacity to manage complex international intergovernmental relations and in many cases rely on the federal government to perform this task. In both Canada and Mexico, lack of interdepartmental communication or unclear ownership of signed commitments can result in a lack of follow-up to meet the agreed-upon timelines. The high turnover among state-level civil servants in Mexico presents continuity challenges, and it is not unusual for international commitments to be abandoned or de-prioritized by new administrations.

Linguistic and cultural differences are clear obstacles to enhanced engagement between Canadian provinces and Mexican states. While English language study is mandatory in almost all secondary schools in Mexico, Spanish language is available for elective study in only half of Canada's provinces and territories, often not until the final three years of public school (grades ten through twelve). While this is likely due in part to the emphasis on encouraging bilingualism in Canada's official languages, the fact that some provinces do not seem actively committed to providing early opportunities for Spanish language acquisition could make it difficult for graduates in these provinces to fully enjoy the opportunities available in an increasingly integrated North America. The need for expanding access to Spanish language instruction in Canadian schools extends beyond the Canada-Mexico relationship: the Pew Research Center projects that the Hispanic population of the United States will triple by 2050, making up 29 percent of the population. It is revealing that the provinces that offer at least six years of Spanish in their public schools (Alberta, British Columbia, Quebec, and Manitoba,) are the provinces that have signed the most co-operation agreements with Mexican states. These provinces are also positioned to produce graduates better equipped to communicate with the growing Hispanic population in the United States.

MOVING BEYOND TRADE:
INCREASING ENGAGEMENT BETWEEN
CANADIAN PROVINCES AND MEXICAN STATES

The final part of this paper will examine new opportunities for government-to-government engagement between Canadian provinces and Mexican states. While the long-term success of these relationships depends on the commitment of states and provinces, there could be a valuable role for existing national associations to demonstrate the importance of subnational dialogue between nations. Both Mexico and Canada have national associations of subnational leaders; these associations could be better used to facilitate contact between states and provinces. A first meeting between the sitting chairs and executive directors of CONAGO and the Council of the Federation would be a very effective way to establish high-level engagement of subnational leaders in Mexico and Canada. Such an encounter could occur on the fringes of a previously scheduled annual meeting of either organization. The Council of State Governments in the United States is very active in bringing US state legislators together with their Mexican counterparts. The National Association of State Treasurers maintains a close dialogue with Mexico's Commission of State Fiscal Officials. Regional meetings of Canadian premiers and US governors take place annually, as do those between US and Mexican governors. Quite simply, the contact between Canadian provinces and Mexican states must be institutionalized if the North American project is to evolve past two and a half relationships.

Second, provinces and states could be encouraged to organize exchanges between public officials in targeted sectors. Ideally, relationships would develop between subnational governments who share common features (geography, economy, etc.) as has been the case with Alberta and Jalisco, British Columbia and Baja California, and Quebec and Nuevo León. These existing relationships can be deepened through a secondment of public officials in areas of shared interest – departments of forestry, environment, and tourism, to name a few. New relationships could be developed between jurisdictions with similar characteristics – Nova Scotia and Nayarit, for example. The benefits to governments would be two-fold: not only would the relationships lead to a greater understanding of organizational and social culture but they would allow the participating officials to network within their respective host governments to identify additional areas of co-operation. This could begin as a pilot project of one or two officials, and could grow incrementally as participating governments evaluate the benefits and costs of the exchanges.

Finally, provinces could commit to providing Spanish programs in their public schools. With a view to long-term relationships, language capacity will be essential to bridging the geographical and cultural distance between the two countries. Six of Canada's provinces and territories offer an elective Spanish language program, and only half of these programs are longer than three years. Altering curriculum is a lengthy and cumbersome process, but the provinces that do not offer Spanish should be encouraged to re-examine this decision during their next curriculum review process.

CONCLUSIONS

A decentralizing Mexico has produced state governments who are actively cultivating relationships around the world. Unlike the other two bilateral relationships, Mexican states and Canadian provinces do not enjoy the same geographical proximity and historical closeness. Developing these relationships will require a more concerted effort on the part of national and subnational governments and associations. The three opportunities identified above are not original; they more or less describe the policies taken by US states and their various subnational associations over the past two decades in Mexico. The success of the North American project depends on the strength of the Canada-Mexico relationship, and the strength of the Canada-Mexico relationship will be determined, in large part, by the cohesiveness of its components.

Everything is Local:
The Growth in Local
Networking Relations

JOSÉ NATIVIDAD GONZALEZ PARÁS

GLOBALIZATION AND FREE TRADE
IN NORTH AMERICA: TOWARD A NEW VISION
FOR NATIONAL AND LOCAL GOVERNMENTS

Mexico and Canada are united by geography and, more recently, by the history of regional economies. They may not be neighbouring countries, but they are close. We belong to the same continental region and the same economic bloc through free trade agreements signed with our common neighbour, the United States, the foremost economy in the world. Canada and Mexico are also united, beyond our shared status as neighbours of the United States, by our aboriginal American and Latin roots, and the similarity of certain cultural values that transcend the tangible.

The free trade agreement has been an asset for all three countries in North America, but the US government has not made closer ties with its neighbours to the north and south a priority for the future. While some see an "Economic Community of North America" like the European Union as the next step after free trade, this is not yet possible. It is not part of the prospective vision of North America. There are also historic structural determining factors of political philosophy that do not include, at least for Mexico, the possibility of being "unconditional allies without restrictions" of the United States on the international scene. Nevertheless, beyond the priorities of the United States, there are two realities that conspire to integrate us and strengthen us as a region. The first is free trade – the economy, so the experts say – and the second is our inexorable proximity, with its implications for populations and reconstituted citizenship, along with common problems and challenges. In this context, Canada and Mexico, with the intangible affinities that bring us together, have a promising outlook that is more than simply the sum of government relations among the three countries.

Relationships between the countries of the world are not limited to relations between national governments. Obviously, international agreements are signed by national representatives, but communication, interlinking, and interaction between countries also flow through connections between people, businesses, academic institutions, non-governmental organizations, opinion leaders, and, of course, state and municipal governments.

The new global economy, in free trade terms, allows capital to flow across borders, searching for markets and attractive places to produce, and in North America all three countries have comparative advantages to share. This has freed up businesses and local governments, outside the scope of national governments and bilateral relations, to interact internationally and to attract productive investment, organize logistical and human networks, and diversify government relations in the local spheres of other countries.

EXPERIENCE WITH STATE-PROVINCE RELATIONS
AND THE NEW MECHANISMS LINKING LOCAL
GOVERNMENTS IN CANADA AND MEXICO

Local government relations between Canada and Mexico have grown in recent years. Business and government delegations go back and forth more often and these sectors have established new patterns of institutional relations independent of those of the national governments. States like Nuevo León, Jalisco, Guanajuato, Campeche, Veracruz, Estado de México, and the Distrito Federal, and provinces like Quebec, Manitoba, Alberta, British Columbia, and Ontario, among others, have been active in this respect. Local governments also participate in trilateral mechanisms (Mexico–United States–Canada) as in the case of NASCO (North American Super Corridor), which integrates vertical axes of trade and logistics, and through forums or meetings for exchange and co-operation, such as the Annual Leaders' Summit on North American Relations, with initiatives led by governors and premiers carried out in the three countries' cities (Monterrey 2005, Gimli-Winnipeg 2006, Dallas 2007, Guanajuato 2008, Quebec 2009, and the International Water Association (IWA) 2010. There are also local bilateral relations between Canada and Mexico created by universities and non-governmental organizations, by the participation of local delegations in international conferences and forums, and by exchanges and agreements (memorandums of understanding) covering cultural, religious, scientific, and technical co-operation issues, among others.

As governor of Nuevo León, an industrial and progress-oriented border state in the north of Mexico, I had the opportunity to contribute to local government relations and witness their dynamics. We interacted in the government sphere, and in promoting exchanges between our regional economies and the provinces of Quebec, Manitoba, Alberta, British Columbia, and Ontario. Premiers Jean Charest and Gary Doer visited Monterrey twice, and I visited various Canadian provinces as the head of delegations of officials and businesspeople. The relationship with Quebec, for example, has been close and edifying. Quebec attended the Universal Cultures Forum of Monterrey (Fórum Universal de las Culturas de Monterrey) in 2007; the universities of Nuevo León and Sherbrooke established a Quebec program at the Universidad Autónoma de Nuevo León and a Nuevo León program in Quebec; the Centre of Quebec Studies was created in Nuevo León, as was the Quebec Business Centre and the International Exhibition Centre, Cintermex. Cultural, scientific, environmental, industrial, and trade exchanges have expanded greatly and continue to grow under my state's new administration.

This new type of relationship has not been sufficiently studied, exploited, and supported in order to strengthen ties between our two countries. There are no systematized records of the work done and agreements entered into at the local level; no institutional mechanisms have been established for associations of government representatives from both countries; no bodies have been created to communicate strategies and activities to national government authorities in charge of foreign policy and the economy; and, so far, no one has managed to describe and measure the advantages and strengths of this new side of the relationship between two countries that are both trade allies and close in proximity.

The challenge is to put the local factor on the strategic agenda of Canada and Mexico as a vehicle for strengthening the relationship between the two countries and for driving proposals that would harness the energy and capacity of local actors.

IDEAS TO STRENGTHEN THE LOCAL SIDE OF THE NEW CANADA-MEXICO RELATIONSHIP

In the first years of the twenty-first century, our experience in several areas – relations in an era of free trade, the integration of geo-economic blocs, virtual proximity brought about by the communications technology revolution, and efforts to share mutual advantages to compete more successfully in the context of globalization – points to an important conclusion. There is a new type of government actor on the scene who moves in both government spaces and local spheres. These actors are already playing an increasingly important role, and can become more effective instruments for exchange and for stronger relations between countries.

The challenge is to find ways to empower these new local agents in order to better channel their efforts and energy, to ensure that their contributions are not lost over time, that, rather than rivalling the foreign ministries and federal agencies, they can create synergies with them and that there can be an interwoven set of relationships that can act as both a platform and springboard for greater understanding and consolidation between the public and private spheres of regions and nations.

Several proposals for empowering local agents have arisen out of expert meetings promoted by the Mexico-Canada Initiative, sponsored by FOCAL and COMEXI.

1 Document the history of an emerging relationship

One of the first requirements is the gathering of documents that testify to what has been accomplished in the last ten years of relations between local authorities and institutions in both countries. This archive must be as complete as possible. It should include agreements and memorandums of understanding, reports of meetings and visits, the conclusions of forums, and the speeches and statements of participating presidents, prime ministers, governors, mayors, association leaders, and opinion leaders.

2 Build canals rather than dams in federal government spheres in order to channel local initiatives

The dynamic between the foreign ministries and federal bodies of our two countries has generally underestimated, overlooked, and sometimes even created obstacles to local initiatives that do not fall under their jurisdiction and are not handled by them. There is a certain resistance to accepting or validating memorandums of understanding or non-binding agreements between local authorities on issues that do not compromise either nation's sovereignty, though this resistance is slowly giving way. The demands and proposals that arise out of non-federal forums make their way with great difficulty, if at all, to cabinet members, and they are rarely considered at bi-national meetings of federal parliamentarians or members of the executive.

Not only should the personnel within the foreign ministries and economic and trade departments responsible for relations between the two countries consider local government initiatives to be of strategic interest; they should go further and become sources of guidance and assistance for these initiatives. There has been some progress in recent years, but it is important to build on that progress and translate this different attitude into public policies within their administrative purview. The embassies' active participation in such processes, which we have seen recently, also provides very important support for these efforts.

> 3 *Reappraise and support specialized forums and non-*
> *governmental mechanisms that contribute to the*
> *relationship between the two countries*

Forums like the North American Hemisphere Summits, organized by local authorities, and NASCO meetings, among others, are very useful opportunities to hear what local actors have to say, and to consolidate relations closer to regional economies and people. In particular, by supporting the Canadian and Mexican leaders of these tripartite initiatives, Canada and Mexico can secure greater involvement on the part of our common neighbour, the United States. The logistical corridors that unite Canada and Mexico are a specific area where NASCO can help make the exchange of goods and merchandise between the two countries more effective.

> 4 *Promote communication between bodies that represent*
> *the local authorities in both countries*

Both Mexico and Canada have mechanisms to represent state and provincial governments. In our country, that mechanism is the National Conference of Governors, (CONAGO), and in Canada, it is the Council of the Federation. In Mexico's case, CONAGO has a Technical Secretariat and an International Trade and Affairs Commission made up of governors. A connection should be established that would follow up on those relations-related issues for which there is universal consensus, and so give weight to proposals made to national governments. CONAGO could invite a Canadian premier to discuss the issue of efforts made in local spheres, in the mutual interest of strengthening the relationship between our two countries.

> 5 *Advance and institutionalize the economic exchange*
> *relationship through strategic production groups or clusters*

There are some sectors that have a greater interest in the relationship with their counterparts in various regions of both countries. Sectors or "clusters" in the aerospace, alternative energy, wood and paper, water use and treatment, biotechnology, and tourism industries, among others, have created networks of members of those sectors. They have sent delegations (public-private groups) to visit different cities in both countries.

It would be worthwhile to document relations in these strategic sectors and to enlist the support of embassies and federal officials to strengthen the communication mechanisms and networks. This strategy of specialized or branch-focused attention could bring in business organizations and chambers of commerce to make relations more responsive and ensure better follow-up of contacts and agreements.

> 6 *Advance and institutionalize relations between academic sectors and science and technology sectors in both countries with the participation of local universities and research centres*

What is true for the economy is even truer for knowledge: it knows no borders. Relations between education sectors, in language teaching and in secondary and higher education, have grown exponentially. It would .be important, with the participation of the foreign ministries, departments of education, science and technology councils, embassies, and university associations of both countries, to develop a more organized and permanent system so as to strengthen the connection in education, science, and technology, and to follow up on agreements and progress achieved in these areas.

> 7 *Advance exchange and co-operation on issues of governance and public administration in state/provincial and municipal spheres*

Canada and Mexico have a great deal to share in the area of administrative management and public service at local government levels. With the participation of the National Institute of Public Administration (Instituto Nacional de Administración Pública, INAP) of Mexico, and the École nationale d'administration publique (ENAP) of Canada, agreements for the exchange of best practices and for the administration of human and financial resources in local management could multiply. Efforts should be made to increase the number of such programs. In so doing, the relationship at the local government level would also be strengthened.

> 8 *Promote and increase the number of student exchanges through regional agreements, and advance the teaching of Spanish as a third language in Canada*

Student exchanges, where students live together for a time and learn a language, help us to understand each other better, and engender empathy, interest, and affection for lands and societies that are different from ours. Achieving these goals creates fertile ground for closeness and connections.

In sum, Mexico and Canada are economic partners through free trade; they are neighbours within the same continental region; they complement each other in terms of geography, roots, cultural values, and tourism. Yet all these features are necessarily predicated on human relationships, which go beyond government institutions. The local level is the foundation and basis of the national and regional levels worldwide.

To understand each other better, to complement each other more, to enrich the lives of our sovereign nations, we must interact at the base of the pyramid, and we must extend and share our vision, and our circumstances as well, from the local level. Only then will we feel that we are truly partners and allies in the building of a better country, a better North America, and a better world.

PART THREE

The Trilateral Relationship

NAFTA: Looking Forward

LUIS DE LA CALLE PARDO

INTRODUCTION

The original rationale for the North American Free Trade Agreement was to further regional integration and to go beyond what was attainable multilaterally. Twenty years later, the same rationale is even stronger. The demographic complementarities of the three NAFTA countries are now more apparent and macroeconomic realities mean that the US will have to move toward a much smaller current account deficit. If this adjustment is not to impose a significant welfare cost in terms of forgone consumption, exports have to increase sharply; for this, Canada and Mexico are called to play a crucial role.

This chapter goes back to the original argument for NAFTA and makes the case for a deeper integration which would take advantage of the region's competitive demographic profile and transform North America into a net exporter. NAFTA was originally conceived as an instrument to deepen regional trade and investment, and now is the time to further arrange trade, investment, and people flows to compete in the world markets.

ECONOMIC INTEGRATION IS DEEPER THAN MOST THINK

Without a doubt, NAFTA has proven to be an effective tool for increasing trade and investment flows among the three partners.

Since Mexico joined the General Agreement on Tariffs and Trade (GATT) in 1986, the expansion of foreign trade has been a key element of Mexico's strategy for sustainable economic growth and macroeconomic stability. Today, Mexico is at the centre of one of the world's most extensive networks of free trade agreements, encompassing forty-three countries.

Similarly, Canada and the US have signed several bilateral and regional trade agreements since NAFTA's implementation. When NAFTA was negotiated in 1993, the central point of the negotiations was to establish conditions to increase trade and investment flows throughout the region. Thus, the agreement's success can be assessed by looking at trade and investment developments of the last seventeen years. The performance has surpassed expectations and done so even in the presence of unforeseen strong competition from China.

- In 2010, NAFTA trilateral trade topped US$878 billion, three times higher than the trade figure recorded in 1993, the year before NAFTA's implementation.[1]
- Mexico's exports to NAFTA partners have increased fivefold, and its market share in total US imports has increased from 5 percent in 1990 to 12 percent in 2010, although most observers believe it has lost ground to China.
- Canada and Mexico have become the largest markets in the world for US exports by a large margin, representing a third of total US exports.
- Canada-US trade is the largest bilateral exchange in the world; it reached nearly half a trillion US dollars in 2010, 137 percent more than in 1993.
- Canada is Mexico's second largest market, larger than the European Union combined, accounting for 3.6 percent of total exports in 2010.[2]
- As of 2008, Canada and the United States' foreign direct investment (FDI) from nafta partners reached nearly US$470 billion. Meanwhile, Mexico FDI from NAFTA economies reached US$156 billion during the first fifteen years of NAFTA.[3]
- Up until 2008, the US economy experienced its longest period of expansion and a significant reduction in unemployment. It would be mistaken to attribute this growth to the agreement, but it indicates that those arguing that NAFTA had a negative effect on the US economy were wrong.

Although trade and investment figures matter, it is worth underlining that NAFTA's most important benefits are more likely linked to the consumer. Thanks to NAFTA, the production processes and quality of goods manufactured in the region have been standardized and consumers have a wider range of quality products at competitive prices all across North

America. In Mexico, stores now offer variety, quality, timing, and credit conditions similar to those offered in the US and Canada.

NAFTA has also induced discipline, a clear legal framework, and a pro-business environment that enhances competitiveness and economic integration in the region. This business environment and economic discipline, achieved since NAFTA took effect in 1994, seems to increase the region's resilience to domestic and external economic shocks and has helped it to weather financial turbulence.

- It helped Mexico recover much faster from the 1994 peso crisis.[4]
- It helped Canada and Mexico adhere to sound monetary and fiscal policies throughout difficult periods and has resulted in a broad political commitment to macroeconomic stability.[5]
- It protected jobs and businesses in all three nafta nations during the Asian financial crisis of the 1990s.[6]
- It contributed to the US's economic recovery after the financial crisis of 2008.[7]
- It has had a profound effect on Mexico becoming a majority middle-class country, in spite of widespread opinion to the contrary. nafta has greatly contributed to the recent expansion of the middle class; it has resulted in unprecedented macroeconomic stability and the absence of wealth-destroying financial crises and it has provided much lower and stable prices for basic goods such as food, meats, dairy products, appliances, cars, and other items that previously were of low quality or were unavailable or too expensive.[8]

DEEPENING NORTH AMERICA'S ECONOMIC INTEGRATION

With NAFTA now fully implemented and with changes in the international trade environment since the original negotiations took place, Mexico, Canada, and the US face common challenges in building a competitive North American export platform.

- Much lower most favoured nation (MFN) duties and the proliferation of bilateral and regional agreements have eroded the original trade preferences among NAFTA partners.
- BRIC countries (Brazil, Russia, India, and China) have taken on an importance they did not have when NAFTA was negotiated. Nevertheless, these economies remain relatively closed to international trade.
- Macroeconomic imbalances mean that the US will have to reduce its current account deficit and China its current account surplus.
- The retirement of the baby boomers has begun.

NORTH AMERICA AS NET EXPORTER

A main factor behind the global financial crisis of 2009 was, unquestionably, the imbalances recorded by all major economies in the world. The US has already begun to reduce its current account deficit and China its surplus, but they have still a long way to go. Most of the discussion has focused on currency manipulation, but the extent of industrial restructuring and changing transpacific trading patterns has received much less attention. Furthermore, the elimination of trade barriers can be much more effective than the competitive devaluations in transforming China, and the other BRIC countries, into large importers. In the same manner that firms interpreted China's accession to the World Trade Organization (WTO) as a signal to export out of the country, a serious lowering of import barriers would be interpreted as a signal toward higher domestic consumption by locals and a growing market for firms.

Of course, Canada and Mexico have a vested interest in a US adjustment that is based on increasing exports rather than lowering imports.

In this new international context, North America is well placed to argue for renewed trade opening across the Pacific and to rediscover its inner competitiveness.

- The three NAFTA countries are relatively open to worldwide trade, so there is little to give in terms of additional concessions.
- The depreciation of the dollar against most currencies makes the region more competitive; the monetary policy and fiscal situation of the US suggest a secular decline of its currency.
- Post-crisis, the shrinking of the financial sector means that its share in total value-added will go down and that value-added in the real economy will be enhanced. This means a partial reindustrialization of the region.
- After years of massive investment in Asia, particularly in China, multinational firms need to diversify to reduce their exposure to Asian and Chinese risk.
- An integrated North America has a much better demographic profile than Asia.

One of the keys to Canada's and the US's industrial competitiveness lies in developing co-production opportunities with Mexico; this offers not only an antidote to Chinese risk on the production side, but also a large and growing market for North American products. In a way, Mexico is now experiencing the demographic bonus that Asian countries had enjoyed in the last twenty years. More North American integration means that the benefits of this demographic bonus can accrue to Canada and the US as well.

When co-producing with Mexico, the US and Canada provide brands, engineering, and parts with high value-added. On the other hand, when plants migrate to Asia, the US and Canada end up providing only the market.

Building a North American platform for worldwide exports can be accelerated by smart government policy, particularly on trade. At the present time, it is politically difficult for the US to propose an ambitious trade agenda, but Canada and Mexico could take the lead. If there was a moment to do it, it is 2011. The United States has not only begun to recognize the need to enhance its exports (the administration has called for doubling exports in five years), but there are no elections and President Obama hosted the Asia-Pacific Economic Cooperation (APEC) meetings in November 2011.

In this context, North America's trade agenda to deepen integration could include three main components: open regionalism that includes the opening of the BRICS, cumulation of origin as a transitory measure, and an ambitious services agenda to facilitate integration of real sectors and to promote free movement of people.

NAFTA'S INTEGRATION AGENDA

Trade Opening for Economic Rebalancing

Canada, Mexico, and the US have relatively low MFN duties and much lower applied rates given the large networks of trade agreements and preferential access. In this way, elimination of import duties for the vast majority of industrial goods does not imply a significant effort in terms of restructuring. On the other hand, some of the countries that could absorb large volumes of imports from North America have fairly major barriers that make penetrating those markets difficult. This is particularly true for the BRIC countries. Canada and Mexico could work together to advance a trade opening agenda in the following fronts:

- APEC: Develop a joint strategy to push for reviving the Bogor goals and to achieve free transpacific trade by 2015. Reinstating the Bogor goals could be discussed in the context of the APEC meetings in the following years.
- Transpacific Partnership (TPP): Canada and Mexico could join TPP to further trade opening across the Pacific. This should be seen as complementary to achieving the Bogor goals. In fact, as a result of the APEC meetings hosted by the US in Hawaii (November 2011), Canada and Mexico have shown interest in joining talks to become a part of the TPP.
- Doha: High commodity prices provide the right conditions to close the agricultural negotiations at WTO. Canada, Mexico, and the US

could push for conclusion in the context of the G20 that Mexico will chair beginning in 2012.

Cumulation of Origin

Cumulation of origin allows the incorporation of regional inputs into exports by one of the NAFTA countries to a third market where they enjoy preferential access.

From the perspective of the WTO, a free trade agreement between country A and country B – in an environment where both countries also have an agreement with country C – is "perfected" by adding cumulation provisions that allow all three trading partners to maximize production efficiencies. Cumulation allows for inputs from the three trading partners to contribute to complying with the origin requirements in existing bilateral agreements.

Cumulation is widely used by the European Union, but not in North America. For the first time, cumulation was introduced on a limited basis in the CAFTA/DR (Dominican Republic-Central America-United States Free Trade) Agreement negotiated by the US as a way to foster the development of an integrated regional supply chain (that includes Canada and Mexico) that would enable hemispheric textile and apparel producers to better compete with Asian suppliers.

Candidate countries where cumulation might be attractive for Canada and Mexico include Chile, Colombia, Israel, Peru, Costa Rica, and, potentially, Brazil. Mexico is already negotiating an FTA with Brazil. Incorporating Canadian inputs in manufacturing in Mexico for the Brazilian market would be an appealing feature to a number of sectors such as electronics, automobiles, appliances, and food. Another interesting country would be South Korea. The US has an FTA pending congressional approval. North American exports to this country stand a much better chance if they are co-produced regionally and benefit from cumulation of origin.

Cumulation is fully consistent with WTO commitments and, once in place, would provide impetus for more ambitious approaches in the non-agriculture Doha negotiations as well as the basis for advancing hemispheric trade integration in the face of a stalled Free Trade Agreement of the Americas. Canada and Mexico can make cumulation a trade priority for regional integration as a temporary measure while MFN duties still apply in many countries.

Movement of People

Canada and the US have complementary demographic profiles with Mexico for the next few decades: Mexico's population is relatively young compared to that of its North American trading partners, but its average age will also increase since fertility rates have lowered dramatically since the 1970s from 7.2 children per woman to 2.1, according to the 2010 census.

This complementary profile is one of the main sources of competitiveness for the region and it has become increasingly important to exploit this structural comparative advantage with respect to other regions.

The European Union faces the very significant challenge of a scarcity of workers, in spite of the recent expansion to Central Europe where fertility rates had collapsed well before the fall of the Berlin Wall. The European demographic challenge is further complicated by integration difficulties and recent and growing migration waves.

Japan faces the most severe challenge of an aging and shrinking population coupled with a tradition of little immigration, while China's main structural weakness has become the lack of young people to support old-age cohorts. Latin America shares a similar demographic profile with Mexico. Macroeconomic conditions that require North America to significantly grow its net exports to reduce unsustainable current account deficits, coupled with aging in Canada, but also in the US, mean that a significant labour force is needed in industry and agriculture to sustain larger exports, and in services, particularly for health care.

Accompanying charts in Appendix 1 help demonstrate how much Mexico contributes to a better distribution of cohorts in North America in 2010 and 2030.

For political reasons, the US can hardly embrace an ambitious agenda that deals with the population imbalances in the short term. However, there is no reason why Canada and Mexico could not advance bilaterally and even become an example by setting a vision for the NAFTA region.

A good starting point is to go beyond the Mexican Migrant Temporary Farm Workers program, but it is clearly not enough; more can be contemplated.

Freer Flow of People

Visas have become an unnecessary obstacle to travel between Mexico and Canada. They are important destinations for each other. However, an opportunity is being missed since travel would only increase in light of the expansion of Mexico's middle class and the growing number of Canadian retirees looking for a warmer climate. Several options could be considered:

- Air connectivity: The efficiency of the transportation network is critical to making the region more competitive. Canada and Mexico could consider open skies, including fifth, seventh, eighth, and ninth freedoms, to foster more air travel and make better use of the privileged location in North America (see Appendix 2). Open skies would not only significantly benefit tourism and business exchanges but also cargo and industrial and agricultural integration.

- A US visa for travel to Canada: Mexico now acknowledges US visas to allow entry into Mexico by tourists coming from countries with US visa requirements. Canada could implement a similar measure for Mexican tourists.
- Preclearance in Mexican and Canadian airports: An alternative to Canadian visa requirements is to have facilities and personnel in key Mexican airports (mainly Mexico City) where migration protocols would be concluded before boarding. In case of doubt, the Canadian officer might just deny boarding to potentially unwanted visitors who would then be required to apply for a visa. Mexico could reciprocate with preclearance in Canada. Flights would become domestic for migration and customs purposes.
- A Can-Mex Border Pass: Canada and Mexico could develop a safe joint border pass with biometric features. The document would allow bearers expedited passage through customs and immigration, modelled on the US-Canadian Nexus and the US-Mexican Sentri programs. Only those who voluntarily seek, receive, and pay the costs for a security clearance would obtain a border pass.
- Expansion of temporary migrant worker programs: Canada's successful model for managing seasonal migration in the agricultural sector should be expanded to other sectors where Canadian producers face a shortage of workers and Mexico may have a surplus of workers with appropriate skills and training. Canadians living in Mexico could be granted working permits since their skills could be useful in management, teaching, training, and other areas.
- From a temporary entry to multiple entry model: Most people would rather choose to have their primary residence in their home countries if given the chance for multiple entries into the host country.
- Mutual recognition of social security contributions: The mechanism for mutual recognition of Canadian and Mexican workers' contributions for health care and pension is not well known and rarely used. The mechanism should be reinforced and promoted.
- Mutual recognition of professional degrees: nafta already encourages the mutual recognition of professional degrees but little has actually been accomplished. Canada and Mexico can move bilaterally for key professions without waiting for the US.
- A major scholarship fund for undergraduate and graduate students: Student exchanges between Canada and Mexico have grown

but are still well below their potential. An agreement between Canadian premiers and Mexican governors could be pursued to multiply the number of exchanges through an ambitious granting of two-way scholarships.

- A major teacher exchange and training program: This would contribute to the transfer of best practices and the upgrading of teaching and it would facilitate and promote student exchanges. It would also allow the recruiting of Mexican language teachers to teach Spanish in Canada.

CONCLUSIONS

For demographic and macroeconomic reasons, the original arguments for NAFTA are more than ever applicable. Now that the agreement is fully and successfully implemented it is time to structure regional trade and investment to enhance competitiveness, not only with a view of increasing intra-NAFTA trade but to transform North America into a net exporter. Canada and Mexico are well positioned to take the lead in proposing trade and further integration measures to enhance regional competitiveness.

It makes sense to recognize that North America's export supply is much richer than the US's, Canada's, or Mexico's alone. To do so the three North American countries must pursue a deeper and real integration of the region, one based on comparative advantages given by a favourable joint demographic profile, the necessary reindustrialization of the region, and the need to diversify Asian and Chinese risk. Paradoxically, the integration proposed in this chapter is premised on open regionalism, with no preferences, but insisting on the opening of crucial markets, particularly the BRICs. The success of the integration also depends on investing in human capital and having the necessary skilled labour force to be truly competitive. To this end, a series of measures can be implemented to allow a freer movement of people in the region. If this goal is unfeasible trilaterally, then Canada and Mexico should move forward bilaterally to foster competitiveness and ultimately improve North America's attractiveness vis-à-vis other regions of the world.

Appendix 1

United States

2010

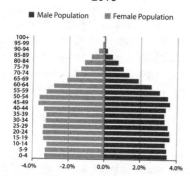

Population (in millions): 310.2

2030

Population (in millions): 373.5

Mexico

2010

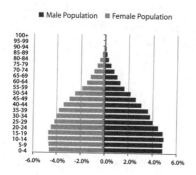

Population (in millions): 112.5

2030

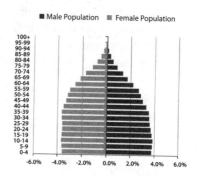

Population (in millions): 135.2

Canada

2010

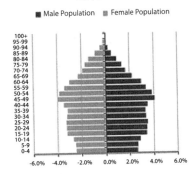

Population (in millions): 33.8

2030

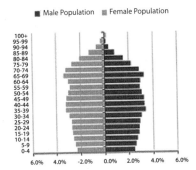

Population (in millions): 38.6

North America

2010

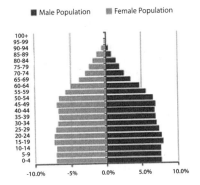

Source: US Census Bureau

2030

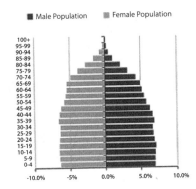

Appendix 2

Freedom	Description	Example
5th	The right to fly between two foreign countries during flights while the flight originates or ends in one's own country	a Mexican company flies from Cancún to Toronto, picks up passengers there, then continues to Chicago or Paris
6th	The right to fly from a foreign country to another one while stopping in one's own country for non-technical reasons	a US company flying passengers from Toronto to Mexico while picking up or offloading passengers in Chicago
7th	The right to fly between two foreign countries while not offering flights to one's own country	a Canadian airline that offers flights between Mexico and the US without offering any to Canada
8th	The right to fly between two or more airports in a foreign country while continuing service to one's own country	a Canadian airline flies from Puerto Vallarta to Guadalajara and then to Toronto
9th	The right to do traffic within a foreign country without continuing service to one's own country	a Mexican airline flies between Toronto and Vancouver

NOTES

1 All NAFTA trade figures in this section were computed by the NAFTA office of Mexico in Canada (Ministry of Economy), using importer's numbers

reported by official sources from the three countries: Banxico, Statistics Canada, and USDOC.

2 Ministry of the Economy with data from Mexico's central bank (Banxico)

3 Source:naftanow.org

4 For further discussion, see David M. Gould, "Has NAFTA Changed North American Trade?" *Economic and Financial Policy Review* 1 (1998): 12–23 at 20

5 "Though monetary tightening (punishing interest rates and an overvalued Canadian dollar) would have short-term negative consequences for the economy, including a deterioration in competitiveness, policy makers believed it would, along with the fiscal adjustments, accelerate the necessary restructuring and strengthen the long-term competitiveness of Canadian business in the new North America." Bruce Campbell, "False Promise: Canada in the Free Trade Era," Economic Policy Institute Briefing Paper (2001): 21–9, at 28.

6 US trade flows with its NAFTA partners increased significantly in 1998; imports recorded an annual growth of 39.8 percent while exports grew 16.7 percent, almost doubling the annual growth rates registered in the previous year, in which US NAFTA imports and exports grew by 9.4 percent and 13.5 percent, respectively.

7 According to US Census Bureau data, US exports to NAFTA partners increased in 2009 by $78,435 millions. Therefore, Canada and Mexico accounted for 35 percent of all US exports growth in that period.

8 For further reading, Luis De la Calle and Luis Rubio, *Clasemediero. Pobre no más, desarrollado aún no* (CIDAC 2010).

Reinforcing North American Co-operation through NAFTA

JOHN M. WEEKES

Twenty years have elapsed since Canada, Mexico, and the United States launched the historic project to build the world's largest free trade area. It is worth reflecting on how NAFTA is doing, to consider whether it has lived up to its potential, and to think about what might be done through trade to improve the economic prospects of the citizens of North America.

NAFTA took down the barriers to investment and trade in goods and services among the three NAFTA countries and it remains the guardian of that achievement. Indeed, the architects of NAFTA recognized that modern business relationships involved a lot more than simply shipping goods from one country to another. Accordingly, they fashioned the first truly modern trade agreement that incorporated provisions dealing with the range of matters relevant to the conduct of international business. There are those in North America who continue to complain about NAFTA and to question its value. Despite this political controversy, however, NAFTA remains the basic model from which all significant trade agreements over the last twenty years have been fashioned.

Certainly businesses are taking good advantage of the opportunities that NAFTA created. In today's world of global supply chains, it is imperative that we in North America ensure that our businesses and entrepreneurs can work together to compete effectively in an increasingly challenging global marketplace. By focusing on how to make North American businesses more globally competitive, we can muster support for such an effort. I will go into these matters in more depth but first I will cite a few statistics,[1] mainly from a Canadian perspective, that serve to illustrate the contribution NAFTA is making to North American prosperity.

- Total trade flows among the three NAFTA partners reached US$942.3 billion in 2008, dropped sharply in the great recession, but grew again in 2010 by 25.6 percent to recover to US$878.2 billion. Since 1993 these trade flows have tripled.
- Within a couple of years it is probable that these flows will exceed US$1 trillion annually.
- The Canada-US economic relationship is by far the largest in the world. Trade between Canada and the United States exceeds that of any other bilateral trade relationship. Trade in goods and services between the two countries totalled $645 billion in 2010 – more than $1.7 billion in goods and services each day. The two economies have become so integrated, so seamless, that countless firms have developed internal production value chains that operate back and forth across the border.
- Canada is the largest energy supplier to the United States. In fact, Canada exports more oil to the United States than Saudi Arabia and Kuwait combined. Canada is also a major supplier of uranium for US nuclear reactors, and Canadian natural gas and electricity are integral to US energy security.
- But what is often not understood or appreciated is that Canada is also a huge market for US exports – in fact the biggest market for US exports. For example, the United States sells more to Canada than it sells to the UK, Germany, Japan, and China combined. The Canadian market for US exports is bigger than that of the entire European Union.
- Very impressive statistics can also be cited to demonstrate the significance of trade between Mexico and the United States. Bilateral trade between these two countries has increased fivefold under NAFTA, reaching a record high of nearly $400 billion in 2010. Indeed, Mexico is the second largest US export market and its third largest trading partner. The US value-added in Mexican manufacturing exports is in the order of a whopping 35 percent.
- Between 1993 and 2010 Mexico-Canada total trade has grown over 6 fold – an average annual growth rate of 12.5 percent
- In 2010 Mexico was Canada's third largest trade partner; Mexico was Canada's third largest supplier and its fifth largest market
- In 2010 Canada's cumulative foreign direct investment in Mexico reached US$9.6 billion, making Canada the fourth largest foreign investor in Mexico

It is hard to understand why NAFTA still has a bad name in many quarters when it has clearly brought such important benefits. How does the situation today match up to Canadian expectations twenty years ago?

The Canadian approach to negotiating the NAFTA was heavily conditioned by our experience in negotiating the bilateral free trade agreement with the United States. That negotiation was rooted in the belief that the Canadian economy would benefit from closer integration with that of the United States, particularly if Canadian access to the US market could be made more certain, more secure. The government of Prime Minister Brian Mulroney touted the significance of the agreement for Canada. A great national debate about the agreement ensued which reached its climax in the 1988 Canadian election in which the agreement became the dominant issue. Passions ran high on both sides. In the end, Canadians gave Mr Mulroney a second consecutive majority government thereby approving the agreement. When the Canadian government finally decided to join with the United States and Mexico to create a North American free trade area the decision was taken to articulate Canada's objectives in a careful manner. The government wanted to ensure that the NAFTA did not put the achievements of the original free trade agreement at risk. A conscious effort was made to define realistic objectives and to avoid exaggerating what the benefits or consequences of the negotiated deal would be. Of course, Canada already had a free trade area with the United States. Canada's relationship with Mexico was tiny in comparison, so it was clear that the impact would not be large, at least for the foreseeable future.

The three key objectives that were articulated by the government were easy to understand and helped keep the debate about NAFTA at a lower decibel level than in the United States:

1. Gain free access to the Mexican market and on the same basis as that enjoyed by Americans.
2. Improve on the provisions of the bilateral FTA between Canada and the United States and protect the achievements of that agreement.
3. Ensure that Canada remained an attractive location for investors.

Clearly these three objectives have been realized. And indeed the statistics above show that NAFTA has brought real benefits to Canada. It has provided a framework within which Canada's economic relationship with the US has continued to flourish. Importantly, NAFTA has also nurtured a significant Mexico-Canada relationship. Canadians and Mexicans rarely thought about each other before NAFTA. Today Mexico is Canada's third largest trading partner. Canada's decision to join with the United States and Mexico in the negotiation of NAFTA, and the decision by Mexico and the United States to accept Canada as a partner in what was initially a bilateral project, stimulated the imagination of Canadians about the potential of Mexico as an economic partner. It also stimulated exchanges in other fields such as culture and education. Coming on the heels of Canada's decision to join the Organization of American States in 1990, the NAFTA experience also contributed to a new Canadian interest in Latin America more broadly. In a very real sense Canada was for the first time recognizing its hemispheric identity.

I now turn to look at NAFTA today and consider its future. The NAFTA is at least as relevant now as it was when negotiated twenty years ago, and perhaps more so. The negative view of NAFTA in some quarters is a challenge we face but it does not alter the significance of this agreement for all three North American countries.

NAFTA continues to serve as the basic agreement that has facilitated the increasing economic integration of our three economies. However, in my view, the NAFTA partners have not taken full advantage of the dynamic factors of the agreement that would have allowed it to be improved over time and to keep pace with changing economic circumstances. We need to think carefully about North America in a challenging global economy and the implications for our prosperity in this neighbourhood of the globe. We need to reinforce the role NAFTA can play in making our businesses more competitive.

When NAFTA was negotiated it was a state-of-the-art trade agreement incorporating the full range of issues important to business in 1991 – trade in goods, trade in services, investment, protection of intellectual property, government procurement, and a range of regulatory barriers that impact on trade. The NAFTA contains provisions that were designed to allow it to evolve and respond to new challenges. Over thirty committees and working groups were established by the agreement with programs designed to deepen and strengthen NAFTA.

Of course, it should be recalled that before President Clinton submitted NAFTA to Congress for approval, side agreements on environmental and labour co-operation were also negotiated. I believe these agreements have served a useful role in promoting enhanced environmental and labour co-operation, while at the same time not detracting from the free trade agreement.

One reason the NAFTA partners have not made full use of the opportunities to strengthen the agreement derives from the controversy surrounding the implementation of NAFTA in the United States and Canada. Neither government was politically interested in drawing further attention to NAFTA through a vigorous work program. In both the United States and Canada new governments arrived on the scene as NAFTA was being concluded and implemented. The Clinton administration saw NAFTA as important and worthwhile but never shared the enthusiasm for the project that the administration of George H.W. Bush brought to the original negotiation. This reality impacted on efforts to both deepen

NAFTA and expand its geographic coverage. In Canada the government of Prime Minister Chrétien brought the NAFTA into force but was reluctant to consider going beyond NAFTA in deepening economic relationships with the United States and Mexico. It did, however, enthusiastically support the idea of bringing Chile into NAFTA and initiated an ambitious program of negotiating free trade agreements with other partners.

In the period since 1991 the way in which business is conducted has changed dramatically. Global sourcing of inputs has become the principal way in which the largest companies organize their production. The production of goods and services has become an international activity involving the trading of various inputs among many countries. Sophisticated products are no longer produced entirely in one country and shipped to another. Production itself has become internationalized. And in this increasingly competitive global environment corporations are trying to increase their competiveness by searching for ways to lower the cost of their inputs.

Reinforcing the impact of this development has been the dramatic rise of new economic powers, particularly in Asia but also elsewhere. BRIC has become a new noun in the language of globalization. Brazil, Russia, India, and China have provided a new vigorous challenge to the American economic dominance that had been a fact of economic life since the Second World War. Of course, the economic integration of much of Europe has also challenged the established order.

These changes did not occur overnight. When NAFTA was being negotiated, it was already recognized that to be relevant for business a trade agreement had to cover more than just trade in goods. However, in 1991 policy makers had not appreciated how fundamentally the organization of production would shift. Fortunately, the NAFTA is sufficiently broad to cover most of the issues that need to be considered as our three countries respond to the challenges posed by these new economic developments.

Finally, the 11 September 2001 terrorist attack on the United States has also impacted the functioning of NAFTA. Dramatic responses to the attack were needed. Unfortunately, efforts to respond to the terrorist threat by making borders more secure also made trade more difficult. Making trade more difficult made production in North America using the new supply chain model more costly. These developments have taken a toll on the competitiveness of production located in North America. They have thwarted efforts to build on the natural competitive strengths of the three North American countries. The result has been diminished economic prospects for the United States and its two neighbours as businesses located in North America shift production to other parts of the globe where quality inputs can be obtained more cheaply. Security has trumped trade and prosperity.

Of course, providing security against attack needs to be the top priority of any government. However, in designing how to provide that security it makes sense to minimize any collateral economic damage. There have been several initiatives since 9/11 to try to reduce the impact of security on the legitimate flow of goods and services. One notable example was the Security and Prosperity Partnership launched in 2005 by the presidents of the United States and Mexico and the prime minister of Canada. This initiative was bold in design but didn't capture sufficient political energy to achieve its purpose. At least in Canada, the failure of this initiative brought into question whether these problems could be better tackled bilaterally, rather than on a trilateral basis. Most recently, in February 2011, President Obama and Prime Minister Harper made a joint declaration at the White House. They launched an effort to design a new approach to border security by looking at how to construct a perimeter security around the two countries. At the same time they established a new Regulatory Cooperation Council to work to reduce regulatory barriers between Canada and the United States. These initiatives are welcome and could well bear fruit. They deserve the full and active support of all those with an interest in increasing the prosperity of North America. But we shouldn't lose sight of the fact that through the NAFTA dynamic Mexico is part of the North American economic integration process. The ultimate objective should be solutions that would contribute to broader co-operation among the three countries and the enhanced prosperity that goes with it.

In this connection I quote from a presentation[2] made by José Luis Paz, the head of Mexico's Trade and NAFTA Office in the United States. He was speaking of how Canada and the Mexico are "competing for US attention."

Our efforts to promote regional integration were further hampered by our countries' policies that sought to "bilateralize" our trade agenda. We are all culprits. In the past years, Mexico and Canada embarked in a race to develop bilateral agendas with the US rather than working together to strengthen a regional framework.

We behaved like teenagers competing for the cute girl's attention. As a result, neither of our countries has made significant progress. Current circumstances dictate that we collaborate, work together, to successfully compete in this new economic order.

He went on to note, "Since President Obama took office, Mexico has laid out a North American competitiveness agenda centered on three pillars: regulatory cooperation, a 21st Century Border, innovation and intellectual property protection." Paz then reported that progress had been registered on all three fronts. These efforts by Mexico are very similar to those undertaken by Canada.

Of course, both Canada and Mexico need to look out for their own interest. Each country will need to take initiatives with the United States to serve interests it considers vital. However, care needs to be taken not to work at cross purposes. In responding to these bilateral approaches, the United States will address them in its own interests. It would make a lot of sense for Canada and Mexico to meet bilaterally at a senior level at regular intervals to exchange views on the management of their relations with the United States in a North American context. During the NAFTA negotiations there were frequent meetings between the Mexican and Canadian chief negotiators. These meetings were very useful in giving each of us a better understanding of where the other stood, and thus a better understanding of the dynamics of the negotiation. It helped us understand where we shared common ground, but equally important where we didn't. Such meetings today would serve a similar purpose and could help all three countries in their quest for solutions to current challenges.

Unfortunately, the "thickening of the border" over the last decade has made doing business in North America more costly and has unravelled much of what NAFTA tried to accomplish. We need to urgently look at how we can rejuvenate the NAFTA project. Part of that process needs to be a political recognition that NAFTA is beneficial and that closer economic co-operation among our three countries will better equip each of us to be competitive in today's world. We need to recapture the dynamic that was built into the NAFTA 20 years ago. We need to be more enthusiastic about the NAFTA and herald its accomplishments.

Without an effort by all three governments we may well witness reduction of the benefits of our partnership. It is worth noting some recent developments in Canada-US trade. The US share of total Canadian trade dropped to 62.5 percent in 2010. That share was 63 percent in 2009 and 76.3 percent in 2000. On the import side, the US share fell to 50.4 percent last year, the lowest figure since before the negotiation of the original bilateral FTA. By contrast, total Canadian trade with China has tripled over the last decade and now accounts for 7.2 percent of Canadian trade.

We urgently need a renewed sense of partnership to help us make the North American economy work better. We have a lot of work to do to overcome many years of neglect. In charting the way ahead, we need to take full account of global supply chains critical to modern business operations. We need to be particularly active in making sure that we root out all unnecessary impediments to allowing North American businesses to participate fully as suppliers throughout the North American region. There are still many barriers and regulatory impediments to trade within our free trade area. And many of these barriers are unfortunately not without their domestic supporters. We need to stop playing the global competitiveness game with one hand tied behind our back. The beneficiaries of a successful effort to strengthen North American co-operation will be the people of the United States, Mexico, and Canada. The beneficiaries of our inaction will be our competitors in Asia and Europe. The choice is in our hands.

NOTES

1 The following statistics are taken from three sources: the website of the Canadian Embassy in Washington, http://www.canadainternational.gc.ca/ washington/commerce_can/index.aspx?lang=eng&menu_id=45; information on "Mexico–Canada Trade and Investment from Canada in Mexico" circulated on a monthly basis by the NAFTA Office of Mexico in Canada; remarks by José Luis Paz, head of Mexico's Trade and NAFTA Office in Washington at the University of St Thomas, 19 April 2011.
2 Remarks by José Luis Paz at the University of St Thomas, 19 April 2011.

New Directions:
Transportation Hub and Corridor

As the 1990s came to an end, a "perfect storm" threatened to disrupt
the course of North American economic integration that had intensified during the previous two decades. In the 1980s and 90s, key sectors of the Canadian, US, and Mexican economies were linked in
cross-border collaboration. Specialized production centres and distribution hubs networked across the continent, enabling firms to select
the most favourable sites to enhance their productivity on a continental and global scale. Effective freight transportation was essential to
these new systems and, during these years, North America's trains,
trucks, and airlines moved growing volumes of goods with increasing
efficiency. But by the end of the 90s the transportation system seemed
on the edge of crisis. Many feared a shift back from more efficient,
low-inventory "just in time" (JIT) production toward inventory-heavy
"just in case" systems.

WHY? WHAT HAPPENED?

The story begins in the early 1980s with crashing oil prices on the one
hand and deepening North American economic integration on the other.
The collapse of oil prices in 1982 dashed Ottawa's and Mexico City's
plans to use the windfall profits from higher oil prices to distance their
economies from the US. Facing soaring debt, Ottawa concluded (and
soon would Mexico City) that the question was not whether there
would be a North American solution but what kind. Trudeau's government looked to Washington for a new trade accommodation, launching

a process that culminated in the Canada-United States Free Trade Agreement (CUFTA) concluded by Brian Mulroney's Conservative Government in 1988.

Studies revealed that, in fact, economic nationalist policies in the 1970s had not slowed the growth of trade and investment linking the North American economies. Instead, significant change in the structure of the North American economy had taken place. Against the background of GATT trade liberalization, tougher international competition, and falling profit margins, many US (and foreign) firms rationalized their operations, reducing excess capacity tied up in Canadian and Mexican branch plants. They constructed integrated North American production, marketing, and sourcing networks – replicating developments since 1965 in the auto industry. The result was much "deeper" integration, with much of the growth in cross-border trade in components, parts, and materials.[2]

Key sectors of the North American economy were restructured with deeply integrated systems of supply chains linking production centres and distribution hubs across the continent. These new production systems enabled firms to link the most favourable sites for production and distribution. This new model of decentralized corporate organization, spread along extended supply chains, was heavily dependent on efficient freight transportation and logistic capacity. During the 1980s and 90s, freight transportation efficiency improved substantially because of the existence of excess capacity, new technology (unit trains, double stacking of containers, larger trucks), and policies of privatization and deregulation which led to consolidation in the trucking and rail industries.

The Canada-US Free Trade Agreement can thus be seen not as the first step toward North American integration but rather as a response to developments already underway in the real economy. The agreement acknowledged the level of integration that now existed and reassured investors that governments would no longer (in most sectors) seek to inhibit trade and investment relations. When Mexico City reached out for a similar bilateral arrangement, Ottawa, fearing the creation of a US-centred "hub and spoke" system, pushed for a three-way accord.

NAFTA negotiations dealt with freight transportation, focusing mainly on regulatory harmonization. Several working groups, set up to continue these discussions after NAFTA was ratified, achieved some success.[3] But critical issues remained unresolved, including immigration restrictions affecting transportation workers, the harmonization of vehicle weights and dimensions and similar standards applying to transport capital equipment, and full liberalization of investment restrictions on NAFTA-based investors in transportation operations. Some agreed-upon arrangements – Mexican trucking for example – remained unimplemented. There was no movement toward free trade in transportation services. The agreement removed the protection offered to trade in goods, but the protection of domestic transportation markets remained unchanged. Nothing regarding infrastructure, including future requirements and maintenance, appeared on the negotiators' agenda. The NAFTA negotiations never strayed beyond the notion of three separate national transportation systems. The agreement provided no commitment to a "North American freight transportation system" and created no institutional arrangements to monitor transportation requirements, identify emerging problems, and suggest possible ways of responding to them.[4]

In the 80s and 90s, these blank spaces did not seem urgent. Following NAFTA implementation, cross-border integration intensified, evidenced by the rapid increase in the movement of goods across North America's internal borders. The entire process of restructuring corporate organization in North America was very much bottom-up, driven largely by individual firms and market transactions rather than top-down government decisions. Companies worked out their own strategies for building new continental systems, and transportation providers met rising demands of users. These developments reflected the liberal milieu of the period and the widespread view that NAFTA should not lead in a "European" direction. The counterpoint to NAFTA-1994 was Europe-1992, the creation of a single European market.[5] What occurred in North America forms a stark contrast to the strategy of the European Commission – to be sure, not always successful – to deliberately use freight transportation systems to enhance integration.[6]

But by the late 1990s, problems were beginning to brew. The rising flow of goods across North America's internal borders (now including rapidly growing Asian imports) was outrunning the capacity of transportation infrastructure and border crossings. Congestion was increasing, escalating fuel use and generating more pollution and emissions. The continued failure to harmonize regulations, the accumulated weight of deferred maintenance, and the impact of post-9/11 measures on borders and ports strained the capacity of the North American freight transport system to serve the economic system that had emerged over the previous decades. A dozen reports on transportation infrastructure carried out in the early 2000s by US, Canadian, and Mexican research centres and government agencies all agreed on the impending infrastructure crisis.[7] The findings are well summed up in a report by the Rand Corporation: "Capacity is overwhelmed by supply chains, disruptions are increasing, the system is 'brittle' with growing risk of continent wide economic damage."[8]

GOVERNMENT RESPONSES

National governments were not unaware of these rising problems of congestion and infrastructure deterioration.[9] As early as 1991, Washington had laid out a program designed to overlay the 1950s Interstate highway system with a more coherent north-south network.[10] Impressive sums were spent on this and follow-on highway programs, and useful results were obtained. But the goal of developing more coherent north-south "corridors" was not achieved. One reason was the localization of highway spending. Congressional earmarks increased from 10 in 1982 to more than 6,300 in 2005.[11] The sense of a coherent national, not to say continental, plan evaporated as control of the authorization of highway funds shifted from the Department of Transportation to Congress.

In Canada and Mexico, transport infrastructure spending was a casualty of deficit reduction strategies adopted by federal (and Canadian provincial) governments in the early 1990s. This resulted in delaying many infrastructure construction and maintenance projects. In Canada, at a time when economic growth, urban concentration, and US border trade were all increasing, government's transport spending as a share of GDP fell from 2.9 percent in 1991–92 to 1.7 percent in 2002–03, opening a wide infrastructure gap.[12] The Toronto Dominion Bank in 2004 underlined that "ongoing neglect of the nation's capital stock presents one of the greatest risks to the country's overall quality of life."[13] Nonetheless, some gains were registered. The privatization of Canadian National in 1995 allowed the company to grow rapidly to become a continental NAFTA railroad with the acquisition of assets in the United States that extended from Canada into Mexico. The Mexican financial situation was much more devastating, and infrastructure construction and maintenance collapsed following the crisis of 1982. In the 1990s, debt reduction drained funding from social and infrastructure programs.

Other transportation-infrastructure initiatives followed, but none was successful in creating a vision of a continentally integrated freight transportation system, let alone building such a system. Indeed, the task became more difficult: the need for a more efficient, better maintained system in the 1990s became a more efficient and secure system after 9/11, and then morphed into a more efficient, secure, and sustainable system as concern over climate change rose.

The Security and Prosperity Partnership (SPP) initiated by the three North American leaders in 2005 raised hopes for a revival of interest and enthusiasm on North American developments.[14] With regard to transportation, the SPP program focused on air transport connectivity and safety planning, border infrastructure planning and coordination, rail safety, short sea shipping, and, once again, harmonizing regulations – though nothing was mentioned about coordinated highway and rail planning or free trade in transportation. Nonetheless, for a brief moment, it looked as though some of the unfinished business of the NAFTA negotiations and other uncompleted tasks might be resumed.[15] Lack of leadership, fears generated by the blowback from groups which claimed that the SPP was a step toward the dreaded North American Union, and the impact of the financial crisis left the partnership dangling until it finally disappeared in 2009.[16]

In 2007, Ottawa and Mexico City both announced major new transportation infrastructure development programs.[17] Both gave nods toward the increasingly integrated North American production system and both contained major projects designed to create a new "land bridge" from expanded or newly constructed ports on the Pacific coast to North American markets. Ottawa's long-term infrastructure program, the Building Canada Plan, stated, "The focus of the Gateways and Border Crossings Fund will be a limited number of national gateway strategies and key intermodal linkages that enhance Canada's trade competitiveness and the efficiency of the national transportation system. This fund will help support infrastructure improvements at and leading to key locations, such as major border crossings between Canada and the US."[18]

Mexican President Calderón unveiled a very ambitious 2007–2012 National Infrastructure Program with a strong emphasis on highways, rail, ports, and air transportation. The program included plans for a new multibillion-dollar deep sea port located 150 miles south of the Tijuana–San Diego border which would, like Prince Rupert Port, create a new rail link to US markets in the Midwest and east coast.

The Canadian Gateways and Corridors project advanced more successfully (at least the Asia-Pacific Gateway and Corridor project[19]) than the Mexican, which was soon mired in funding and coordination problems. What is noteworthy in both cases, however, is their firmly national structure. Neither project involved in-depth planning with US agencies on connections with US railroads and highways, enhanced cross-border connections, potential increases in congestion, or the impact on border crossings.

The February 2011 meeting of Prime Minister Harper and President Obama announced several reconditioned initiatives – a "Beyond the Border Working Group" would implement and oversee work on an "action plan" to ease border flows (and perhaps create a continental security perimeter) and a new US-Canada Regulatory Co-operation Council made up of officials from both countries would seek to streamline regulations governing product safety and quality. While nothing was said regarding transportation infrastructure, these initiatives could affect transportation flows – if, of course, they were actually advanced.

CONCLUSIONS

Despite congestion, decay, and thickened borders, the North American production system has continued to function. Companies learned to cope with these conditions, building delay and additional costs into their business calculations. Cross-border movement of goods has continued to recover from the recession downturn. But this has been a defensive operation, and while transport users and suppliers have continued to muddle through, little progress has been made even in thinking about what kind of freight transportation system will be required to maintain North American competitiveness in the global economy in the next decades.

Creating a North American freight transportation system remains more a dream than a reality, even as reality appears to demand such a system. Railway systems have become more North American, inter-modal linkages have improved, and the volume of goods carried on North America's railways has increased after the recession plunge. But there is little sense of what happens next, except the expectation that as the recession passes, key choke points will experience more congestion. Moreover, while railroad performance has been greatly improved over the past two decades, particularly on major (Class 1) lines, less has been done to prepare for the changing demands (for example, changing economic geography and shifting production systems) of the twenty-first-century economy.[20] Highways remain fragmented. What Susan Bradbury observed in 2002 still largely stands: "Although the individual national [highway] transportation systems of the three countries are linked together, they are not truly integrated with each other."[21] There is little doubt that highway congestion will intensify and, given cuts in spending, that maintenance problems will worsen. Successive biennial report cards on US infrastructure by the American Society of Civil Engineers gave US roads and bridges no better than a D- and, in 2009, calculated a $550 billion shortfall in maintenance investment over the past five years.[22]

Even with increasing continental and global integration of production and distribution systems in many sectors of our economy, there is no evidence of planning for a North American transportation framework. Infrastructure programs enunciated by the three national government show little sense of cross-border connectivity, and reveal little collaborative North American consultation behind them. Conceived as national programs, they do not make up an interconnected continental project. Discussions continue among the three national transportation departments on a wide array of issues. But they focus overwhelmingly on regulations. No agency has been mandated to develop a vision of an efficient, secure, and sustainable North American freight transportation system for the twenty-first century. Our inability to develop and coordinate freight transportation planning in a continental perspective poses serious obstacles to the creation of more efficient, competitive North American industries.

Lack of coherence at a continental level reflects the lack of coherence in national transportation planning in each of the North American nations. Transportation planning in all three countries is fragmented among an array of federal-executive and legislative agencies and between federal, state/provincial, and even municipal entities as well. Although the challenges differ in each country, neither the Canadian, the US, nor the Mexican federal government currently has the capacity to deal with infrastructure problems as they arise, or to develop complementary processes for facilitating the integration of national transportation systems where necessary to unplug major bottlenecks in each country or at national borders.

The US experience strongly indicates that in the absence of a clear vision of a wider national-continental transportation infrastructure, local interests will play dominant roles in shaping policy outcomes, and that this will produce fragmented outcomes. As we saw earlier, highway legislation in the 1990s became a source of funds gifted by earmarks rather than a strategy for strengthening the US (not to mention the North American) economy. The same holds true for Canada and Mexico.

Even before the 2008 crash, national programs all acknowledged problems of funding infrastructure construction. In fact, funding goals seem unrealistic in light of estimated costs of providing needed new capacity and dealing with the impact of delayed maintenance. The amount of investment promised in the national infrastructure programs is dwarfed by an infrastructure funding gap reaching trillions of dollars.[23] As a funding "solution," the national programs all emphasized the need for new forms of "innovative financing" and for creating a broad array of private-public partnership programs – just as the worst financial crisis since the 1930s was breaking. The most comprehensive US report on surface transportation concludes that underinvestment in transportation infrastructure will almost certainly continue.[24]

Meanwhile, the politicization of infrastructure spending in the US Congress (Is infrastructure a vital investment or discretionary spending? Should infrastructure planning be carried out at the national or state levels? Is infrastructure a governmental or private sector responsibility?) has greatly slowed, if not halted, the process of infrastructure renewal in the US.[25]

LOOKING FORWARD

The transportation infrastructure crisis arrives at a moment full of uncertainty arising from what scenario builders call "known unknowns" – that is, factors which are known to exist but whose impact cannot be estimated. For example, we assume that the "Great Recession" tracks "normal" patterns and that economic activity is recovering (or will recover in the near, certainly not distant, future). The crisis might represent, however, emerging structural changes in the global economy, and normal patterns may not resume. Technology-driven changes in fuel, engines, and the design of ships, planes, trains, and trucks could alter transportation infrastructure requirements and patterns. Global production and trade patterns may change – perhaps with a crisis in China, less trans-Pacific trade, or more trade from Latin America. New environmental regulations already affect freight transportation costs, routes, and infrastructure needs and their impact is likely to increase in the near future. The era of easy linear projections for transportation planning is surely over.

Meanwhile, mistrust has increased along the internal borders of North America. Some Canadian leaders have backed away from trilateralism and press for bilateral deals. Immigration and drug-related violence have coloured all else on the US-Mexico border and here, and battles still rage over the implementation of the NAFTA trucking accord.

Economic slack should have provided the opportunity to launch significant maintenance and construction projects. In Canada, competition between East-West national visions and North-South continental visions continues to create uncertainty about infrastructure planning. In the US, substantial stimulus funding was sprayed in this direction, but overwhelmingly it went to immediately available "shovel-ready" jobs and not to longer-term strategic projects. Moreover, some US groups no longer on the fringe of politics seem prepared to tear down government structures, dump the Department of Transportation, and give up federal involvement in transportation.

Is there no good news? As noted above, cross-border supply chains have continued to function. Companies have been able to manage border constraints without collapsing JIT programs. Metropolitan leaders together with some state and provincial officials understand how cross-border ties create jobs and have continued to support cross-border regional development efforts, although lack of funds is eroding some of this. Substantial efforts have been registered by trucking firms and railroads to improve efficiency and fuel performance. Despite frightening violence in several areas, some production may be relocating from China to Mexico. But these individual achievements, however worthy, do not add up to a North American infrastructure program.

Some transportation observers believe that only when the crisis becomes severe enough will attention be focused on these issues. This does not, however, seem a good plan for success. For the time being, we are destined at best to muddle through, patching and mending as we go. More, of course, can be done. The smaller railroads can be much improved, following the lead of the Class 1's, and some new routes can be explored (perhaps, for example, a southward rail corridor from Halifax or a new intermodal exchange in southern Michigan). The highway system is the most serious issue with vast maintenance and congestion problems. Congestion is not spread evenly, however, and a finite number of choke points can be improved. Better border management – moving more of the security procedures away from the border itself, for example – would diminish congestion and pollution. Overcoming the regulatory inhibitions on short sea shipping and reviving barge traffic on inland waterways should be a key transport goal.[26] The danger, however, is that without a broader vision, vast sums can be spent on local and regional upgrades without advancing toward a more integrated continental structure.

What – ideally – is needed is to begin with alternative visions of an efficient, sustainable, and secure North American freight transportation system for the next decades, starting as Roberto Newell puts it, with a blank sheet of paper and trying to relate the impact of new technologies, changes in global production and trade flows, and demographic patterns. This is what the European Community has tried to do over the past decade.[27] The key is less what they have accomplished than the emergence of a vision as target and baseline for performance. The most serious lack in North America is the kind of institutionalization of these discussions (and supporting research) that informs stakeholders and constituencies and climbs beyond the repetitive ad hocism that characterizes our approach. The Europeans know well that it is a long way from word to deed, and building policy consensus and financial resources is tough. But in Europe there is at least a process. The creation of a North American Commission on Freight Transportation, not isolated like the Commission for Environmental Cooperation (CEC) and Commission for Labor Cooperation (CLC), but with a more aggressive mandate and deep ties to existing transportation research agencies, would be a useful start.

In the second decade of the twenty-first century, we understand that transportation infrastructure will be a critical element in shaping our competitiveness in the global arena. But it is also clear that in our national and the continental economies, North America continues to face significant transportation infrastructure deficits. We lack a vision of an efficient, sustainable, and secure North American freight transportation system for the next decades and we have failed to create a mechanism to think about, to say nothing of putting in place, such a system. Recent Canadian efforts to push once again on regulatory harmonization would help, of course, but without similar efforts to collaborate on infrastructure planning and execution, these partial initiatives cannot cure the comprehensive problems that threaten our supply chain systems.

NOTES

1 Malcolm Cairns, Graham Parsons, Barry Prentice, Juan Carlos Villa, and I drafted several papers on North American freight transportation during the past few years. This essay builds on our collaboration, though my colleagues are not responsible for any errors found in this article. I am indebted to Stephanie Golob for her advice on the paper.

2 See Stephen Blank and Jerry Haar, *Making NAFTA Work: U.S. Firms and the New North American Business Environment* (Published by Lynne Rienner for the North-South Center, University of Miami, 1998).

3 See "Initial Five-Year Plan for Increased Cooperation in the Field of North American Transportation Technologies" signed by Canada, Mexico and the US on 12 June 1998, http://www.tc.gc.ca/pol/nafta-alena/en/plenaries/plenary_1998/TCG4.htm.

4 See Mary Brooks, "NAFTA and Transportation: A Canadian Scorecard," Centre for International Business Development, Dalhousie University (Research Paper 177, August 2000), http://cibs.management.dal.ca/Files/pdf%27s/DP-177.pdf.

5 See Stephanie Golob, "Background: NAFTA as the Anti-Europe" in her case study "'Three Strikes and You're Out?' The Security and Prosperity Partnership of North America (SPP) and the Future of North American Integration," Portal for North America (July 2008), http://www.portalfornorthamerica.org/teaching-resources/%E2%80%9Cthree-strikes-and-you%E2%80%99re-out%E2%80%9D-security-and-prosperity-partnership-and-future-nor.

6 Directorate General for Energy and Transport, *A Sustainable Future for Transport: Towards an Integrated, Technology-Led and User Friendly System* (Luxembourg: Publications Office of the European Union, 2009), http://ec.europa.eu/transport/publications/doc/2009_future_of_transport_en.pdf.

7 Guy Stanley, "Review of Recent Reports on North American Transportation Infrastructure," North American Transportation Competitiveness Research Council, Working Paper 3 (September 2007).

8 David S. Ortiz, Brian Weatherford, Henry H. Willis, Myles Collins, Naveen Mandava, Chris Ordwich, *Increasing the Capacity of Freight Transportation – U.S. and Canadian Perspectives*, RAND Corporation, Conference Proceedings, (2007), http://www.rand.org/content/dam/rand/pubs/conf_proceedings/2007/RAND_CF228.pdf.

9 On national transportation infrastructure policies, see Stephen Blank, Graham Parsons, Juan Carlos Villa, "Freight Transportation Infrastructure Policies in Canada, Mexico & the US: An Overview and Analysis," North American Transportation Competitiveness Research Council, Working Paper No. 5 (March 2008).

10 See "Intermodal Surface Transportation Efficiency Act of 1991 – Summary," http://ntl.bts.gov/DOCS/ste.html.

11 "Review of Congressional Earmarks within Dept of Transportation Programs," US Department of Transportation, 9 July 2007, http://coburn. senate.gov/public/index.cfm?FuseAction=Files.View&FileStore_id= 85049145-abf0-4af9-83c4-9189944808f7.

12 See Western Provincial Transportation Ministers Council, *Western Canada Transportation Infrastructure Strategy for an Economic Network* (March 2005).

13 TD Bank Financial Group, *Mind the Gap, Finding the Money to Upgrade Canada's aging Public Infrastructure* (Toronto, 2004).

14 See Golob, "Background: NAFTA as the Anti-Europe."

15 See Stephen Blank, Stephanie R. Golob, and Guy Stanley, "SPP and the Way Forward for North American Integration" (2006) *Faculty Working Papers*, http://digitalcommons.pace.edu/lubinfaculty_workingpapers/57.

16 A remarkable uproar emerged over the so-called North American Super Highway, a fear-fantasy cobbled together from several different directions. See Jerome Corsi, "Bush Administration Quietly Plans NAFTA Super Highway" (12 June 2006), http://www.humanevents.com/article.php?id=15497.

17 For more detail on these developments, see Blank, Parsons, and Villa, "Freight Transportation Infrastructure Policies in Canada."

18 Canadian National Policy Framework for Strategic Gateways and Trade Corridors (2007), 14.

19 See the Gateway website at http://www.gateway-corridor.com/index.htm.

20 See National Rail Freight Infrastructure Capacity and Investment Study, final report, prepared for Association of American Railroads, prepared by Cambridge Systematics, Inc. (September 2007), http://www.aar.org/~/media/ aar/Files/natl_freight_capacity_study.ashx and Association of American Railroads, America Needs More Rail Capacity Now (March 2011), http:// www.aar.org/KeyIssues/~/media/aar/Background-Papers/America-Needs-More-Rail-Capacity.ashx.

21 Susan Bradbury, "Planning Transportation Corridors in Post-NAFTA North America," *Journal of American Planning Association* 68, no.2 (Spring 2002), 3.

22 American Society of Civil Engineers, Report Card, America's Infrastructure, http://www.infrastructurereportcard.org/.

23 "Future Highway and Public Transportation Finance; Phase I: Current Outlook and Short-Term Solutions" prepared for National Chamber Foundation, prepared by Cambridge Systematics, Inc (2005), 1, http://www. camsys.com/pubs/ChamberStudy.pdf.

24 For one example, see Final Report, National Surface Transportation Policy and Revenue Study Commission, "Transportation for Tomorrow" (December 2007) 1: 4, http://transportationfortomorrow.com/final_report/index.htm.

25 Much of the debate in the winter of 2010–11 focused on high-speed rail which is basically irrelevant to freight transportation and, some argue, may actually diminish investment funds for freight transportation.

26 See Mary Brooks, "NAFTA and Short Sea Shipping Corridors," AIMS
    Commentary (November 2005), http://www.aims.ca/site/media/aims/
    AtlanticaBrooks.pdf.
27 Newell was the CEO of the Mexican Institute of Competitiveness. In a
    personal interview with the author. See "European transport policy for
    2010: Time to Decide," http://ec.europa.eu/transport/strategies/doc/2001_
    white_paper/lb_com_2001_0370_en.pdf, and Commission of the European
    Communities, "Towards a Better Integrated Transeuropean Transport
    Network at the Service of the Common Transport Policy," Green Paper:
    Ten-T: A Policy Review (Brussels, 4 February 2009) (http://eur-lex.europa.
    eu/LexUriServ/LexUriServ.do?uri=COM:2009:0044: FIN:EN:PDF).

Expanding Energy Co-operation[1]

LOURDES MELGAR

As North American partners, Canada and Mexico can build bridges to a better future through the transformation of bilateral energy relations. The energy sector plays a central role in defining the outlook of our shared future in North America. Energy is not only the motor of an economy; it defines its competitiveness. More importantly, the current paradigm shift in energy matters opens up an array of opportunities to reignite the dynamism of the North American region and position it to reclaim its leadership role in the world economy.

As a result of climate change concerns, energy policy has become central in the definition of strategies for a low-carbon economy. Canada and Mexico share the dilemmas of being producers, consumers, and exporters of fossil fuels, who are now called upon to mitigate their greenhouse gas (GHG) emissions. In addition to their hydrocarbon resources, both countries have significant untapped potential in renewable energies. The time has come to widen the focus and uncover new alternatives for bilateral and trilateral co-operation. Fostering clean energies and technologies is a precondition to enhancing the competitiveness of the North American region. A brighter future is in sight. Yet, this clean energy revolution will not take place unless Canadian-Mexican energy relations are restored.

Indeed, the bilateral energy relationship is currently at an impasse. The Canadian redefinition of North America as including just the United States and Canada has precluded constructive work at the trilateral level. Bilateral work has centred on limited interaction with provinces in traditional areas of collaboration, primarily the oil sector. The level of Mexican commitment to approved programs has been disappointing at times, discouraging further efforts. Rebuilding trust and defining a shared view of the future are preconditions to the development of an agenda of co-operation in energy issues.

This paper advances a proposal for co-operation between Canada and Mexico in energy matters. It argues that much is to be gained from a shift in focus toward clean energies and technologies and the restoration, when appropriate, of a trilateral approach. First, the evolution of Canadian-Mexican energy relations over the past decade is assessed. Then, the shift in the energy paradigm is considered, as climate considerations are turning previous understandings upside-down. Finally, the paper presents a comprehensive agenda, defining short- and medium-term objectives, bilateral and trilateral approaches, and traditional and new sectors, including conventional and non-conventional oil and gas, nuclear, and clean energies and technologies.

BUILDING BRIDGES OF MUTUAL UNDERSTANDING

Mexican public officials, scholars, and some Canadian businesspeople share the view that bilateral energy relations are at an impasse. Canadian officials seem puzzled by this perception and tend to point to existing interaction, particularly with the provinces of Alberta and Quebec. The profound differences in assessing the state of the relationship is a sign that, at least for some of the parties involved, expectations about the potential of bilateral energy co-operation are not being met.

After a decade of productive and mutually beneficial bilateral and trilateral energy relations, Mexicans are left with the impression that the current stalemate lies with Canadian disinterest in having a close energy relation with Mexico. The fact that no bilateral encounter on energy matters has taken place at the ministerial level over the past five years is cited as proof of indifference.[2] That Canada is held responsible for having stalled the trilateral effort does not improve this assessment. Mexico seems to have lost a significant partner, a valuable one in dealing in a constructive manner with its northern neighbour on a highly complex issue.

Canadian officials tend to minimize the negative outlook on bilateral energy relations. Off the record, however, some have expressed frustration at the slow pace at which Mexico responds to Canadian proposals and the lack of commitment to take full advantage of co-operation programs already underway. The dismal use of the training program for mid-career petroleum engineers offered by the University of Alberta to Petróleos Mexicanos (Pemex) is cited as an example of minimal Mexican involvement. In addition, delayed payments by Pemex to Albertan oil contractors have damaged the image of Mexico among its strongest supporters in Canada. Some acute observers point to the lack of continuity of public officials within Mexico's energy sector, calling attention to changes among high-level officials and the high rotation at the middle level, which preclude a fluid exchange.

In order to advance in the development of a low-carbon, energy secure North America, the productive exchange of ideas and high level of co-operation in Canadian-Mexican energy relations must be restored. And this will require better mutual understanding.

As in any relationship, issues have to be brought to the forefront. Diplomatic accounts of past deeds cannot replace required frank dialogue. At some level, there is an urgent need to go back to basics: Mexicans must recall how to deal with the complexities of Canadian-specific federal-provincial relations on energy issues, while Canadians have to keep in mind that, although they share the understanding of sovereignty issues and of public ownership of hydrocarbon resources, when it comes to oil, Mexico has much more restrictive legal and political frameworks. In addition, situations have to be clarified. The relationship is not well served by awkward explanations. The straightforward approach is most productive in this case. Allow me to illustrate the point.

The prevalent view among Mexican officials and analysts is that, at least when it comes to energy and climate change issues, Canada has redefined North America to include only Canada and the United States. This conclusion is based on the lack of Canadian interest in pursuing work at the trilateral level, as well as on statements from high-level Canadian officials referring to North America as only the two northern countries.[3] Officials at the US Department of Energy (DOE) share the view that, at least for the time being, Canada is not interested in trilateral work.[4] Nonetheless, at the latest meeting of the Working Group of the Canadian-Mexican Initiative,[5] which is not a bilateral governmental meeting but an effort by civil society to find ways to strengthen the relationship, a Canadian high-level official responded that such interpretations were unfounded and offered an ardent defence of the state of the bilateral relationship. Four months later, the US diplomatic cable disclosure known as WikiLeaks revealed that "Canada prefers meeting the US without Mexico," or, as a Canadian newspaper put it, "Three is a crowd."[6]

It would be fruitless to argue about whether certain perceptions are correct or not. The easiest and most comfortable stance for Mexico is to feel ignored; the entire responsibility for the deterioration of the relationship then lies elsewhere. Mexico does not have to face up to its shortcomings in its dealings with its Canadian counterparts or to the impact of the disappointing nature of its energy reform. Canada, on the other hand, could continue to pretend that nothing is wrong. The stalemate remains.

A bridge of understanding needs to be built based on the realization that energy policy and energy relations have become increasingly complex; a paradigm shift is underway, bringing to the forefront enticing opportunities but also great challenges.

Canadian distancing from the trilateral approach on energy matters has a simpler explanation: currently the country is absorbed by the significant challenge of developing its vast unconventional hydrocarbon resources in a sustainable manner, while facing potential trade barriers in the United States. Canadian commercial energy stakes are high. Significant investments have taken place to develop oil sands with the expectation of exporting the product to the United States. The delays in the approval of the Keystone XL pipeline, on the grounds that its development undermines US pledges to a clean energy economy, have become a priority in US-Canadian relations. In addition, the potential exclusion of Canadian hydropower generation from renewable portfolio standards at the state level threatens the competitiveness of power exports to the United States and the health of an established market. Addressing such pressing issues trilaterally would be highly inefficient.

Canadian disengagement has internal causes as well. In 2006, under the leadership of Stephen Harper, the Conservative party won a minority government. Domestic politics took precedence over international affairs, leaving foreign policy on the side, with the exception of bilateral relations with the United States. The prime minister rarely travelled abroad and the Department of Foreign Affairs underwent significant budget cuts. "Hard power" politics were favoured over diplomacy.[7] Some observers believe that now that Prime Minister Harper heads a majority government, he will be more active in the international arena.

Over time, Canadian diplomacy has gone through phases of isolationism and internationalism, with some chapters of "Continentalism." Some of the most productive moments in the bilateral energy relationship have come about when the pro-North American spirit of the leaders has been complemented by a shared personal interest on the part of the ministers of energy.

A case in point is the period between 2001 and 2003, when the North American Energy Working Group was established. At the time, Minister Ralph Goodale and Secretary Martens[8] shared a common view of the value of strengthening the bilateral relationship and building a trilateral approach to balance the demands of the United States on both countries, as it faced an energy security crisis.

Given the deterioration of the bilateral relationship, particularly after the visa requirement was imposed in 2009 and the Trilateral Summit was cancelled in 2010, diplomacy aside, Mexican officials do not seem to have an incentive to strengthen the relationship with Canada. There is a lingering view that priorities will not be realigned until after the change of administration in Mexico, scheduled for December 2012. This outlook is based on the top-to-bottom approach that Mexicans favour. As long as the president of Mexico does not set Canadian-Mexican relations as a priority for his administration, the current state of affairs will remain, even in energy matters.

Nonetheless, bilateral energy relations can be assessed on the basis of a wealth of information, proposals, and shared experiences, not solely on recent developments at the federal level. Two phases in bilateral energy politics can be identified over the past decade: the first extends from 2001 to 2004, with the creation of the North American Energy Working Group (NAEWG), an initiative that came about from an understanding of the strategic value of the bilateral relationship, while the second runs from 2004 to the present, with the establishment of the Canada-Mexico Partnership (CMP), an effort aimed at restoring the relevance of the relationship.

It is worth recalling the origins of the NAEWG. Early in 2001, the United States entered an energy security crisis, epitomized by the power shortage in California. The newly inaugurated President Bush called upon the United States' NAFTA partners to provide the required energy to fuel the US economy. During his campaign, George W. Bush had advanced an energy security scheme based on the rapid development of resources in Canada and Mexico. The rhetoric of the US president, as well as his demands on his counterparts, generated political tensions and raised concerns over sovereignty issues both in Mexico and in Canada. The situation became fraught. Mexico was pressed to increase its sales of electricity to California, something technically unfeasible given the limited capacity of transnational transmission lines. The search for ways to deactivate a potential political crisis led Mexico to propose to Canada the creation of a trilateral energy commission. Canada amended the proposal, favouring the establishment of a technical working group. An agreement was rapidly reached and a Mexican-Canadian proposal was presented to the United States.

In March 2001, NAEWG came into existence, with the aim of conducting the technical work needed to advance sound policy on energy issues. The NAEWG worked on three specific areas: the mapping of resources and infrastructure, electricity and natural gas regulation and interconnections, and energy efficiency norms and standards. The goal was to use hard data to determine the energy balance of each country and the real possibilities for increasing exchanges throughout the region, while developing areas of opportunity in non-contentious sectors such as energy efficiency.

At its second meeting, held in Washington, DC, on 28 June 2001, to the astonishment of both Canadian and Mexican delegations, President Bush visited the DOE precisely on the day of the meeting. In an unusual move for a technical meeting, Secretary Abraham inaugurated the session and extended an invitation to the delegates to attend the gathering with the president the next day. The delegations were taken aback in view of the fact that for weeks they had been negotiating with their DOE counterparts for a low-profile visit with no press. The initial session was wrapped up rapidly so delegations could inform their governments of this turn of events.

In his speech, President Bush acknowledged the delegations and referred to the relevance of their task,[9] hence giving a high profile to the NAEWG. This anecdote is worth recalling since, under the aegis of the NAEWG, Canada and Mexico worked closely, at the technical level, to balance out US interests and demands. Members of the US presidential task force in charge of defining the National Energy Policy informally consulted the NAEWG on parts of the content, something unheard of until then, at least in Mexico.

The Security and Prosperity Partnership (SPP) of North America, a US-led initiative, absorbed the NAEWG. By 2006, with changes of government in Canada and Mexico and under a different set of conditions, the NAEWG lost its relevance.

Currently, bilateral interaction takes place under the Energy Working Group (EWG) of the Canadian-Mexican Partnership.[10] Established to enhance the strategic relationship, the CMP provided an innovative mechanism to convene key actors and decision makers from the private and public sectors of both countries. Recently the EWG of the CMP was restructured to include an Oil and Gas Technical Committee and an Electricity Committee. The 2008–2009 CMP report indicates that areas of opportunity were identified, mostly in the oil sector. But, as a 2010 ProMexico report[11] notes, thus far many projects agreed upon have not been executed and others, which were initiated, were not followed up to achieve results.

The CMP has the merit of providing a framework to foster the bilateral agenda. Mexico has benefited from its interaction and co-operation with specific provinces, given their expertise on distinct energy issues. However, current arrangements narrow the nature of the relationship; Mexico asks for co-operation while Canada plays the provider role. This approach, perhaps acceptable in the short term, hinders the possibility of kindling a more dynamic and mutually beneficial relationship, which is a precondition for moving North America forward in its transition to a low-carbon economy.

Since 2007, the North American Competitiveness Council has stressed that greater energy integration would enhance energy security in the region and improve the international competitiveness of North American countries.[12] A shared vision and joint efforts are needed to spur the region's untapped potential in clean energies, transforming environmental challenges into opportunities and turning North America into a leader in the transition to a low-carbon economy.

The shared vision of the future will determine whether the energy relationship between Mexico and Canada has a primarily bilateral or trilateral dimension. A narrow and short-term focus on traditional areas of co-operation will respond to a low-priority approach where no common dilemmas and goals are identified. A more ambitious outlook, one that sees the North American region as an exemplar of sustainable development and growth based on a low-carbon economy, would undoubtedly require a trilateral approach. As Joe Dukert asserts in his contribution to this volume, "a complex 'energy bridge' *already exists* between Canada and Mexico. It's called the United States of America." Energy markets and integration between Canada and Mexico cannot be realized and regional GHG emissions mitigation objectives cannot be met unless the US is part of the equation.

BUILDING BRIDGES TO A NORTH AMERICAN LOW-CARBON ENERGY SECURE FUTURE

Climate change concerns have transformed the manner in which energy issues, in particular energy policy, are considered. Given the contribution of energy production and use to greenhouse gas emissions, a paradigm shift is underway to bring about a "low-carbon energy revolution."[13]

The year 2005 marked a turning point in the discussion on energy issues. The Intergovernmental Panel on Climate Change produced a somber report on the dimension of climate change and the limits of current response. As the Kyoto Protocol entered into force, it became evident that the agreed reductions would not be met. Oil prices were high, reflecting supply and demand tightness as well as the impact of hurricanes on energy markets and infrastructure. Concerns over energy security and climate change brought about an international response. The G8, of which Canada is a member, invited five emerging economies, including Mexico, to a dialogue on climate change, clean energies, and sustainable development, starting a trend of major economies summits on these issues. In Paris, a global ministerial meeting marked the return of nuclear energy as a policy option. For the first time, energy security and climate change mitigation objectives converged, challenging to its core the formulation of energy policy.

Until 2009, consideration of energy issues in the context of climate policy took place mainly at the political level, whether in the realm of international negotiations or of domestic politics. Now, countries and businesses alike are seizing the opportunities offered by the shift toward a low-carbon economy to increase their competitiveness. The North American region is losing ground to regions such as the European Union and competitors in China, India, South Korea, and the United Kingdom that are adopting aggressive strategies to capture new markets and creating green jobs, particularly in the area of clean energies and technologies.

North America is called on to take a leadership role in the transition to a low-carbon economy. It is currently responsible for 21.95 percent of the world total yearly emissions and for 26.99 percent of the world total cumulative emissions between 1990 and 2005; Canada accounts for 1.96 percent and 2.17 percent respectively of these world totals, while Mexico accounts for 1.71 percent and 1.54 percent.[14] In a business-as-usual scenario, the trend shows a significant increase in GHG emissions in the three countries in the years to come.

At the last Trilateral Summit, held in Guadalajara, Mexico, in 2009, North American leaders agreed to work together to reduce the region's greenhouse gas emissions. The effort entails trilateral action on energy issues, given the significant contribution of fossil fuel production and use to the region's emissions level. In their joint statement, Presidents Calderón and Obama and Prime Minister Harper made the following declaration:

> We recognize climate change as one of the most daunting and pressing challenges of our time and a solution requires ambitious and coordinated efforts by all nations. Building on our respective national efforts, we will show leadership by working swiftly and responsibly to combat climate change as a region ... We also recognize that the competitiveness of our region and our sustainable growth requires a greater reliance on clean energy technologies and secure and reliable energy supplies across North America. Today, in agreeing to the "North American Leaders' Declaration on Climate Change and Clean Energy," we reaffirm our political commitment to work collaboratively to combat climate change.[15]

In spite of the shared vision and clear intent of the leaders, thus far rhetoric has not translated into firm action. In practice, there has been little effort to coordinate policy across countries. Currently, the difficulties of advancing regional governance on climate policy have less to do with the limits of NAFTA institutional arrangements than with the intricacies of building domestic consensus. Within both the United States and Canada, climate policy has emerged as a highly divisive political issue. In Mexico, presidential activism on climate change has been translated into policy proposals that advance minor changes at the margins, without threatening vested interests or representing significant costs, at least in the short run.

Much is to be gained from increasing understanding of the dilemmas each country faces as the world moves toward a low-carbon economy. A dialogue on challenges and opportunities could open up unforeseen alternatives to renew Canadian-Mexican relations and restore the commitment required to implement an innovative energy agenda.

Canada and Mexico share the significant challenge of reducing greenhouse gas emissions while relying heavily on hydrocarbons, as sources of both primary energy and export revenues. Canadian and Mexican energy supplies are derived mostly from fossil fuels, 85 percent and 93 percent respectively. Canada is a net exporter of oil, natural gas, coal, and uranium, and has significant potential to increase production. Mexico, on the other hand, has declining oil production and is a net importer of natural gas and coal. The Canadian power sector is mostly based on hydro and nuclear generation, while Mexico's electricity production is dominated by hydrocarbons, particularly natural gas. Both countries show interesting potential in renewable energies but thus far have limited installed capacity. In terms of fossil fuels, they share the challenge of exploiting non-conventional resources in a sustainable manner. Mexico is exploring new frontiers, such as ultra-deepwater crude production and shale gas development, whereas Canada has been producing oil from tar sands since the early 2000s.

Under current climate policy constraints, the abundance of fossil fuel resources represents a challenge in terms of their exploitation and use. Both countries have announced GHG emissions reduction targets under the Copenhagen Accord: Canada has set a 2020 target of 17 percent economy-wide reduction from 2005 emission levels aligned to a US pledge, whereas Mexico has committed to a 30 percent reduction from business as usual by 2020, contingent upon receiving international financial and technological support.[16]

Meeting these targets will require a profound transformation in the production and use of energy. The transition to a low-carbon energy sector includes measures such as the implementation of energy efficiency programs; the diversification of the energy mix, including the promotion of renewable energies; research, development, and deployment of clean energy technologies; and the establishment of a cap-and-trade emissions market and/or of a carbon tax to finance this transition.

Canada represents a fascinating case in terms of the difficulties of complying with GHG reduction commitments, notwithstanding sharp awareness of the issue. Very early on, Canada took a leadership role at the international level, adopting national actions plans on climate change and agreeing on mitigation targets. Yet, as Peter J. Stoett states, in 1987, Prime Minister Mulroney "started a fairly consistent pattern of Canadian rhetoric outweighing policy formulation and implementation on climate change."[17]

Canada's dismal results in terms of reducing its GHG emissions have several layers of explanation. Politically, Canadian federalism renders compliance extremely difficult, given that provinces are responsible for environmental policy. Financially, in most provinces and territories, resource extraction remains the main source of income generation.[18] Shareholders are numerous and diverse. Each province defines its climate policy in agreement with the structure of its local economy, its possibilities for alternative options, and its vested interests. This explains the divergence in positions, ranging from a highly committed British Columbia that adopted ambitious mitigation targets and implemented a carbon tax in 2008, to an oil sands producing Alberta with a clear anti-Kyoto Protocol stand.[19]

Concerns about the economic impact of taking action on climate change and its political consequences are at the core of the Harper government departure from Kyoto-based policies. It is clear that Canada will not meet its Kyoto engagements. The federal government has not acknowledged the fact. Yet, it has taken the road of "less Kyoto, more Washington,"[20] aligning its international commitments to those of the United States.

In November 2009, in a speech to the Edmonton Chamber of Commerce, Jim Prentice, then Minister of the Environment, elaborated on the logic of the shift in Canada's position, adopting a strategy that made sense from an economic and political viewpoint, leaving aside "moral leadership" stances. It is worth reviewing the text both from the perspective of Canadian climate change policy as well as for its view of North America, which clearly excludes Mexico. In it, Minister Prentice made the following argument:

> If the US does not make a substantial effort going forward, there is nothing Canada can do. Our own mitigation efforts will be futile – as a practical matter, we should probably focus on adaptation. If we do *more* than the US, we will suffer economic pain for no real environmental gain – economic pain that could impede our ability to invest in new clean technologies. But if we do *less*, we will risk facing new border barriers into the American market.
>
> In short, we need a substantial effort from the United States; and a comparable effort from Canada, so we can create an effective North American climate change regime with national policies that are harmonized, consistent and free from conflict. A continental system composed of national policies and regulations that are equal in value and of similar effect, so we foster fair competition and maintain free trade in the integrated North American market.[21]

As somber as this approach may seem given the lack of legislation in the United States, it is worth noting that Canada is taking measures to reduce emissions and exploit resources in a more sustainable manner. The recently published *A Climate Change Plan for the Purpose of the Kyoto Protocol Implementation Act*[22] details actions to address climate change, most of them in the energy sector.

Mexico has also defined a blueprint for action in order to comply with its Copenhagen Accord pledge. The National Ecology Institute-McKinsey report[23] presents areas of opportunity for abatement by sector and through 2020 and 2030. It also identifies barriers to implementation in key measures.

The comparison of both documents reveals similar areas of opportunity for abatement. In some cases, measures will have a local application, but could develop into best practices to be shared between countries. In others, the definition of joint solutions, standards, or labels, could become an instrument for increasing North American competitiveness and integration. The transition to a low carbon economy opens up new areas for co-operation in Canadian-Mexican energy relations.

BUILDING BRIDGES TO A NEW ERA
IN CANADIAN-MEXICAN ENERGY RELATIONS

Opening a new era in Canadian-Mexican energy relations requires the formulation of a comprehensive vision of the future. If the outlook is limited in scope and time, it will not respond to the fact that the countries are NAFTA partners who share a geographic space and common challenges. Given the current state of the relationship and the political intricacies of moving toward a low-carbon economy, choosing a more ample view of the possibilities of bilateral co-operation requires a certain leap of faith. Nevertheless, the goal of a dynamic and fruitful relationship that leads to greater regional integration is not without foundation. The past demonstrates that, given the right conditions, Canada and Mexico can develop a powerful and mutually beneficial partnership.

The innovative outlook needed for a North American low-carbon energy secure future will require imagination that is grounded on technical analysis. The point of departure includes the mapping of the energy balance of the three countries, an inventory of infrastructure, and an accounting of GHG emissions. The regional potential for clean energies also has to be assessed taking into account proven as well as incoming technologies. A trilateral effort is needed to define alternatives based on existing and foreseen resources. In addition to updating the North American energy picture on a regular basis, the effort should include an emissions prediction and policy analysis model of the North American region in order to devise the most effective and least costly path to move toward a low carbon energy future.

Sound technical work is a prerequisite to policy dialogue. A common vision of the potential for a North American low-carbon energy secure future would allow forecasting markets development and infrastructure investments. Turning an idea into a reality requires many small steps, which could become part of a bilateral and trilateral agenda of co-operation.

Even in the most ambitious transition to a clean energy sector, hydrocarbons will continue to play a significant role in the North American energy mix over the coming years. In this regard, traditional areas of co-operation between Mexico and Canada should be maintained, while adding an emphasis on sustainability. Bilateral co-operation could be enhanced in the area of environmental and safety regulation and best practices in the oil and gas industry, particularly in the context of exploration and production of non-conventional sources.

Natural gas will play an increasingly significant role as a transition fuel. Canada is the world's third largest producer and exporter of natural gas. Mexico, on the other hand, is a net importer of the fuel, despite existing reserves. Canadian companies already participate in the downstream gas market in Mexico, and there is significant exchange on regulatory issues. Currently, the Mexican constitution does not allow for private or foreign participation in gas exploration and production; nonetheless, gas producing Canadian provinces could share with Mexico their experience of turning natural gas into a valuable commodity.

Since natural gas has proven to be far more abundant in North America than previous forecasts indicated, a trilateral dialogue on enhancing the natural gas market should be encouraged to maximize benefits to the region. Natural gas could become a cornerstone in transforming the transportation sector, which is a major source of GHG emissions in the region. In addition, abundant supply could support the development of a pipeline to Central America, a project which has been on the drawing board since the 1990s.

Nuclear energy has been called upon to play a major role in reducing GHG emissions in the power sector. The Fukujima-Daiichi nuclear power accident has generated a worldwide debate on the future on nuclear energy. In Mexico, discussions on increasing nuclear power generation have been truncated and conditions will not be right for exploring this option anew for some time to come. However, Mexico does have a nuclear power plant. Thus far, the generated nuclear waste has been confined in the pools of the reactors. Canada produces uranium and is a pioneer in nuclear power generation and fuel production. In 2002, Canada established the Nuclear Waste Management Organization (NWMO) with the mandate of studying alternatives for managing used nuclear fuel, which presents long-term hazardous risks to people and to the environment. Canada could share with Mexico the experience of NWMO and the best practices it is developing.

Energy efficiency is the preferred policy option to reduce GHG emissions at a negative cost. Both Canada and Mexico have established targets in a wide variety of sectors to reduce their energy intensity.

Canada is a leader in energy efficiency programs, as well as in the development and analysis of indicators. It has produced extensive regulations for buildings, appliances and equipment, lighting technology, transportation, and energy utilities, at the federal and the provincial levels. Given its national commitment to achieving a 20 percent increase in energy efficiency by 2020, it aims to maximize opportunities for energy savings particularly in buildings and road transportation, two areas of relevance to Mexico.

Since the 1990s, Mexico has had positive experiences in working with Canada on energy efficiency programs, regulation, and standards and labelling. Currently, joint work is underway in green buildings and zero energy homes. An aggressive bilateral and trilateral agenda should be developed in this area, with the aim of harmonizing standards and issuing North American labels in as many sectors as possible. In addition to the contribution to mitigating emissions, stronger NAFTA standards and labels would increase the competitiveness of goods produced in the region.

Excluding hydropower, Canada has small installed generation capacity in wind, solid biomass, and photovoltaic energy. Mexico has a similar profile with an even smaller percentage of wind generation, but greater installed capacity in biomass and geothermal energy. With the exception of hydro and ocean energy, provincial governments have jurisdiction over renewable resources in Canada. Both countries have significant potential to develop their renewable energy capacities.

Research and development and policy dialogue on renewable energies should become a strong part of the bilateral agenda between Mexico and Canada. Given their individual expertise in this area, each country has something to contribute. In addition, a dynamic North American clean energy market could be developed. The infrastructure would need to be put in place. Efforts are already underway in the definition of smart grids, a requirement to optimize the use of renewable energies. Despite the leaders' pledge at their Guadalajara Summit, thus far most of the co-operation has taken place at the bilateral level. Building on the positive experience of the past, Canada and Mexico should join forces again to influence the definition of the infrastructure and regulation needed to accelerate a North American clean electricity market.

The countries which have been most successful in deploying renewable energies have coupled renewable energy generation to the local production of equipment. Spain is perhaps most notable; wind generation became an industry and the motor of development of a region. But similar examples are arising elsewhere. China, for instance, is increasing its installed capacity at an accelerated pace while becoming a leader in wind turbine and solar PV manufacturing. US companies are taking a share of the market, as well as Canadian solar, which holds 3 percent of the solar FV market.[24] Countries such as China, South Korea, and even the United Kingdom have clear policies and strategies to acquire a part of the emerging clean energy market. Taking advantage of NAFTA, Canada, Mexico, and the United States could develop a competitive and cutting edge clean energy industry.

In this regard, the Trilateral Agreement for Cooperation in Energy, Science and Technology, signed in 2007, should be implemented. Trilateral research, development, and deployment could be undertaken to produce clean energy products. For wind power, Mexico could bring its manufacturing competitive advantage, as well as the support of the Oaxaca-based Centro Regional de Tecnología Eólica, which has expertise in testing and improving wind generation equipment. The centre could eventually evolve into a NAFTA certification lab. A similar approach could be taken for solar panels and FV equipment.

A profound transformation of the region's energy sector can only be sustained with the appropriate human capital. Currently, North America faces a rapid decline in numbers of qualified professionals and technicians in the energy sector. Setting up a bilateral training program could become a top priority. In light of the complexities of implementing an effective program, different agencies and stakeholders need to collaborate in its design and implementation. Yet, the benefits could go well beyond the specific area of expertise. Through their participation in this program, technicians and engineers could become ambassadors for change and integration, and a central piece in building bridges to a better future in Canadian-Mexican energy relations.

NOTES

1 This article presents some of the findings of research on "Defining a North American Low-Carbon Energy Security Regime" carried out in Mexico and in the United States since July 2010. The author would like to acknowledge the support of a Woodrow Wilson International Center for Scholars-COMEXI scholarship in conducting this research. The article draws in part on the content of a FOCAL Policy Brief published under the title "In search of relevance for Canadian-Mexican relations," in March 2011, http://www.focal.ca/en/programs/research-forum-on-north-america/canada-mexico-initiative. The author wishes to thank FOCAL for permission to use this material.

2 Since Prime Minister Harper took office, no bilateral encounter has taken place between the Minister of Natural Resources Canada and the Secretary of Energy of Mexico, with the exception of the trilateral meeting held in Canada in 2007.

3 A review of Environment Minister Jim Prentice's (2007–2011) speeches shows that when it comes to climate change and energy issues, the concept of North America does not include Mexico. A particular example is his speech of 13 November 2009.

4 Interviews conducted by author in Washington, DC, July-August 2010.

5 The Canadian-Mexican Initiative was launched by COMEXI and FOCAL "to develop solutions and develop public support for positive changes in

the bilateral relationship." The meeting referred to in this paper took place in Veracruz, Mexico, in November 2010. http://www.focal.ca/en/programs/research-forum-on-north-america/canada-mexico-initiative.

6 "Three is a crowd" in *Macleans.ca*, 3 March 2011, http://www2.macleans. ca/2011/03/03/three%E2%80%99s-a-crowd/. "Sorry, amigo: WikiLeaks shows Canada prefers meeting U.S. without Mexico," in the *Globe and Mail*, posted 2 March 2011, http://www.theglobeandmail.com/news/politics/sorry-amigo-wikileaks-shows-canada-prefers-meeting-us-without-mexico/article1927720/.

7 According to Canadian sources, between 2007 and 2009 the Department of Foreign Affairs underwent a budget cut of $639 million while the Department of Defense saw a budget increase. "Foreign Affairs Hit with $639 Million in Cuts," 18 March 2009, http://www.embassymag.ca/page/view/foreign_affairs_cuts-3-18-2009.

8 Having attended high school in Canada, Ernesto Martens (Secretary of Energy of Mexico December 2000 to April 2003) had a deep understanding of Canadian politics and sensitivities. He was able to quickly identify opportunities for bilateral and trilateral co-operation, and had a personal interest in furthering this bilateral relationship.

9 This was the first visit of a president of the United States to DOE's headquarters in over twelve years. Both the Canadian and Mexican delegations were taken by surprise. They were told that the visit had not been planned in advance. Both delegations had insisted on a low profile visit with no press. "President Bush visits Department Headquarters" in DOE *This Month* (Washington DC: Department of Energy Office of Public Affairs 24, Issue 6, July 2001): 8-9, http://www.hss.doe.gov/deprep/facrep/workshop2001/2000FROTHY/DOE_This_Month_jul01.pdf.

10 Canada-Mexico Partnership. *Annual Report 2008-2009*. Ottawa: DFAIT, 2009, http://www.canadainternational.gc.ca/mexico-mexique/assets/pdfs/CMP%2008-09%20Annual%20Report.pdf.

11 ProMéxico, *Síntesis de la Relación Comercial México-Canadá* (Mexico City: Proméxico,2010), http://promexico.gob.mx/work/sites/Promexico/resources/LocalContent/2221/2/nb_canada.pdf.

12 North American Competitiveness Council, *Enhancing Competitiveness in Canada, Mexico, and the United States: Private Sector Priorities for the Security and Prosperity Partnership of North America (SPP)* (Washington, DC: NACC, 2007), http://coa.counciloftheamericas.org/files/editor/image/grp_10_4.pdf.

13 This phrase was coined by the International Energy Agency in its *2009 World Energy Outlook*.

14 Climate Analysis Indicators Tool (CAIT) Version 8.0. (Washington, DC: World Resources Institute, 2011).

15 Joint Statement by the North American Leaders, 10 August 2009, http://pm.gc.ca/eng/media.asp?category=3&id=2723

16 UNFCCC, "Copenhagen Accord," http://unfccc.int/files/meetings/cop_15/ copenhagen_accord/application/pdf/canadacpaccord_app1.pdf, http://unfccc. int/files/meetings/cop_15/copenhagen_accord/application/pdf/ mexicocpaccord_app2.pdf.

17 J. Peter. Soett, "Looking for Leadership: Canada and Climate Change Policy" in *Changing Climates in North American Politics,* ed. Henrik Selin and Stacy D. VanDeveer (Cambridge: MIT Press, 2009), 51.

18 Ibid., 48.

19 This paragraph draws on the work of Peter Soett.

20 Ibid., 53.

21 Speaking Points, The Honourable Jim Prentice, PC, QC, MP, Minister of the Environment, to the Edmonton Chamber of Commerce, Edmonton, Alberta, 13 November 2009, http://www.ec.gc.ca/default.asp?lang=En&n= 6F2DE1CA-1&news=757C0154-3353-4BB4-B2F3-9E095A0DA33E

22 Environment Canada. *A Climate Change Plan for the Purposes of the Kyoto Protocol Implementation Act,* May 2011, www.climatechange.gc.ca/ Content/4/0/4/4044AEA7-3ED0-4897-A73E-D11C62D954FD/COM1410_ KPIA%202011_e%20-%20May%2031%20v2.pdf.

23 *Potencial de Mitigación de Gases de Efecto Invernadero en México al 2020 en el contexto de la Cooperación Internacional.* México D.F.: SEMARNAT-INE, 28 de octubre de 2010, http://www2.ine.gob.mx/descargas/ cclimatico/Potencial_mitigacion_GEI_Mexico_2020_COP.pdf.

24 *Renewables Gobal Status Report 2010.* REN 21, September 2010, http://www. ren21.net/Portals/97/documents/GSR/REN21_GSR_2010_full_revised%20 Sept2010.pdf.

Energy: The *Continental* Bridge

JOSEPH M. DUKERT[1]

This chapter is qualitatively different from some others in this book. The book is about *building* bridges overall; but a complex "energy bridge" *already exists* between Canada and Mexico. It's called the United States of America.

Co-operation between Canada and Mexico in both energy and environmental initiatives (which themselves often intertwine) will be limited in both scope and effectiveness, however, unless all three countries appreciate more fully its value.

The "energy bridge" includes a workable and still-growing network of pipelines, power lines, interacting investment, electronic communication, environmental interests, and simple habit. Credit for reinforcing it so solidly during the past two decades goes as much to the private sector as to the respective national governments.[2] But its future efficacy, as all three countries struggle to find the right models for sustainable energy systems within each, deserves renewed and closer government attention.[3] This attention is difficult to attract right now. As of late 2011, Canada had yet to fully digest the results of its most recent national election. Both Mexico and the United States were stalled in anticipation of their 2012 presidential elections. In respect to energy (and climate change), it was especially hurtful that 2010 had been the first year in a decade that the top leaders of the three countries did not hold a North American Leaders' meeting and that the following trilateral summit (announced for November 2011 with only two weeks' notice) was cancelled because a helicopter crash in Mexico took the lives of several top government officials just as the meeting was about to start.

Prime Minister Harper and President Obama dined together in November after President Calderón cut short his stay in Hawaii, where the trio had planned to confer as an add-on to a broader international conference; but the less formal Harper-Obama meeting yielded no actions in regard to energy. And when the top US and Canadian leaders met again in Washington a few weeks later to reveal "joint border action plans to boost security, trade and travel" the prime minister committed a perhaps revealing faux pas that was diplomatically ignored. He referred to the potentially significant *bilateral* agreement as "moving security to the perimeter of our continent" (overlooking for the moment the fact that Mexico is *also* part of the continent).

Political minds and political will are easily distracted from energy matters – and certainly from continental energy co-operation – unless they are wrapped in popular goals: international competitiveness, quality of life, and measurable progress toward some relief from enervating threats to either one. The North American energy bridge is actually relevant to *all* these goals, but this is not widely understood.

Political conditions make the continuation and expansion of trilateral co-operation in energy an especially tough sell. Yet, if we stress the links between energy and environmental protection, current conditions contain the seeds of opportunity too. This requires conscious effort because both are priorities in each country but with different (and sometimes antagonistic) constituencies of support.

The honest regional and global outlook for both is bleak and uncertain, thanks to tensions among the multiple problems facing "conventional" energy sources and the disturbing tick of the climate change clock. We are all in the midst of a generational restructuring of the ways we produce, deliver, and apply energy. Massive change takes time, and we should not have to wait until 2013 (after Mexican and US elections) for stepped-up efforts.

Government leaders seeking to hold or extend electoral control instinctively deny the reality that some shorter-term costs and frustrations are in store for virtually all of us between now and at least 2050. If we can get officials to admit this, it will become much easier to understand and explain that sustainable trade-offs in respect to energy and environment come more easily within a larger area of population, resources, and skills – where interactions can follow natural paths that have already been complemented by the artificial "bridge" that serves all three (quite distinct) countries.

Fossil fuels will be an essential part of North America's energy mix for decades. Major hydroelectric installations will continue to operate almost indefinitely. The unheralded but basic role for nuclear power won't disappear soon here either, regardless of Fukushima's psychological aftermath and Germany's noisy vacillation over shutting down reactors;[4] but the possibilities of continental co-operation in the field of nuclear generation of electricity are limited by the fact that new projects will continue to be sparse in all three countries.

Canada, Mexico, and the United States have barely begun to restrain our consumption of non-renewable and polluting energy in practical ways, such as sweeping retrofits and the introduction of more efficient equipment in all sectors; yet energy efficiency isn't a complete solution in itself. Both supply and demand need to be addressed. Unbiased analysis shows that the most attractive "new renewables" (wind, advanced biofuels, and various types of solar installations) cannot penetrate the market in meaningful volume without enormous cost overall.[5] In one way or another, though, bilateral (and sometimes trilateral) co-operation can strengthen each country in respect to *all* energy sources, as well as in making energy use more efficient and reducing environmental insult along the way.

There must be winners and losers as a transformation takes place. Thus, unanimous consent is impossible for any one of the thousand labyrinthine courses we might take.[6] Instead, we need to target consensus and to welcome it whenever and wherever it comes, so long as it fits into a general but ever-changing vision of future improvement.

TO BEGIN, LET'S FACE FACTS

It raises some hackles in all three countries to admit that North America already *is* a single energy market and that common environmental interests also dictate co-operation within it. However, no amount of nationalist posturing will change the underlying situation. That is why "market sense" has succeeded in maintaining and strengthening continental energy co-operation – even when "official" trilateral efforts such as the North American Energy Working Group (NAEWG) and the Security and Prosperity Partnership (SPP) have failed to carry through their initial promises.[7]

Canada and Mexico have more bargaining power in this situation than they seem to realize. For reasons of politics as well as economics, the energy/environmental interrelationship among the three is different from other topics of ongoing conversation (such as security and immigration). Co-operative solutions in this instance are rarely zero-sum games.

The two US neighbours understandably fear being smothered in three-way (or even two-way) negotiations with the giant that lives between them. Canada's population will remain a fraction of that in the United States. For the foreseeable future, Mexico will be poorer on a per capita basis than either of its continental partners (although the GDP gap between Canada and Mexico is narrowing). Yet Canada and Mexico have the opportunity to help set future agendas on energy and environment as full partners with the United States if they face facts and summon the courage to act boldly.

Since energy *inter*-dependence among the three offers net benefits to all three, many of the conscious efforts toward optimizing energy policy risk falling short if they fail to consider a continental, as well as a national, perspective. This applies to bilateral as well as trilateral contacts. It also applies to a surprising number of global issues involving energy/environment relations with OPEC (the Organization of Petroleum Exporting Countries), the BRICS (Brazil, Russia, India, China, and South Africa), and Third World countries of all types. Despite appreciable differences among the countries of North America in national interest and patterns of governance, an objective continental viewpoint also affects and is affected by energy activities *within* each.

WHO SETS THE ENERGY COURSE? AND HOW?

None of these three countries has a clear-cut energy policy that emanates from a single source. (I define "energy policy" as the complex of factors that guide suppliers, transporters, and consumers of energy in what they tend to supply, transport, and consume.) Like Canada (and, to an increasing degree, Mexico), the US embraces divided control as a major practical factor in governance.

On three occasions I have drafted the actual text of a document that was popularly known as our "national energy policy" and referred to as such by presidents; but in the real world US national energy policy goes beyond any single document coming from or directed to the White House. First, US national energy policy must be implemented by bodies such as the Federal Energy Regulatory Commission, the Department of Interior, the Nuclear Regulatory Commission, the Environmental Protection Agency, the Federal Reserve Bank, the Office of Management and Budget, and so on. These often act independently and sometimes at cross-purposes in respect to energy or environment. Each responds to a different set of constituent appeals.

US "policy" is amorphous and many-sourced, also developing in large part outside the federal executive branch. It goes beyond excruciatingly detailed statutes that members of the US Congress hail as "comprehensive energy legislation." It is even broader than the judicial decisions (ultimately affirmed or denied by the US Supreme Court) that sometimes block or reinforce the manner and degree of interaction between national statements of policy wishes and what actually goes forward at state and local levels. For example, various state authorities decide currently whether Canadian hydroelectricity is to be identified as "renewable energy," although this might be contested eventually by congressional action or in court. Other subnational actors – such as the Electric Reliability

Council of Texas (ERCOT) or the Conference of Western Governors – also influence the feasibility of electricity exchanges between the United States and Mexico.

Somewhat analogous conditions prevail within Canada (whose provinces control natural resources[8]) and even within Mexico (where state governors have gained historic influence, independent power producers of one sort or another rival the national electricity monopoly in some respects, and Petroleos Mexicanos – Pemex – aspires to act like a "super-major" in hydrocarbons rather than a completely docile government department).

This is not to deny that the top leaders of the three countries have considerable power by themselves to push or pull national movements in respect to the flowering or floundering of continental energy interdependence. On 10 August 2009, Prime Minister Harper, President Calderón, and President Obama agreed on a multi-pronged program to achieve low-carbon development goals and pledged that "In order to facilitate these actions, we will work cooperatively to develop and follow up on a Trilateral Working Plan and submit a report of results *at our next North American Leaders Summit in 2010*"[9] (emphasis added). If they had carried through, the situation would be far brighter than it is; but Canada defaulted on hosting the promised 2010 follow-up summit.

The leaders also pledged at that 2009 summit in Cancun to complete a "North American Carbon Storage Atlas" by April 2012.[10] When and if it is completed, such a report should offer a framework for the pursuit of a harmonized continental strategy in carbon capture and sequestration. And Presidents Obama and Calderón also "reiterated their commitment" to "conclude ... negotiations by the end of 2011" on an "agreement on transboundary reservoirs" in the Gulf of Mexico.[11] Because deepwater drilling for gas and oil has become so significant in maintaining continental energy production, removing uncertainties about potentially rich but untapped sources there would be meaningful to all three nations.

Actions to nurture interdependence implicitly harbour potential controversy. Thus, strong and informed leadership is essential in each country to operationalize a national vision for the energy future. This might encourage the tradeoffs among intragovernmental competitors and among subnational players required to face such challenges as oil price volatility, the threat of climate change, and an energy infrastructure that must continue to adapt – at daunting expense – to both the opportunities and penalties of "doing more with what appears to be less."

WHAT MAKES UP "ENERGY NORTH AMERICA"?

Limited space permits only the briefest highlights of what North America looks like in energy terms,[12] followed by some advice for each member of the triad and the partnership as a whole.

Canada is the richest of the three countries in energy resources (oil, natural gas, and electricity, especially hydro) as compared with domestic energy requirements. The capacity for high net exports counts more in measuring a nation's energy clout than production by itself. Yet Canada depends on links to the US power-grid to optimize its load balancing during diurnal and seasonal variations in demand. Some of its highly profitable exports southward of natural gas ultimately even reach Mexico, by virtue of electronic markets that permit the United States to be a net supplier of gas to that country.

Canada's gas exports can be maintained at current levels or expanded only if the US, now awash in the newly burgeoning "unconventional" source of shale gas within its own borders, determines to expand its own use of natural gas steadily during the decades needed to switch its enormous delivery and consumption infrastructure to even "cleaner" forms of energy in sufficient quantity. It should! Fortunately for Canada, the wisest course for the United States is to expand use of natural gas - perhaps by as much as 30 percent or more within the next two decades. The US Energy Information Administration, (EIA) in its latest edition of *Annual Energy Outlook*[13], no longer assumes that a gas pipeline will be built between Alaska and the Lower 48 States before 2030, so the US will continue to be Canada's prime gas customer.

Liquefied natural gas (LNG) will continue to be used throughout North America, so the LNG receiving facilities each country has built (though underused at present[14]) will find renewed use in the future. Nevertheless, North America will continue to be a pricemaker for itself in natural gas rather than a pricetaker (as it is in petroleum). The continent's virtual self-sufficiency in gas can sustain this enviable position; and the interplay of geography and economics makes it likely that some US natural gas will be *exported* as LNG.

Oil supplies within North America are more complicated in some ways than those for natural gas. Without its oil sands, Canada would be a net importer of petroleum today. It already imports refined products, primarily for its populous eastern provinces. Canada is justly proud of ranking third globally in proved oil reserves (behind Saudi Arabia, and now Venezuela, since the authoritative industry monitor, *Oil & Gas Journal*, recently accepted the latter country's reservoirs of "heavy" oil also as "proved"). But that is not the whole story – which is almost never told.

Neither Canada nor Venezuela actually approaches Saudi Arabia (or Iran, or even Iraq and Kuwait, for that matter) in importance to the world oil market during the near- to mid-term. Average production costs from a combination of Canada's oil sands and its dwindling conventional oil reserves make it a marginal-cost supplier. "Proved" reserves consist of identified deposits that can be produced by available technology at current prices. This means that the gross number for proved reserves should be continually adjusted, at least from year to year. Persistently higher prices worldwide could open up fresh exploration in OPEC countries with budget pressures of their own, including many regions where "lifting costs" are a fraction of those anywhere in North America; and production quotas can be adjusted to crowd out non-OPEC competition. Conversely, sharply falling prices would also be bad news for Alberta, whose oil sands would not have reached their present status without a huge, ready market just across its international border.

Nevertheless, make no mistake: The United States must recognize Canada and Mexico (also suffering depletion of conventional on-shore and shallow-water oil fields) as vital suppliers. The combination of reliability and proximity entitles both neighbours to some preference.

USING WHAT WE HAVE WISELY

The lineup of US oil suppliers varies slightly from month to month; but Canada perennially tops the list and Mexico is often second. The level of Venezuelan exports to the US occasionally vies with Mexico's, but the former have dropped continuously since 2004, while Mexico has managed to keep its sales to the US fairly steady in volume despite the falloff in production from traditional fields such as Cantarell.

A wild card is that all three countries in North America (and most in the world) hope to limit oil demand; and their efforts will succeed to some extent. Total demand is bound to increase in developing countries because of rapid population growth and the pressure to raise living standards, so the world price is likely to remain high enough to support continued oil sands development. Still, there is the additional problem of environmental complaints about oil sands development because of water use, land use, and life-cycle emissions of potentially global warming gases. More will be said about this below. Meanwhile, let's take a brief continental look at electricity.

Canada's topography, its concentration of population along its southernmost latitudes, and the independent policies of its provinces have created a trade pattern for electricity that favours north-south rather than east-west connections. Mexico's transmission system has failed to keep pace with urban development, especially in the north; but the country has done an admirable job of replacing dirty and wasteful old oil-burning power plants with modern, natural gas-fueled turbines (including many combined cycle units for high efficiency and some that are designed for combined heat-and-power applications). The United States built its multiplicity of electric networks to satisfy local needs, with hundreds of guaranteed monopolies interested almost exclusively in specified utility service territories and protected until recently by politically regulated and non-competitive rate schedules from pressures to maximize efficiency. A number of steps (at the national level and by interested states) are changing this. There is greater co-operation among regions, so price competition now tends to even out rates to a lower average level than might have prevailed under earlier practices. Still, states favoured with very low-cost coal, hydro, and nuclear facilities resist broader power trade – to the detriment of the nation and continent as a whole.

Today it is imperative that each country move toward "smarter grids" as technology and capital availability permit. In their fullest potential, such systems involve beefed-up transmission, distribution, storage (to the extent technically feasible), and essentially instantaneous two-way digital response that reaches generally from the point of generation to individual households and even single pieces of equipment. Besides making it possible to tap the most efficient generation sources and to use "demand-side management" in conserving energy overall while reducing monthly bills to consumers, this is the most practical way to integrate intermittent sources of electric generation such as wind and solar energy. However, such a system will take decades to develop, and it will be incomplete unless it completes and perfects the trilateral coordination represented by the North American Electric Reliability Corporation (NERC).

NERC is a public-private, essentially self-regulating entity of long standing that has grown much stronger in recent years. Generation sources quite distant from one another find increasing net benefits in exchanging supplies, and reliability can also enhance cost-effectiveness. The mandatory reliability standards and procedures NERC develops are enforceable with stiff fines and other sanctions, depending for their effectiveness in the case of Canada on memoranda of understanding with its National Energy Board (NEB) and individual provinces.

NERC works through eight interconnected "regional entities." One includes all of British Columbia and Alberta, the northern part of Baja California in Mexico, and all or part of more than a dozen US states in between. Two other NERC regional entities straddle the rest of the US-Canadian border. Within each "reliability region," wholesale electricity flows through AC (alternating current) connections that are synchronized to permit exchanges in either direction between neighbouring states and provinces. NERC also involves Quebec, although that province maintains only DC (direct current) connections with the US and the rest of Canada.[15] There are also parts of northern Mexico in which the Comisión Federal de Electricidad co-operates voluntarily with ERCOT.

Shunning federal regulation of any sort, ERCOT itself has intentionally limited the capacity of its electricity to cross state boundaries or even to link into all parts of Texas; but its studied isolation could finally be ending as the old electricity paradigm is replaced. A new project called Tres Amigas[16] is seeking to establish an electricity hub near adjacent grid borders, and that may finally unite the essentially separate eastern, western, and Texas networks in practical terms.[17] This has ramifications for future US trade with both Mexico and Canada because it would create the weak beginnings of a truly continental grid.[18]

Vulnerability to attacks on the system by terrorists, organized criminals, or plain hackers is a special concern that NERC must address. Federal Energy Regulatory Commission chairman Jon Wellinghoff has acknowledged that "security for the US grid is meaningless without similar measures in Canada."[19] We are mutually vulnerable, and only a harmonized approach to a solution is reasonable.

Consultations take place about every four months among the staffs of three key national regulatory groups for energy across the board – NEB, Mexico's Comisión Reguladora de Energía (CRE), and the US Federal Energy Regulatory Commission (FERC). These may be the most important ongoing exchanges about energy that now take place among the respective governmental sectors. There is no thought of adopting a single regulatory agency for North America, but the meetings let each country give the others a timely "heads up" about problems, solutions, new technology, and changes that are taking place for natural gas and all electricity sources and delivery systems.

WHAT'S AHEAD?

As the smart grid evolves, interoperability standards will be critical. AC-DC-AC connections, though still expensive, will become more common. This will facilitate exchanges between areas that are not synchronized and will make long-distance contributions from intermittent renewable energy sources more practical. Thus far, only meager government resources[20] have been put into any trilateral effort to push the smart grid as a co-operative project that can help all three countries in terms of both energy policy and environmental policy. Broad trilateral initiatives could arise, however, from bilateral discussions – such as the "Clean Energy Dialogue" between Canada and the United States and a counterpart series of similar information flows and joint projects that link the US and Mexico.

Most such initiatives still exist largely on paper, although one exception is the North American Synchrophasor Initiative. This is a highly technical effort aimed at facilitating all sorts of communication within a smart grid through significantly more rapid system measurement, from perhaps once every half-second to thirty times each second. Intermittent sources face difficulties in integration to the grid, but so will baseload plants as daily load curves change. We can tolerate the fact that it now takes one to three minutes to switch a combined cycle turbine system on or off; but in order for batteries, flywheels, and other storage devices that are already available to fill in smoothly, even during reasonably steady operation, we must enter a whole new era of speed in response times.

Renewable energy is a sub-area where opportunities for co-operation abound[21] and where pledges by the respective national governments can make them easier to achieve. California is only the most extreme example of US states that have adopted targets (sometimes legally binding ones) to obtain shares of renewables-fueled generation by specified future dates that simply will not be met by new installations within their own borders. We can look for more wind farms[22] in Mexico (and perhaps in some parts of Canada) that are called upon to fill such quotas through exports that will be economically beneficial on both sides of each border.

In the second half of the current decade, an integrated industry for wind, solar, and distributed generation in general is likely to arise among the three countries. Impetus for this will come largely from the private sector, but it can be encouraged by governments through regulatory co-operation, and also in certain cases by assistance with up-front investment that promises attractive returns over time.

The outlook for alternative fuels of various types is less certain. If it proves cheap and plentiful enough in the long run, natural gas cannot be ruled out as a feedstock for methanol, which has some advantages as a vehicle fuel but few backers at present. US subsidization of corn-based ethanol will ultimately contribute relatively little except for the forced introduction of flexible-fuel vehicles taking place now (potentially a boon to all) and a slowly growing infrastructure for ethanol distribution. Eventually, if biofuels of some sort pass the tests of economics and life-cycle environmental acceptability, most relatively modest installations to produce them will tend to be regional because of cost and difficulty in transporting bulky feedstocks. Cellulosic ethanol, if and when it arrives commercially, might draw feedstock from Canada's forests. In the far south, there have been experiments with Mexico's maguey and some plants that otherwise have low or no commercial value.

A major interest in North America is the use of combinations of renewable and clean energy to replace coal plants (especially the older and less efficient ones) as they are phased out. Even prevailing breezes are unpredictable and variable, so wind generation usually supplies only about one-third of its peak capacity. Complementary power in substantial amounts is needed on a regular basis for wind farms, and natural gas turbines have become the generally accepted choice to provide such backup. But that means we may have to do more than install many more gas-fired turbines; in some areas we will also need to modify existing pipeline networks and even build new natural gas pipelines to fuel them. The designed-in ability to reverse flow as conditions change will be a commonplace requirement.

Coal is arguably still one of the keys to North America's sound energy future, but only if an economical means is developed to isolate its byproduct of carbon dioxide (before or after combustion, depending on the technique used) and "sequester" it, meaning to use it in some form (for example, to enhance recovery of oil and gas from existing wells) or to lock it away for good. The US and Canada have long co-operated in research, development, and demonstration for CCS (carbon capture and sequestration), and the Alberta government is spending prodigiously in the hope of reaching some breakthrough. Most technically sophisticated observers believe that commercializable CCS is many years away. Achieving it at some distant point (when restrictions on CO_2 emissions may have to be far stricter than those now being discussed, in order to reach the now-visionary goal of 80 percent reduction by 2050) may be applicable to natural gas as well as coal.

SOME IMMEDIATE TASKS

A thirty- to forty-year planning horizon is needed for changes of these kinds. That calls for short-term, medium-term, and long-term targets. Actions along the way will surely have to be taken regionally, but it would help enormously to keep a continental vision in mind. Since environmental goals and energy goals are both important, life-cycle impacts must be evaluated and monitored as well.

NAEWG was urged for years to sponsor an annual North American Energy Outlook report, developed along the lines of EIA's *Annual Energy Outlook* and *International Energy Outlook*.[23] Not only has NAEWG failed to do so; it has not even updated its *North American Natural Gas Vision*, which itself was delayed by bureaucratic lack of resolve and thus was already out of date when it appeared in January 2005.

The time has come for objective analysts within the private sector to develop at least an initial North American Energy Outlook (NAEO) to illuminate the difficult path that lies ahead. Although budget stringencies still deter NAEWG, this document would not be a hugely expensive private undertaking for an international team of think tanks, academics, and NGOs. Its obvious utility should attract adequate financial support – even at the tail-end of an economic recession. Most North American energy statistics for 2009 and 2010 are now in hand. The widely respected National Energy Modeling System (NEMS) (and roughly compatible versions in Canada and Mexico) are available for serious research of this type. The fact that EIA already tabulates data on GHG emissions that could be integrated into the document is a bonus.

Eventually, without any threat to individual sovereignty, it is easy to envision a "North American stance" at future meetings of COP (Conference of Partners on Climate Change). Focal points at future meetings of COP will undoubtedly include the modes and practicalities of monitoring, measuring and verification (MMV). This continent's experience with each would be impressive to others. If we could agree to consider combined North American emission targets rather than individual ones for each country, this would further facilitate efficiency. Alberta might feel free to expand its own refining capacity for bitumen, rather than send much of it to the Gulf of Mexico. The result would be a higher-value-added product for Canada, more efficient and effective application of natural resources, and a minimization of total emissions into the global atmosphere.

We need "continental thinking" about energy and environment, but the United States (the largest producer and consumer of energy by far) has been slow to foster it. In inspiring future action, Canada and Mexico both have more "soft power" vis-à-vis the United States than has been recognized, and it need not be exercised jointly. But we all need to "think outside the box" as we "think across borders."

Mexico's success as an innovator during the 2010 global climate change discussions at Cancun showed that its own commitment to serious change in energy mix and environmental concern (over both the short and long haul) earns respect. But its value as an energy partner within the North American triad depends also on some demonstration of its recognition that fossil fuels will continue to dominate and that it still has the ability to be a reliable supplier.

Assuming (as I do) that Pemex will continue to be strapped for liquid capital for some time because of constitutional restrictions and incomplete tax/fiscal reforms, it could still remain a "player" by bidding on deepwater leases in the US sector of the Gulf of Mexico through partnership in drilling with another national oil company (Brazil's Petrobras comes to mind) or even a US- or Canada-based private company. Some Mexican officials and other energy specialists in that country have told me they believe this type of joint venture would pass constitutional scrutiny (after a certain amount of debate); and it could certainly provide needed technological experience at relatively lower cost than a full-blown solitary effort.

The special significance of Canada's oil sands (and, to a diminishing extent, its role as a natural gas supplier) give Canada extra weight in discussions of the most appropriate balance for North America among the ever-relevant but often-conflicting goals of affordability, reliability, what we deem adequacy of supply, environmental protection, and realistic timing of a move toward a more stable situation. Yet exaggerated voluntary restraint in oil sands output could turn Canada into a net oil importer.

172   Joseph M. Dukert

What are the political realities? Canada faces opposition from some members of the US Congress in sales from oil sands, and the proposed new Keystone XL pipeline for bitumen is in for rough sledding. The US State Department recognizes its value, but the final decision promised now for 2013 will surely be litigated. All three branches of the US federal government, as well as multiple states, will be involved. In what appeared to be a power battle between the State Department and the Environmental Protection Agency, the EPA returned State's "Supplemental Draft Environmental Impact Statement" on the pipeline as "inadequate." That meant delay and uncertainty, and thus risk to potential investors.

Is there another course? Yes. How much does Canada value its own moral authority, when doing so has a price? Canada could have far more influence on US policy by becoming more serious about responses to the risks of climate change. Ottawa would be in a stronger position to exercise its vaunted "soft power" in government-to-government discussions if the new government could muster the co-operation of the provinces and enunciate a clear-cut joint resolve to take several steps unilaterally: 1) internalize the externalities of CO_2 emissions on its own in a way of its choosing, but without waiting for a US lead; 2) put a price on unrecyclable water use; and 3) push oil sands developers to speed their transition to in situ production methods (which will be necessary in time anyway to tap 80 percent of the oil sands reserve because of its depth below the surface).

Each of these steps would be costly in the short run from a purely dollars-and-cents standpoint; but consolidating Canada's moral high ground might be worth it. It would demonstrate Canadian power that was heretofore latent. True, US oil imports from Canada could be replaced from other sources; but this would not be done without palpable costs.

Although the Harper government has been unenthusiastic (to say the least) about moving ahead unilaterally in respect to serious climate change efforts, it could move ahead on the basis of a "transitional policy" of its own along the lines of one suggested by a long-standing group whose members at the time Prime Minister Harper himself had appointed – the National Round Table on the Environment and the Economy. In its recent report, *Parallel Paths: Canada-U.S. Climate Policy Choices*, the NRTEE recommended, among a number of national measures, "a 'price collar' that limits carbon price differentials between Canada and the U.S." It said that "Such a 'made-in-Canada' policy would allow Canada to achieve significant greenhouse gas reductions even in the face of uncertain U.S. policy, address competitiveness concerns for industry, and pave the way towards greater harmonization later as American policy direction emerges."[24]

It is easy (and, in my opinion, justified) to remind the US constantly of its oil addiction. But, to press the analogy of "addiction," Canada's policies and pronouncements have made it both an "intervener" (to a modest extent) and (for understandable self-interest) an "enabler" and "facilitator" to the addict. The ready availability of Canadian oil eases US concerns, thus weakening the case for frugality in oil use. At the same time, Canada is not about to renounce its role as a profitable oil exporter. Perhaps "shared sacrifice" is a solution, if it is recognized to be in the joint interest.

Many in the US resist steps that should be taken in the interest of its own national security, such as more strenuously and imaginatively pushing substitutes for oil use (including automotive efficiency) and adopting various other measures to reduce CO_2 emissions. Being nudged in a "proper" direction by Canada or Mexico (rhetorically and by example) might stress relations to some extent in some quarters. But it would underscore the US position as a "dependent variable."[25] Overall US power is affected (indirectly) by the condition of the country's energy security.

CONCLUSIONS

Patterns of governance within and among the three countries of North America in respect to energy and environmental protection are not likely to change in the foreseeable future. Yet there is no need for a hierarchy of junior and senior national partners in regard to energy ideas. What would serve all parties best is a blend of technical, economic, and political/geopolitical analysis. The energy market will not and should not be totally free because there are market imperfections. Externalities such as limits on free entry and exit, tendencies toward monopoly, and pollution need to be internalized in various ways and according to a balance of public aims. This could encourage discrete, step-by-step changes toward a Paretooptimal arrangement of conceptually equal neighbours in their individual and joint pursuit of reliable, affordable, and environmentally acceptable applications of energy resources in a timely fashion.

I believe it would be counterproductive for either Canada or the United States to press Mexico officially for additional energy reform. Academics and NGOs should not hesitate to do so, though, sometimes in bilateral or trilateral concert. The private sector might hope to do so also, by setting successful examples. Unless and until Mexicans undertake energy reforms on their own, however, Pemex and CFE (Comisión Federal de Electricidad) can be treated in these analyses as if they were hyper-majors in their respective fields.

The potential rewards of gradually increasing energy links across North America's borders are many: 1) greater certainty of an adequate supply of energy to satisfy the requirements of an interactive general economy with restored vigour; 2) a competitive stance for each country in world trade that is better fitted to divert competition with the BRICS into the sort of mutual economic growth that was envisioned as far back as David Ricardo in the eighteenth century and as recently as optimistic heralds of globalization in the twenty-first; 3) something closer to a common stance vis-à-vis OPEC and IEA (International Energy Agency) alike; 4) energy prices that are lower than they otherwise would be; 5) a fighting chance to cope with anthropogenic climate change, in case the self-healing attributes of Earth itself do not forestall it.

Each country's status and actions in regard to the energy/environment future may be viewed as dependent variables. As each country's energy patterns change, the others are nudged (inevitably, if not always abruptly) in some direction. There are risks of common failure; but this reality grows out of the very definition of "interdependence." The secret is to make it succeed for everybody as often as possible.

NOTES

1 Dr Dukert welcomes questions or reactions to this commentary at dukert@verizon.net.
2 Although "energy" is basically a government monopoly in Mexico, some elements of that country's energy sector display private-sector characteristics. Self-generation of electricity by private companies and by ad hoc consortia of firms is common. Natural gas is distributed locally in ways that resemble private utility franchises. Pemex (the national oil, gas, and petrochemical enterprise) is still treated domestically as a "cash cow" for federal revenue; but it can be viewed like a "super major" company – with self-interest in making decisions that make sense from a "business perspective" wherever it can.
3 The private sector's interest in stimulating and reinforcing continental cooperation in all forms of energy goes back more than a decade, as evidenced in the US Energy Association's publication in October 2001 of a white paper entitled *Toward an International Energy Trade and Development Strategy* and USEA's ongoing partnership since then with business, industry, and government counterparts in Canada and Mexico via the World Energy Council.
4 Adverse public reaction to the mismanaged nuclear power plant disaster in Japan following an earthquake and tsunami was surprisingly mild around the world, and its major result may well be just to tighten regulatory oversight and improve safety provisions - especially at older reactors. Even the political pledge in Germany to phase out all nuclear power plants within a relatively short time is likely to falter, as attempts to replace their output prove far more difficult and economically disruptive than assumed.
5 Criticism of these "soft" energy sources on economic grounds is often as exaggerated as the claims of their supporters, and this is not the proper venue for a detailed refutation of either. They generally fit into niche markets and should be evaluated on a case-by-case basis.

6 The *Annual Energy Outlook* is published by the US Energy Information Administration, which is enjoined by statute to remain "policy neutral." Its latest edition (released on 26 April 2011, and available at http://www.eia. doe.gov) uses fifty-seven different sensitivity cases to demonstrate how projections of future US energy production, energy use, emissions of global warming gases, etc., may be materially altered by essentially unpredictable circumstances. Even this range does not consider the cause-and-effect of actual policy *changes* if they should come.

7 NAEWG, staffed mainly by mid-level bureaucrats, started vigorously in 2001; but it lost momentum after the terrorist attack of 11 September and wars in the Middle East, and has been moribund for some time. SPP - which covered far more than energy - was supposed to have the advantage of close attention from cabinet-level officials; but in the US that promise was quickly forgotten. US emphasis on security outweighed that on prosperity. Meanwhile, wild and unjustified attacks on SPP as a plot to produce a super-government led to its quiet official death as soon as a change in the US presidency made that convenient without embarrassment. For what SPP might have accomplished if it had been faithful to its original charge, see Joseph M. Dukert, "North American Energy: At Long Last, One Continent," Center for Strategic and International Studies, Washington, DC, William E. Simon Chair in Political Economy, Occasional Contributions (October 2005, Number 2).

8 In July 2011 a pan-Canadian Energy and Mine Ministers' Conference produced what the participants called a "National Energy Plan" that acknowledged interrelationship with the United States, and Alberta's Energy Minister (Ron Liepert) voiced a hope that the framework might develop into more of a joint energy-environment venture.

9 "North American Leaders' Declaration on Climate Change," accessed via the website of the White House Press Office on 8 June 2011.

10 White House Press Office, "Fact Sheet: Enhancing U.S.-Mexico Cooperation," 3 March 2011.

11 Ibid.

12 Unfortunately, no single, joint summary of the current energy status and energy interrelationships of the three countries is remotely up to date. NAEWG's *Energy Picture II* was released in January 2006, using earlier data. EIA's annual *International Energy Outlook* has combined the three countries in some of its tables, and individual sections have discussed North America as a region, but without "continental analysis." EIA's *Monthly Energy Review* is an invaluable source in regard to imports and exports of natural gas and petroleum, but electricity exchanges must be tracked elsewhere. Even EIA's "Country Analysis Briefs" (CAB) are useful only to show fragments of the story, belatedly. The ones for Canada and Mexico frequently employ statistics that are several years old, and a periodic CAB for the United States has apparently been dropped for budgetary reasons. Little wonder that a

"North American Energy Vision" is inevitably somewhat fuzzy in the eyes of policymakers.

13 Released on EIA's website (http://www.eia.gov) 26 April 2011, and scheduled for publication subsequently in hard copy.

14 LNG receiving facilities represent far lower capital investments than either liquefaction facilities at the source or the fleets of huge, refrigerated tankers used for intercontinental delivery. Thus, receiving facilities can survive economically with relatively low throughputs.

15 This was a rarely needed advantage to Quebec in August 2003 because its lights stayed on during the blackout in NERC's Eastern Interconnection that affected service otherwise as far west as Manitoba. NERC recognizes Quebec as a distinct "interconnection" in itself, so the province is also able to develop its own reliability standards as needed in addition to those enforced by NERC.

16 For the current status of Tres Amigas, see www.tresamigasllc.com.

17 The Eastern and Western Interconnections are already linked by half a dozen high-voltage DC transmission facilities, but their total capacity is insufficient to treat them as a single grid. More electricity traffic in all directions is promised in the future as renewable energy sources such as wind and solar farms are built in areas favourable to their development but remote from centres of residential, commercial, and industrial demand.

18 For practical reasons, Alaska would still be unconnected by power lines with the rest of the continent.

19 Chairman Wellinghoff made the statement during a question-and-answer period at a forum sponsored by the US Energy Association in Washington, DC. on 7 October 2010.

20 In 2009 the National Electrical Manufacturers Association (NEMA) was assigned the lead role (in conjunction with Canadian and Mexican partners) to begin to develop common standards for smart grid components over a three-year period.

21 See Duncan Wood, *Environment, Development and Growth: U.S.-Mexico Cooperation in Renewable Energies,* Woodrow Wilson International Center for Scholars, December 2010, which lays out the history of some modest successes over two decades and proposes a number of specific bi-national actions that could build on the current base.

22 Solar installations in Mexico to supply cross-border power are also technically feasible but less attractive in the near future because such facilities of sufficient size to make much of a contribution are far from commercialization.

23 EIA has announced quietly that budget cutbacks will force it to end its long-time publication of its annual *International Energy Outlook* with the 2011 edition, but it might be hoped that protests from policymakers and analysts will force a reversal of this shortsighted decision.

24 NRTEE news release of 25 January 2011, headed "NRTEE Recommends Phased-In Climate Harmonization Policy with U.S." For a full copy of the report, see www.climateprosperity.ca/parallel-paths.

25   This portion of the chapter originated some months ago in an electronic conversation with Professor Stephen Clarkson. It started when he asked me to review a draft of his since-published book, *Dependent America? How Canada and Mexico Construct and Constrain US Power* (University of Toronto Press, 2011). By stressing North American energy interdependence in my own writings since the early 1990s, I had long accepted the idea that each partner was *dependent* on the other in this particular field, but it was only in framing my requested critique of Clarkson's manuscript that I conceived and suggested the link with "soft power." I am grateful to my colleague for triggering this idea, which I fully expect some to challenge. Based on a follow-up draft I saw later, however, I believe he may agree with me – at least in broad strokes.

North America in 2020:
Two Visions

ROBERT A. PASTOR

It is not hard to imagine the future. Indeed, there is a market for "futures," and risk managers and investors make decisions every day based on what they think the future portends. While the methodology used by futurologists is sometimes quite complex, essentially, predictions about the future rely on one of two techniques. The most popular approach is to look backwards, extract the critical trends, and project those trends into the future. Usually, the adviser will warn the investor that the past is no guarantee of the future, but nonetheless, most people will rely on this approach.

A second approach is sometimes used if the first approach does not yield a desired outcome. If the recent past is dismal or simply failed to meet expectations, the futurist will look for another period, country, or region, or he/she will extract positive elements from the past and explain how negative trends can be overcome. In short, the first approach predicts the future by looking clearly and unromantically at the past, while the second approach rearranges the multiple variables of the past, and drawing pertinent lessons, shows how the future can be made better.

In predicting North America's future in 2020, I will rely on both techniques, and I will be aided by using the last two decades as the points of reference. The first vision of "North America as Three Bilateral Relationships" will project from this past decade. Since 2001, while there have been a few rhetorical gestures about the continent, the three countries have concentrated their energies on addressing problems on a bilateral basis. Vision 1 will assess the effectiveness of this approach and speculate about where that will leave North America in 2020.

The second, less likely, vision is one that looks back to the first decade of NAFTA – from 1990 to 2000 – and asks whether the three governments can recover the initial promise of the North American idea. The first decade was one of rapid expansion of trade and investment. Economic and social integration accelerated on multiple tracks. This second, "North American" vision requires more imagination. It does not suggest that we should simply return to 2001 and get back on the NAFTA road anymore than Mexico could return to the strategy of import-substitution-industrialization in order to return to high rates of economic growth. Rather, this vision recognizes that NAFTA was a spent force by 2001 and incapable of dealing with the new North American agenda. The second vision therefore extracts elements from other experiences and periods to suggest a new approach to reach a more competitive, secure, and respectful North America.

VISION I: TRIPLE BILATERALISM

With the signing of the North American Free Trade Agreement (NAFTA) in 1992, Canada, Mexico, and the United States dismantled the trade and investment barriers that had segmented the North American market, and the result was the emergence of a vast and unregulated continental market. The logic of economic and social integration extended across the waterfront of interaction – trade, investment, tourism, migration, phone calls – and the growth in each area among the three North American countries exceeded the region's interaction with the rest of the world, meaning that integration was deepening almost as much as it had in the European Union after fifty years.

By 2001, however, NAFTA's advantage had diminished. The growth of trade, which soared in the first seven years of NAFTA, slipped to about one-third that initial rate. New problems emerged. Some stemmed from the after-shocks of 9/11, others from the commercial success of China, but the single most important reason that old problems were exacerbated and new ones surfaced was the failure of the three governments to find the will and imagination to govern the space and plan a continental future.

The three governments made a few efforts to deepen North American integration. The most notable was the Security and Prosperity Partnership (SPP) launched in 2005. This initiative elicited a nativist reaction, particularly in the United States. Though few in number, the opponents were determined to halt any initiative. Instead of defending North America or the SPP, President George W. Bush and his counterparts decided to keep their efforts incremental and private. After a decade, the only progress that could be measured was in "declarations" and "bureaucratic meetings," of which there were many. At the same time, the borders became more restrictive, integration declined, illegal migration and drug-trafficking worsened, and one-third fewer people were crossing the borders on a routine basis. The North American share of the world's gross product, which had soared from 30 percent in 1994 to 36 percent in 2001, sank to 29 percent by 2009.

The truth is that soon after NAFTA came into effect, the three governments stopped proposing North American initiatives and returned to the traditional default option – dual bilateralism – the United States and Canada and the United States and Mexico.

Technically, Canada became the father of the "new" North America when it asked to be included in the Mexican-US trade negotiations, but its motives were more defensive than ambitious. Canadian Prime Minister Brian Mulroney wanted to make sure that none of the provisions in the recently negotiated Canadian-US Free Trade Agreement would be diluted in the Mexican agreement, and the best insurance was to join that agreement.

Having brought NAFTA into being, however, Canada soon became a "dead-beat dad." When Mexican president Vicente Fox asked Canadian prime minister Jean Chretien to work together to establish a Cohesion Fund similar to Europe's in reducing the income gap among the countries, Chretien said "non." When Raul Rodriguez, the first president of the North American Development Bank, asked Canada to join, he was rebuffed. When Jim Kolbe, an influential Republican Congressman from Arizona, asked Canadian legislators to join with US and Mexican legislators in order to form a North American Parliamentary Group, the Canadians turned him down. When Mexican Foreign Minister Jorge Castañeda asked Canadian Foreign Minister John Manley to work together for a single "smart borders" agreement in the aftermath of 9/11, he too was rejected.

North America did not disappear, and indeed, the three leaders met periodically at summit meetings. Most recently, in August 2009, Prime Minister Harper, President Obama, and President Calderón met in Guadalajara and discussed a wide agenda, including the environment, border security, economic competitiveness, and regulatory policies. One specific decision was that Canada would host a follow-up summit in 2010. Harper failed to fulfill that pledge. Instead, President Obama met separately with each leader and established parallel organizations to address the key issues of the border, the environment, and regulation.

The real energy of the three governments was invested in the two principal bilateral relationships, but these also failed to show any progress. Despite a long, hard-fought, negotiated agreement, Canada and the United States are still at odds on softwood lumber. Border co-operation has not yielded border efficiency. US-Mexican relations have been focused on drug-related violence. Trade, trucking, and competitiveness have taken a back seat.

With this past decade as the prologue, "path dependence" would suggest that we will see the continued decline of North America and the proportional rise of a chronically dysfunctional dual bilateralism.

However, there was one important change in the past years, and that was the emergence of Canadian-Mexican relations. After NAFTA, both Canada and Mexico expanded their diplomatic missions in each other's country, and trade and investment increased at a much faster rate, though admittedly a very low level, than each country's trade with the United States. Canadians began to vacation in Mexico, and Mexicans began to emigrate to Canada.

Still, the new bilateral relationship was a bit testy as is evident from the various Canadian rejections noted above. With the inauguration of President George W. Bush in 2001, Canada and Mexico competed with each other to see which leader could get to the White House first. They acted like jealous siblings trying to capture the attention of the United States, and they repeated the same dance both before and after Obama's inauguration.

The symbolic rivalry became more serious in July 2009 when Canada announced a change in its visa policy for Mexicans at the very moment when the foreign ministers of all three countries were meeting in Washington. The Mexicans viewed this as a calculated insult. Canada was responding to internal pressures on the refugee issue and acknowledged the insensitivity of the decision, and both countries tried to mend relations by promoting research and other exchanges. But this disagreeable incident suggests that the emerging, third leg of the bilateral triangle might prove almost as problematic as the other two.

By 2020, we can expect more of the same with the three countries wrestling with the same problems that have frustrated them for decades. Moreover, if there is another crisis like 9/11 or the auto crisis, we can predict that the United States will react unilaterally without consulting or even informing its neighbours. This future is like the past.

VISION 2: A NORTH AMERICAN VISION

A second North American vision is trilateral; all three governments see themselves as partners – not competitors or sibling rivals – in dealing with common challenges of development and security and in addressing transnational issues like the environment and climate change, migration, the border, and drug-related violence.

The essence of a North American community is that each of the three sovereign states has a stake in the success of the other, and each will pay a price if one fails. That is the first principle – interdependence – of a community. The second is reciprocity – that each nation should treat the others as it wants to be treated, and each should want to learn from the experience of the others. The third principle is a community of interests; instead of seeking a quid pro quo - every concession by one government would require similar ones from the others – all three governments would share responsibility for problems and contribute to solutions.

These basic principles seem obvious, and the leaders of all three countries often refer to them, most recently as "shared responsibility," but few leaders, if any, act on these principles. The usual approach is that the strongest nation insists or ignores, and the weaker ones persist, resist, or accommodate. If, however, the leaders adopt this vision, how might they apply it?

The most immediate security issues relate to border management. The Canadian government has preferred the bilateral approach because it contends that the two borders are very different and that it could solve the problems faster with just the United States. Despite a decade of bilateral discussions, the US-Canadian border situation is no better than it was before 9/11, and while some of the problems differ from those encountered at the US-Mexican border, the truth is that both borders are dysfunctional for similar reasons – inadequate infrastructure, multiple security requirements imposed by the US government, and a fragmented approach by agencies within and between the three governments. All three countries need to design a single approach with similar rules and requirements and jointly trained personnel to manage the borders. Canada and Mexico would benefit from a single set of rules, and the United States would benefit from not having to repeat the same exercise twice. What kind of rules?

First, instead of having multiple "fast" cards, the three governments could agree to a single North American pass or passport that would be cleared by all three countries and allow the individual to use the fast lane at both borders. Second, instead of three sets of customs forms and officials, they would agree to one set of forms and a single team that would include individuals from all three governments. Third, instead of having different standards for the weight, length, and height of trucks, there would be a single standard. Fourth, instead of cabotage, which restricts trucks from picking up cargo at different sites, they could agree to allow certified "North American trucks" to deposit or retrieve cargo anywhere in the three countries. The US Congress would be more likely to approve a system if its two neighbours were united in proposing a fair scheme.

The same pattern applies to other issues. To narrow the development gap between Mexico and its northern neighbours, it would help if all three designed a plan and agreed about what each would contribute. To address the dual problems of energy security and climate change, it would be desirable for the three countries to design a unified cap-and-trade system and ask the North American Commission on Environmental Cooperation to measure the problems and the progress. While most prefer a global system, if the three governments of North America found a functional and effective formula for reducing carbon emissions at a regional level, they could provide the model.

The three leaders should begin to articulate the North American vision and embody it with two simple, inexpensive initiatives. First, they should ask their ministers of transportation to work together to prepare a North American Plan for Transportation and Infrastructure with new trade corridors that go from northern Canada to southern Mexico, new ports, and more efficient inter-modal transportation networks. The plan would respond to the tripling of trade and anticipate an even larger surge in the future. The second step should be directed at the continent's students. The countries should offer a North American Scholarship Fund to encourage students of each country to study in the others and expand their support for existing regional studies centres to include ten North American centres. These centres would prepare options for North American collaboration and infuse a consciousness of being North American in all three countries.

Why should the three governments pursue their interests trilaterally rather than bilaterally?

- With two sides negotiating, there is an inevitable tendency for each to see its approach as the only right one. Add a third perspective and new ideas, and a more productive negotiation, becomes possible.
- A trilateral approach is more likely to yield an outcome that is based on rules than one based on an imbalance of power.
- Canada and Mexico are more likely to feel as if they have a stake in the region's future if agreements are fair and binding on all.
- Each country brings a different perspective to these and other international issues – that of a superpower, a middle power, and a developing country. To the extent that the resulting policy integrates those different approaches, the final result is most likely to have the widest influence in the world.
- If all three governments agree to a single approach to a problem, they would have additional leverage to overcome the pleading of special interests.

Some Canadians believe that their "special relationship" with the United States, combined with a similar level of development, means that their interests would be more efficiently served by bilateral talks. But the United States is moving more rapidly in its negotiations with Mexico than with Canada in the two parallel groups on the border, environment, and regulatory policies that have been set up in the past year. Of course, this does not mean that the Mexican talks will conclude first. The probability is that neither will conclude without the converging of the two paths.

Mexico has a large, growing, and increasingly influential constituency of Mexican-Americans in the United States and the American concern with violence in Mexico has assured Mexico that it has the attention of the US government in a way that Canada is unlikely ever to equal. If Canada were to find new ways to work with Mexico and the United States, its value would actually increase in the American marketplace. In brief, both the outcome and the process are more likely to advance in a trilateral than in a bilateral framework.

The paradox is that the leaders of all three countries have been cautious because they think the public is resistant to North American integration, but an analysis of public opinion surveys suggests that the public is actually ahead of its leaders. Frank Graves, president of Ekos, a leading Canadian polling firm, has conducted many surveys in all three countries. He found, in the summer of 2005, majority support in Canada (57 percent) and Mexico (59 percent) and a plurality in the United States (45 percent) for forming a common market or economic union like Europe. In the case of the United States, the same question asked three years before yielded 58 percent support. Not only do the people favour an economic union; 61 percent of Mexicans, 58 percent of Canadians, and 51 percent of Americans believe that it is very or somewhat likely that a North American Economic Union will arrive by 2015.[1]

That seems unlikely, but the more concrete point that leaps from the surveys is that the public wants much more trilateral collaboration. In an explicit question about whether people in each of the three countries would prefer separate or integrated policies on twelve sets of issues, a majority of the citizens of all three countries preferred more integrated, trilateral policies on the environment, transportation, defence, and the economy. On immigration, currency, foreign policy, banking, and culture, a slight majority favoured independent policies.

While the leaders want to proceed incrementally and slowly, the public is ready for bolder initiatives. One-fourth of Canadians and Americans feel their governments are providing a bold vision for the future, but 56 percent of Americans and 61 percent of Canadians wish their governments would do so.

It is true that a minority of the public – about 15 to 20 percent – oppose any collaboration among the three governments of North America, and that this group is more intense than the majority. Perhaps the reason that the three governments have not moved more quickly toward a North American Community is that the governments, especially the United States because of its porous and pluralistic political system, are reluctant to antagonize this more salient group of sovereignty-defenders. Hence the stasis. To overcome it requires a vision, leadership, and institutions.

NORTH AMERICA THROUGH BI-FOCALS OR HIGH DEFINITION

Historically, "divide and rule" has been the strategy of the strong against the weak. In North America, however, the country that has pursued this strategy most vigorously has been one of the two weaker partners, Canada. It has pursued it because it has believed its interests would be better served by a bilateral than a trilateral approach, but the evidence suggests that a bilateral approach has failed, and while a trilateral approach has not succeeded, the reason is that it has not really been tried. The virtue of a trilateral approach is that one does not have to wait for the United States. If Canada and Mexico were to indicate an interest in collaborating, then the United States under a Democratic president would probably join, and if the United States were to wait for the outcome, it would be in a weaker position to resist it.

None of the many proposals that have been advanced for the region – whether incremental ones like harmonizing a single regulation or bold ones like a customs union – has much chance of being achieved without a North American vision. Americans and Canadians will not provide funds to narrow the development gap with Mexico without a convincing vision of how Mexico's growth will benefit their countries. There is little prospect of a transportation plan, an agreement on labour mobility, a unified approach to climate change or the environment, or any other proposal that would cost money or change the status quo unless there is a vision of a wider community that could attract the support of the people and their legislatures.

Even with a vision, the governments need to organize themselves internally and create lean, advisory institutions among them if they are to offer concrete and realistic policy options. That is why a North American vision is necessary but not sufficient to advance an agenda for the region.

The North American Leaders' Summit in Guadalajara in 2009 underscored both the promise of North American co-operation and the chronic difficulty. The three governments are trained to think in bilateral terms, and thus our imagination of what North America could become is limited. A genuine three-sided dialogue could introduce new ideas to chronic problems, but it could also create a sense of community that would handle future problems more effectively. North America's potential awaits leadership in all three countries and the political will to place an agenda before the three publics.

In summary, we are at a crossroads. One path is well-trodden. It will lead to three bilateral relationships. None will be satisfactory, but because all three governments understand their mutual importance, they will seek to avoid a breakdown. A second path needs to be blazed. It is to create a sense of community among the people and the three governments of North America. This could lead to the most productive region economically in the world. It could enhance cultural diversity and security at the same time. It could create a model that other countries and regions would want to emulate.

NOTE

1 For an analysis of these and other surveys, see Robert A. Pastor, *The North American Idea: A Vision of a Continental Future* (New York: Oxford University Press, 2011), chapter 3.

PART FOUR

Regional Partnerships

The Canada-Mexico Relationship in a Latin American and Transpacific Configuration

CARLOS HEREDIA ZUBIETA[1]

CANADA AND MEXICO: PARTNERS OR COMPETITORS?

Mexico, Canada, and the United States became trade partners with the enactment of the North American Free Trade Agreement on 1 January 1994. However, over seventeen years later it has become evident that the three countries have decided to prioritize their bilateral relationships (US-Canada, US-Mexico, and Canada-Mexico) instead of investing in a long-term vision for the future of their trilateral partnership. Neither Canada nor Mexico has been able to satisfactorily resolve the essential asymmetry of power vis-à-vis the United States of America. Moreover, the current relationship between Mexico and the United States is characterized as one of sustained dependence and dominance.[2]

A 2010 CIDE (Centro de Investigación y Docencia Económicas) survey[3] shows that Mexicans continue to rate Canada highest among the countries of the world. However, as José Carreño notes in his article, we know very little about what Canadians and Mexicans actually know about each other. While there has been a significant set of proposals on the North American idea,[4] there is no appetite on the part of the respective governments to push the trade pact forward. Ottawa, Washington, and Mexico City obviously have not put North American integration at the top of their agendas.

The yearly North American Leaders' Summit (NALS) – which is undoubtedly the most important decision-making compact in an agreement that lacks permanent institutions – was scheduled to take place as a "side dish" to the Asia-Pacific Economic Cooperation Forum (APEC) leaders' summit in Hawaii for 13 November 2011. It was postponed because President Felipe Calderón cancelled his trip to Hawaii following the sudden death of Mexico's number two official. This inaction illustrates that NALS is not seen as a self-standing event worth the time of President Barack Obama, Prime Minister Stephen Harper, and President Calderón.

Without a strategic vision, the question of whether to go on a bilateral or trilateral track is a false dilemma. Mexico and Canada are now each other's third largest trade partners after the United States and China. However, it appears that the NAFTA era has come to a close, and that another instrument will be needed to serve as the road map for North American integration. The Security and Prosperity Partnership (SPP) was too cumbersome and failed because a building-block approach does not work when there is no overall vision of where the region wants to go. North America lacks a joint plan to compete vis-à-vis the Asian and European blocs in the global economy.

As the three NAFTA partners diversify their political and economic relationships in reaction to the changing economic and political land-scape and the growing presence of China in the Western Hemisphere, several questions arise:

- Are Ottawa and Mexico City prepared to upgrade their activities in the Latin American subcontinent from distracted co-operation to strategic partnership?
- Does the Canada-Mexico relationship have a regional economic dimension in Latin America?
- Are Canada and Mexico on different paths when it comes to regional integration, or are there areas of common interest and collaboration?
- Can we construct mutually beneficial regional partnerships between Canada and Mexico in Central America, the Caribbean, and South America?

While bilateral trade and investment have grown, both Canada and Mexico have diversified their relations with other economies, such as the United States, Europe, China, and Latin America. The United States is by far each country's largest trading partner. Canada is the third larg-est destination for Mexico's exports, while Canada is the fourth largest importer of Mexican products.

THE PERSPECTIVES OF NORTH-SOUTH
VIS-À-VIS EAST-WEST TRADE AND INTEGRATION

Since the onset of the twenty-first century, the People's Republic of China has become a major actor in trade, investment, and political partnerships

Mexico's top trading partners in 2010 (Percentage of total)

Exports		Imports	
By main destination		By main origin	
1. United States	80.7	1. United States	48.1
2. European Union (27)	5.1	2. China	13.9
3. Canada	3.6	3. European Union (27)	11.9
4. Colombia	1.1	4. Japan	4.9
5. Brazil	1.1	5. Korea, Republic of	4.7

Source: http://data.worldbank.org

Canada's top trading partners in 2010 (Percentage of total)

Exports		Imports	
By main destination		By main origin	
1. United States	75.0	1. United States	51.2
2. European Union (27)	8.3	2. European Union (27)	12.4
3. China	3.1	3. China	10.9
4. Japan	2.3	4. Mexico	4.5
5. Mexico	1.3	5. Japan	3.4

Source: http://data.worldbank.org

throughout the western hemisphere. Although important global players such as the European Union, Japan, India, Russia, and South Korea are increasingly present, China trails only the United States in the volume of trade in Latin America. It aims to become a major if not the main supplier and partner to North America in the near future.

China has emerged as Canada's and Mexico's second largest trading partner immediately after the United States, while it has also become their main competitor in the US market. The fact that Canada and Mexico share their most important trading partners means that both countries rely on the same dynamics – i.e., what happens in the US and Chinese economies is absolutely critical for both Canada and Mexico. The trade pattern is quite different in South America, where trade relationships are more diversified, but China's appetite for commodities has translated into long-term contracts of huge imports of soya from Argentina, iron ore from Brazil, and copper from Chile, among other raw materials.

In the aftermath of NAFTA there was talk of adopting its framework as a model and extending it to the whole hemisphere. There were two attempts: the Initiative for the Americas and the Free Trade Area of the Americas (FTAA). Neither prospered because a different strategy gained ground instead: relying on bilateral trade relationships and negotiating trade agreements with individual countries.

In Latin America, Canada has signed free trade agreements with Chile, Colombia, Costa Rica, and Peru, while it has a non-reciprocal preferential trade agreement known as CARIBCAN with the fifteen-nation[5] Caribbean Community (CARICOM). Mexico has signed trade agreements with Bolivia, Chile, Colombia, Costa Rica, the triangle of the north (El Salvador, Guatemala, and Honduras), Nicaragua, Panama, Trinidad and Tobago, and Uruguay. In mid-2011 the Mexico-Peru agreement had yet to be ratified by the Mexican Senate and discussions on an agreement with Brazil had stalled.

However, Latin America is not a unified bloc that acts in a concerted manner. The Latin American Community of Nations (CELAC) is the most recent effort to establish such a bloc, but it does not translate into a unified strategy for trade negotiations or for trade policy.

As difficult as it may be for Latin America to act in sync, the NAFTA partners have yet to implement the nuts and bolts of their own agreement. Again, seventeen years after NAFTA entered into force, it is still not possible to drive a truck from Ottawa to Oaxaca in a non-bureaucratic, hassle-free environment. The July 2011 memorandum of understanding signed between Mexico and the United States – meant to end the long-standing trucking dispute and to make the United States abide by the road transportation provisions of NAFTA[6] – is still to be implemented.

In the 1980s, firms in North America used inputs from the region almost exclusively. Three decades later, the internationalization of production and supply chains has facilitated inputs from many different countries, as the production process has spread itself geographically. Currently, complex supply chains depend on efficient transportation and logistical systems, an area in which North America lags behind East Asia. Congested railroads and ports are unable to handle ever-increasing amounts of cargo and containers. As Stephen Blank has stated in his chapter in this book, North America does not have a secure, efficient, and sustainable transportation system that reduces transaction costs, allows the use of cumulative wisdom, and responds to market needs.

Economic and trade co-operation between Canada and Mexico in a NAFTA context is still underdeveloped, considering the existing potential benefits between two countries that are trade partners.

The North American Pacific coast has many dynamic ports that serve commerce with Asian economies – Prince Rupert and Vancouver in Canada; Seattle, Oakland, Los Angeles, and Long Beach in the United States; and Manzanillo and Lázaro Cárdenas in Mexico, for example. Another key hub for ocean trade within the hemisphere is the Panama Canal; as it is broadened, trade will increase on both sides of the Pacific Ocean.

Both Canada and Mexico have a strategic interest in developing their trade links with Asia-Pacific. The sheer volume of trade between the Asia-Pacific basin and the western hemisphere means that the demand for port facilities and shipping capacity will remain for years to come. Canadian, US, and Mexican ports on the Pacific coast will need to handle more cargo than they can now manage separately. Multimodal transportation corridors across the Pacific are needed, as well as from the Pacific coast to consumption centres inside and across the continent.

Since transoceanic trade represents about 80 percent of world trade, shipping lines, port operators, port authorities, as well as importers and exporters have become key players. There are two initiatives that are fundamental to a better synergy among the NAFTA partners in their Asia trade. The first is the NAFTA Rail, which departs from the port of Lázaro Cárdenas in the state of Michoacán on Mexico's Pacific coast. It is a seamless, double-stack railway connection that hauls incoming Asian cargo from the Pacific coast to the heart of the United States market in Kansas City, Missouri. It continues all the way to Winnipeg, Manitoba, located halfway between the port of Vancouver and the major economic hubs of Toronto and Montreal in eastern Canada. The city of Winnipeg plans to re-establish itself as a major transportation hub; it is developing CentrePort Canada, an 8,000-hectare inland port as a one-stop shop for air, truck, and rail shipments designed to reroute North American trade through the middle of the country.[7]

The second initiative is the North American Super Corridor Coalition (NASCO), an association of cities, counties, states, provinces, and private sector representatives. Spanning almost 4,000 kilometres through the mid-continent in central United States, eastern and central Canada, and deep into Mexico, the NASCO trade corridor is a multi-modal transportation network that connects 71 million people and supports $1 trillion dollars in total commerce between the three nations. It is geared to help increase trade flows between North America and other trade regions such as Asia-Pacific and Latin America.[8]

CANADA-MEXICO: THE OUTLOOK FOR POSSIBLE FUTURE CO-OPERATION IN THE HEMISPHERE

Mexican and Canadian interests in foreign policy are distinguished by their contrasting history and traditions. México has strong links with

Latin America by means of a common history, language, culture, and religion. This has led the country to have an active stance toward the south, joining regional organizations such as the Latin American Economic System (SELA), the Latin American Integration Association (ALADI), the Organization of Ibero-American States (OEI), the nascent Community of Latin American and Caribbean States (CELAC) and acting as an observer at the Andean Community of Nations (CAN), the Southern Common Market (MERCOSUR), the Central American Integration System (SICA) and the Union of South American Nations (UNASUR).

On the other hand, Canada is more focused on the European Union in light of its historical links with France and the United Kingdom, and also on the Asian economies, in particular Japan and China. Canada's interests are explicit in its participation in the Euro-Atlantic Partnership Council (EAPC), the European Bank for Reconstruction and Development (EBRD), the Paris Club, the Organization for Security and Cooperation in Europe (OSCE), and its role as an observer at the Southeast European Cooperative Initiative (SECI).

At the same time, Canada is advocating the participation of Asian economies in regional agreements in several ways: as a dialogue partner of the Association of Southeast Asian Nations (ASEAN), as a non-regional member of the Asian Development Bank (ABD), and as a member of the ASEAN Regional Forum. Notwithstanding the Asia Pacific Foundation of Canada (APFC), which studies Canada's relationship with Asian economies, a poll of Canadian attitudes toward Asia revealed that Canadians feel that they are affected by Asia but do not consider themselves to be part of the Asia-Pacific region.[9]

NAFTA and (APEC) are the two existing regional agreements that provide a framework for economic co-operation between Canada and Mexico in the hemisphere.

APEC jump-started the Transpacific Partnership (TPP) in 2006; its original members were Brunei, Chile, New Zealand, and Singapore. Australia, Japan, Malaysia, Peru, the United States, and Vietnam were to negotiate to join. Canada, Mexico, the Philippines, South Korea, and Taiwan have expressed interest in TPP membership. The TPP is seen as a blueprint for the proposed Free Trade Area of the Asia Pacific (FTAAP).

However, there are other new initiatives that can potentially be used to broaden and deepen this collaboration. In 2007, Alan García, president of Peru at the time, proposed the Latin American Pacific Arc, a new regional trade integration mechanism that would include all Latin American countries on the Pacific coast.[10] On 28 April 2011, four countries within the Pacific Arc – Mexico, Colombia, Peru, and Chile – signed the Pacific Alliance. These four countries have at least two common features: they are located on the Pacific Basin and they have signed trade agreements with the United States. Some analysts have seen the Pacific

Alliance as a counterweight to MERCOSUR, and particularly to Brazil,[11] although the new government of President Ollanta Humala in Peru may shift gears and nurture a closer relationship with Brazil.

Since the second half of the 1990s, many US manufacturers have set up shop in China, attracted by the low cost of production. However, ten years later, both the increasing cost of labour in China and the higher cost of fuel used by megacarrier ships have prompted a slow but significant return of manufacturers to the western hemisphere. Moreover, the 2008 global financial crisis has marked a turning point. In 2010, President Barack Obama set up a high-level panel of American chief executives in his effort to double US exports over the next five years.[12]

This call for the US to curtail its trade deficit by reducing its imports from China and increasing its exports to the world is intimately related to the need for Americans to enter their own age of austerity. This implies increasingly relying on goods that have a significant regional (North American) content.

Canada and Mexico are geographically positioned to prosper as the crossroads between North America and the growing Asian economies, such as China, India, Korea, and Japan. A new tri-national production and logistics platform is needed if North America is to compete with the other two mega-blocs: the European Union and the East Asian bloc. There is a trend to consider North America as a joint productive and exporting platform, in which Mexico concentrates on manufacturing, the United States and Canada provide process engineering, design, technology, branding, financing, and marketing, and all three countries contribute strategic energy resources.

CONCLUSIONS AND RECOMMENDATIONS

The economic relationship between Mexico and Canada is determined by the role that each country plays in the world's economic system and as part of the North American region.

Mexico promised to become an active ambassador for Latin America when it joined NAFTA in 1994, but in practice its presence and political influence in Central America and in South America have decreased. De facto, Latin America is divided into a northern region – Mexico, Central America, and the Caribbean, which share the fact that the United States is their largest trade partner and the source of remittances of their migrant workers – and a southern region – the economies of South America, which have diversified their trade and now export large amounts of commodities to China and other markets. Mexico, Argentina, and Brazil are expected to jointly represent Latin America in the Group of 20.[13] However, in light of the international financial crisis, Mexico has not yet coordinated its actions with the two largest economies in

South America, while the UNASUR countries have agreed to boost intra-regional trade, coordinate the use of monetary reserves, and strengthen the regional financial institutions.[14]

Although in 2010 Canada had a GDP considerably larger than Mexico's,[15] current projections for the next decades show a dramatic shift in their respective position. Mexico is projected to have a population of 148 million in 2050, compared to Canada's 41 million,[16] while by the middle of the twenty-first century Mexico's GDP will be US$6.682 trillion, twice Canada's projected GDP of $3.322 trillion.[17] Moreover, in 2050 almost 25 percent of the total population of Canada's biggest trade partner – the United States – will be of Hispanic background, and two thirds of those will be of Mexican descent.[18]

The outlook for further regional integration in North America is explored by Professor Robert Pastor in another chapter in this volume. As Alex Bugailiskis and Edward Dosman correctly assert in their essay, joint regional co-operation has little logic or sustainability unless it is grounded in strong national interests. However, as Pastor so clearly demonstrates, in the long run each country's national interest is best served by interdependence instead of dependence, reciprocity instead of unilateralism, and negotiations based on the common interest rather than on a quid pro quo.

Rather than simply continuing to import Chinese goods, Mexico, Canada, and the United States have much to gain through co-operatively building a new production and logistics platform to make the North American region more competitive at a global level.

Immersed as it is in a deep ideological dispute over how to manage its own economy, Washington is ill-prepared to envision the future of the region. Mexico and Canada must take the leadership within APEC, leading the drive to bring in Colombia as a member economy and exploring export alliances with the Asia-Pacific region.

Mexico City and Ottawa can also advance their national interests, propel economic growth, and reap economic and political benefits by looking at North America as a unified business region, relying on the combined production and trade advantages of the three North American partners. Their ability to pursue common goals in Latin America will depend on a new vision that helps realize the notion that the whole is greater than the sum of its parts.

NOTES

1   I am grateful to Alexis Rivera for his highly qualified research assistance.
2   Sidney Weintraub, *Unequal Partners: The United States and Mexico* (Pittsburgh: University of Pittsburgh Press, 2010).

3 Guadalupe Gonzalez, Jorge A. Schiavon, David Crow, and Gerardo Maldonado, "México, las Américas y el Mundo 2010 – Política Exterior: Opinión Pública y Líderes" (Mexico City: CIDE, 2011).

4 Robert A. Pastor, *The North American Idea: A Vision of a Continental Future* (Oxford: Oxford University Press, 2011).

5 Trinidad and Tobago, Bahamas, Jamaica, Haiti, Barbados, Guyana, Antigua and Barbuda, Surinam, St Vincent and the Grenadines, St Lucia, Saint Kitts and Nevis, Belize, Grenada, Dominica, and Montserrat.

6 Firman México y Estados Unidos memorando en transporte transfronterizo (Mexico and the United States sign a Memorandum of Understanding on transborder transportation) www.t21.com.mx, 6 July 2011.

7 Siri Agrell, "Winnipeg working to regain role as transportation 'gateway to the West,'" *Globe and Mail*, 22 May 2011.

8 www.nascocorridor.com.

9 Paul Evans,"Canada faces a simple choice: open up to Asia, or be left behind," Liu Institute of Global Issues, University of British Columbia, 2010, http://www.ligi.ubc.ca/?p2=/modules/liu/profiles/profile.jsp&id=1.

10 Samuel Logan, "Pacific Arc Plan: Innovative but Challenging," (International Relations and Security Network), www.samuellogan.com, 24 September 2007.

11 Farid Kahhat,"Del Arco del Pacífico Latinoamericano al Acuerdo del Pacífico," www.americaeconomia.com, 29 April 2011.

12 Edward Luce, "Obama sets up export growth panel," *The Financial Times*, 7 July 2010.

13 Mexico will host the G20 leaders' Summit in June 2012.

14 Alejandro Rebossio, "América del Sur hace frente común contra la crisis – la amenaza al crecimiento económico impulsa la ansiada integración regional" (South American countries coalesce against the crisis – the threat of lower economic growth triggers regional integration), *El País*, Madrid, 14 August 2011.

15 According to the International Monetary Fund, in 2010 Canada's GDP was US$1.574 trillion, ninth largest in the world, while Mexico's was US$1.039 trillion, the fourteenth largest.

16 United States Census Bureau – International Data Base, July 2011.

17 "GDP projections from PricewaterhouseCoopers: how China, India and Brazil will overtake the West by 2050," 7 January 2011, www.guardian.co.uk.

18 See "Population Profile of the United States" in www.census.gov.

Shared Interests
in an Expanded Regional Agenda

ALEX BUGAILISKIS AND ED DOSMAN

INTRODUCTION

A number of the contributors to this book lament that the Canada-Mexico relationship has failed to reach its potential. It is true that the loftier visions of a North American Community that greeted the signing of NAFTA have yet to be fully realized. However, as many of the articles in this volume illustrate, the relationship between Mexico and Canada has expanded significantly since their "shotgun wedding" in 1994. The marriage has blossomed over the years, spawning significant increases in trade and investment and expanding academic and people-to-people linkages. In this chapter, we focus on the positive by looking at what Mexico and Canada have accomplished and assessing how they might take that accumulated experience and knowledge and leverage it in support of their larger hemispheric interests. This paper seeks to explore the potential and prospects for more innovative regional policy collaboration between Mexico and Canada. We argue that stronger hemispheric co-operation by Mexico and Canada will advance their national interests while also strengthening their bilateral relations and even their trilateral relationship with the United States. In examining the potential for that engagement, we identify their common interests and assess their combined capacity to act in the current geopolitical environment.

MEXICAN AND CANADIAN FOREIGN POLICY PRIORITIES

Converging Interests and Approaches

At first glance, the comparison of Canadian and Mexican foreign policy in the Americas appears elusive since it is difficult to imagine two countries with more divergent histories and diplomatic traditions. Mexico has been a vital and core Latin American culture for centuries, with long-established diplomatic relations in the region. This includes a close yet tumultuous relationship with the US that has encouraged and enshrined the principle of "non-intervention." The Mexican revolution of 1910 has inspired generations of students, academics, and political leaders in the region and made it the destination of choice for political refugees. In the years following the Second World War, Mexico became a strong advocate for Latin American independence and economic and social development and was a founding member of regional bodies like the Organization of American States (OAS) and the Rio Group.[1]

In contrast, Canada, with its very different Anglo-French lineage, remained outside the inter-American system. Following the Second World War it tied its future prosperity and security to Europe and the US, forging strong political/military and economic relations through institutions like NATO, the UN, and NORAD (North American Aerospace Defense Command). During the Cold War, Canada saw the region as a potential hotbed and sought to avoid confrontation with the US in "its own backyard." Nevertheless, Canadian businesses became active in the region, including as investors, as early as the nineteenth century. Canadian banks followed, but interest waned following major losses during the regional financial crisis of 1982. Thus, apart from sharing borders with the US, Mexico and Canada lived in very different diplomatic worlds.

The NAFTA Effect

Mexico was an early and active advocate for regional integration. Mexico (unlike Canada) was a founding member of both the Latin American Free Trade Agreement (LAFTA) in 1960 and its less ambitious successor the Latin American Integration Association (ALADI). However, both failed to achieve regional integration and what emerged instead was a series of bilateral and subregional agreements with limited scope.[2]

In 1990 the Mexican government astonished Ottawa with a proposal to form NAFTA, a free trade area encompassing Mexico, the US, and Canada. It would be a unique regional free trade agreement, encompassing a developing and two developed economies. NAFTA would redefine North America and permanently alter Canadian relations with the largest Hispanic country in Latin America (and the world). Mexico's decision to opt for NAFTA reflected the reality of a growing economic and trade relationship with the US which had continued to deepen after 1945. It also heralded Mexico's geopolitical reorientation toward North America and the narrowing of a shared Latin American integration strategy and vision.

While initially hesitant, Canada was propelled into the negotiations by the need to protect the benefits acquired under its earlier (1988) Free Trade Agreement with the US. Canada's decision to join the OAS and, soon after, NAFTA would prove historic in moving it from its singular focus on Europe and the US toward greater engagement with Latin America. With the demise of the Cold War, converging interests and trade opportunities with Mexico and the region provided the underlying rationale for this shift of Canadian foreign policy toward Latin America.

Transition in Mexico: Fox and Calderón

There has been much debate surrounding the impact of NAFTA on Mexico, but the free trade agreement undoubtedly further integrated its economy into the North American production matrix. President Fox's election and the return of multiparty democracy led to a more assertive foreign policy and a closer alignment of Canadian and Mexican interests in promoting prosperity through open markets and free trade and strengthening democratic institutions to support sustainable development and the security of citizens. However, Mexico has remained constrained by a constitution and a "foreign policy doctrine of non-intervention, respect for people's self-determination and interdiction of the use of force"[3] that limits its ability to actively participate in conflict situations. For example, while Mexico is a member of the "Friends of Haiti"[4] it has declined to participate in peacekeeping operations, unlike Brazil, which now heads the military force for the United Nations Stabilization Mission in Haiti (MINUSTAH).

The election of Felipe Calderón in 2006 heralded a return to a more traditional Latin American foreign policy orientation. President Calderón placed a renewed emphasis on strengthening relations with the region and rebuilding bridges with governments in Nicaragua, Cuba, and Venezuela. He provided a new vision of co-operation with Central America, replacing the old Plan Puebla-Panamá program with a new Mesoamerican Project based on eight jointly agreed priorities.[5] Calderón also initiated his own models for regional integration, proposing and hosting the first meeting of the Community of Latin American and Caribbean States (CELAC). Unlike the Brazilian-led initiatives (such as the Union of South American Nations [UNASUR] and the South American Defence Alliance)[6] the CELAC brings Mexico, Central America, and Caribbean countries together with their South American counterparts (although it still excludes Mexico's two North American neighbours, Canada and the US). In April 2011, President Calderón signed the Lima Declaration – along with fellow presidents from Chile, Colombia, and Peru – creating the Pacific Alliance, aimed at deepening economic integration. In a less than veiled challenge to Brazil, Calderón noted that the Pacific Alliance countries combined value of $872 billion well exceeded the $543 billion represented by the MERCOSUR market.[7]

CANADA AND THE REGION:
THE AMERICAS ENGAGEMENT STRATEGY

While Canada's commercial linkages with Latin America date back centuries, serious and sustained political engagement in the region really began with Canada's participation in the Central American peace process in the late 1980s. As the Cold War drew to a close in the late 1980s, then foreign minister Joe Clark took the momentous decision following a visit to the region (and encouraged by a very active Canadian civil society presence in Central America) to engage directly in the peace process. The peaceful end to the long and bloody civil conflicts in Central America reinforced an ongoing democratic transition in the region, leading Prime Minister Brian Mulroney to conclude that it was time for Canada to take up its seat at the OAS. As Dr Brian Stevenson notes, "it is important to see Canada's entry into the inter-American system from a historical perspective, as part of a long-term movement towards integration with the hemisphere."[8] In the decade after joining the OAS, Canada was an active host and participant in regional meetings and initiatives where it promoted an ambitious concept of hemispheric integration that included a Free Trade Area of the Americas (FTAA). While it had been hoped that NAFTA would be the first decisive step toward achieving a hemispheric trade agreement, the FTAA negotiations proved as unsuccessful as the previous regional initiatives of LAFTA and ALADI.

Canada developed an activist inter-American agenda, hosting numerous regional events and promoting co-operation on human rights, democracy, and development. The Inter-American Democratic Charter adopted at the Quebec Summit of the Americas was signed by regional representatives in Lima on 11 September 2001. The events of that fateful day would compel Canada to turn its focus to the protection of its border and economic lifeline with the US. The "War on Terrorism" would reduce the priority and resources devoted to engagement with the region.

However, on 6 February 2007, marking the first anniversary of his government, Prime Minister Stephen Harper announced his intention to "re-engage relationships throughout the Americas, with our partners in Mexico, the Caribbean, and Central and South America."[9] This renewed focus on the hemisphere led to the development of the "Americas Engagement Strategy" – a "whole-of-government" effort based on three interrelated goals that seeks to build prosperity, enhance security, and strengthen democratic institutions and practices in the hemisphere through co-operation with regional partners and organizations.[10] The initiative has spawned a new dynamic in relations with the hemisphere starting with a three-fold increase in high-level visits to the region by the prime minister and foreign minister and a dedicated minister of state for the Americas. In lieu of the FTAA, the Canadian government has committed resources to a robust program of bilateral trade negotiations which has succeeded in concluding FTAs with Peru, Colombia, Panama, and Honduras.[11] At the Fifth Summit of the Americas in 2009, Prime Minister Harper announced a $4 billion temporary infusion of capital for the Inter-American Development Bank (IDB), which IDB president Luis Alberto Moreno credited with providing vital liquidity for the region at a critical moment during the global financial crisis. The Canadian International Development Agency (CIDA) announced significant increases of development assistance for Haiti and the Caribbean which, along with Honduras, Bolivia, Peru, and Colombia, have become countries of focus. CIDA has also provided a three-year $20 million contribution to the OAS to support its efforts to modernize and more effectively promote democratic practices and enhance security in the region. Following the devastating 2010 earthquake in Haiti, Canada took immediate leadership in convening a high-level meeting of donors and "Friends of Haiti" in Montreal to begin working on a framework for long-term recovery and reconstruction.[12] Canada has also made hemispheric security a key priority, using its role as host in 2010 to place the issue firmly on the G8 agenda and establishing a new Anti-Crime Capacity Building Fund to build regional capacity to combat crime. Furthermore, Canada is expanding people-to-people linkages through new scholarship programs and student mobility agreements.

NATURAL PARTNERS WITH COMMON INTERESTS AND COMPLEMENTARY CAPACITIES

This brief historical overview, along with other articles in this book, highlights the commitment made in both words and actions by Mexico and Canada to deepen engagement with the region. While the degree of this engagement waxes and wanes in response to global and domestic developments, the overarching trend line is clearly positive. This should not be surprising. There has been a parallel evolution in Canadian and Mexican foreign policy since 1990 where we have seen closer alignment on key issues and shared values that include international law (US trade embargo on Cuba, Law of the Sea, the International Criminal Court); security and disaster-relief; multi-party democracy and human rights; humanitarian issues; open markets and free trade; conflict resolution (Central America, Colombia); and multilateralism (OAS, UN Security Council, G20). Indeed, this high degree of convergence on multilateral and regional issues is in stark contrast to Brazil where Ottawa and Brasília are separated by major differences on issues like UN reform, climate change, Iran, and the Middle East. This bodes well for enhanced collaboration with Mexico in global forums (as discussed by Enrique Berruga-Filloy and Philip Oxhorn) and for greater regional co-operation.

Mexico and Canada share a similar approach and reputation for quiet but effective multilateral diplomacy. In 2010 Canada successfully hosted international meetings on Relief and Reconstruction in Haiti, the G20, the G8, and the Arctic. Mexico has also had considerable international success in recent years including chairing and hosting the successful COP 16 climate change meetings, leading the establishment of the new UN Human Rights Council, chairing the OECD, and completing an effective term as a non-permanent member of the Security Council (2009/10). They will also host the G20 meeting in June 2012. Canada and Mexico have worked closely and constructively on sensitive issues in the region including successful efforts to lift sanctions barring the membership of Cuba and Honduras from the OAS and to mitigate various border disputes. They have also been active in promoting greater regional collaboration through the OAS and subregional organizations to combat organized crime and to strengthen democracy. These shared interests and networks could be applied to support an even more robust regional agenda.

Most foreign policy theorists agree that the strongest motivating force in the conduct of foreign relations is the pursuit of economic prosperity and security. When it comes to prosperity, our colleague Carlos Heredia and others in this book illustrate in a very convincing manner the primordial importance of the US relationship to both Canada and Mexico. There is no need to repeat or debate the figures, and despite a relative decline in the wake of the recent financial crisis and economic recession, the US will continue to be the key market for Mexican and Canadian exports well into the future. What is not as well appreciated is the growth in Mexican and Canadian commerce. Trade between Canada and Mexico has increased six-fold since 1994, but even this is vastly underestimated due to difficulties in capturing the transhipment of goods through the US and the increasing level of intra-firm trade. While trade diversification is a good risk management practice, at least in the short term, it must be seen as a complement rather than a substitute for strengthening existing trade links in the region.[13] Mexico and Canada share a common interest in attenuating the negative impact of a move toward greater regional protectionism and in managing increased competition from new actors like China. As Heredia points out, China is now the second-largest (following the US) trading partner of both Mexico and Canada. However, these two relationships differ considerably since Mexico and Canada are net exporters to the US and net importers from China. They therefore share an interest in addressing this financial imbalance by increasing North American productivity and working together in such forums as the G20 to encourage responsive and responsible Chinese economic policies. They also need to actively promote economic models that can better leverage their existing FTAs in both North America and the region (and in the case of Canada protect significant investments).[14] Even relatively small advances in achieving greater harmonization or convergence on existing trade agreements could bring enormous benefits to both, as well as to their NAFTA partner, the US.

Regional security has become an increasingly important and inter-related interest of both Mexico and Canada. The growth of transnational crime, frequently fuelled by illegal drug trafficking, has led to significant increases in violent crime and homicides (see articles by Reid Morden and Raúl Benitez Manaut). From 2006 to 2010, President Calderón's "war on drugs" is estimated to have resulted in more than 40,000 drug-related homicides in Mexico. As frightening as these statistics are, homicide rates are even higher in Brazil and other parts of the region. Central America now has the lamentable distinction of being the most violent region in the world (aside from actual war zones) with homicide rates six to eight times the global average. With smaller economies and less robust democratic institutions, these countries are less capable of protecting their citizens and absorbing the immense costs and economic losses. The web of globalized crime networks makes its way up to the streets of Toronto and Vancouver and across the ocean to West Africa where related gang members are actively engaged in importing both their drugs and their violence. In 2010 Canada placed the issue of transnational crime in Latin America on the G8 agenda for the first time and in June 2011 it was the focus of two high-level regional meetings: the Annual General Assembly of the OAS held in El Salvador and the Central American Integration System (SICA) in Guatemala City where Mexican foreign minister Patricia Espinosa and the Canadian minister of state, Diane Ablonczy, committed their respective governments to work with Central American officials to combat transnational crime networks.

Together, Mexico and Canada have something unique to offer the region. First, they provide an example of positive, mutually beneficial north-south co-operation. While critics complain that the bilateral relationship has failed to reach its full potential, when measured in relative as opposed to absolute terms, there has in fact been a fundamental change in both the breadth and depth of Canadian-Mexican relations. Twenty years ago no one imagined the density of economic, political, and societal linkages that now exist between these two countries. The strengthening of Canadian-Mexican relations since 1990 provides a durable example of community building. Step by step, and often ignored, transnational and subnational linkages between the countries have gradually deepened – beyond the unprecedented expansion of bilateral trade – to issues of labour, health, education, training, technology, and tourism, to name a few. Contributing authors to this book, like Jon Allen and Julian Ventura, Isabel Studer, and David Parks outline an impressive record of engagement, much of it informal, yet no less important.

CHALLENGES AND OPPORTUNITIES FOR JOINT ENGAGEMENT

The Changing Regional Context

We now turn to the challenges and opportunities facing Canada and Mexico in pursuing their regional goals. The current hemispheric conjuncture holds enormous promise but also significant challenges. Emerging from decades marked by economic instability, authoritarian governments, and civil wars, the hemisphere has witnessed a democratic surge and an unprecedented period and rate of economic growth that is producing a burgeoning middle class with aspirations for a more prosperous and secure future. President Moreno of the IDB has called this the "Decade of Latin America" and influential magazines, including the *Economist*, have joined the chorus.[15] Despite these gains, however, the region continues to be plagued by huge pockets of poverty and inequality, although some countries like Brazil, Mexico, and Peru have made important advances.[16] While most countries in the region are expected to come close to meeting the goal of universal primary education by 2015, several studies have been critical of the poor quality of instruction and the high rates of desertion.[17] High levels of corruption and impunity further impede the region's ability to lift up its poor through sustainable economic growth.

The combined threat of high food and energy prices and climate change will disproportionately affect the smaller and more vulnerable states in the region. Recent exponential increases in violent crime in Mexico (and particularly Central America) threaten economic growth

and could unravel the relatively fragile democratic fabric of these countries. There has also been a geopolitical reshaping of the Americas in the
past decade which is transforming the post-1945 landscape. The relative
power of a still dominant US is declining while new international actors
like the EU and China have become active in the region. With the eighth-
largest economy in the world, Brazil has become a regional power with
global status. Beyond its sheer size and resource endowment, sixteen
years of consistent leadership behind a strong economic and regional
vision and effective self-promotion have served to project Brazil as the
regional leader in South America. While Latin America remains extremely
diverse in structure, endowment, ideology, and regional memberships,
Brazil has taken the lead in promoting a new complex of diplomatic,
trade, and security networks focused on strengthening South American
integration and independence. Canada, which has invested heavily in
the OAS and its agencies, is concerned that the growth of alternative
forums may undermine the authority of the OAS and disperse limited
resources. Moreover, Canada's exclusion, along with the US and at times
even Mexico, from these new "regional" organizations is limiting their
ability to expand their engagement in the region. Overall, the "reshaping" of the Americas has narrowed both Mexico and Canada's diplomatic space in the region.

The relative political and economic decline of the US in Latin America
is a particularly important issue for Canada and Mexico. Despite efforts
to diversify, both continue to depend heavily on the US as a key market
for their exports. In the case of Mexico, diaspora linkages with the US are
expanding almost exponentially, with both economic (remittances) and
political implications.[18] Mexico and Canada's shared concern in protecting their significant interests in the US can sometimes conflict with their
desire to take a more active regional leadership role. Despite compelling
examples of their ability to take "independent" positions from the US
(e.g., Cuba, the Contadora Peace Process, Iraq), both Mexico and Canada
have been vulnerable to accusations that their "special" relationship with
the US constrains their capacity to vigorously promote regional interests.
As the US embarks on the road toward the 2012 presidential elections, we
can expect it to become increasingly disengaged from the region, which
may provide Mexico and Canada with greater room for manoeuvre.

The changes underway in US-Latin American relations create both
the imperative and the context for a more active engagement by Canada
and Mexico in the region to protect and promote "North American"
interests. Brazil's growing weight in the region may also open doors to
Mexico and Canada, who would be seen as a balancing influence by
countries that share a more inclusive hemispheric vision. As will be discussed in the next section, a more strategic and collaborative regional
engagement by Mexico and Canada at this critical juncture could

advance their interests, including their primordial relationship with the US. Their combined experience (and resources) could provide a compelling example of regional collaboration and make an important contribution to addressing key challenges in the hemisphere.

A Regional Agenda for Increased Collaboration

In the following section, we propose a short list of areas where Mexico and Canada could use their considerable experience to good effect in jointly pursuing common interests in the region. The following proposals for enhanced joint regional engagement by Mexico and Canada have been selected on the basis of the combined experience, interests, and capacity of the two countries. Naturally, the success of this engagement will be predicated on

- the degree of political savvy, capital and 'mutual confidence invested by both sides;
- the regularity and intensity of high-level consultations;
- joint outreach and engagement with other government and opinion leaders in the region;
- effective communication to promote a regional vision that engages citizens; and
- the willingness to commit sufficient, long-term resources, both financial and human.

ENHANCED POLITICAL ENGAGEMENT WITH CENTRAL AMERICA AND THE CARIBBEAN

Canada and Mexico share a strong reputation in the region given their mutual support for the Central American peace process. Canada also has a "special" relationship with the Caribbean based on its shared Commonwealth heritage and Westminster traditions. A concerted effort by Mexico and Canada to both engage and champion issues of priority to the Caribbean (climate change, food security, and the impact of globalization) and Central America (security, economic integration, and trade) could bring returns in garnering their support in key regional forums like the OAS (where together they represent twenty of its thirty-five members) on issues and important candidacies.

HEMISPHERIC INTEGRATION

Canada and Mexico provide a positive example of north-south collaboration. Despite asymmetries, both have achieved significant benefits from NAFTA. Together they can make a compelling case for increased economic integration that can benefit from the inclusion of both developed and developing economies. They should lead on efforts to expand the rules of origin and cumulation[19] provisions that would broaden the range and movement of allowable goods from and through countries in the region. This would enlarge the benefits accruing from existing free trade arrangements and make the case for deeper integration. They should be even bolder, as Heredia proposes, in pursuing new initiatives like the Pacific Alliance or their more recently announced interest in joining the Transpacific Partnership (TPP) that could expand trade between the countries in the region bordering the Pacific coast and Asia.[20] To be successful, Canada must be prepared to bring greater offers of technical assistance to the table while Mexico will need to champion Canada's seat at the table. The creation of a joint innovation centre open to Latin America partners would be one way in which they could strengthen their role in designing and implementing strategies of collaboration to buttress the integration process at a practical working level.

STRATEGIC PARTNERS IN REGIONAL FORUMS

Mexico and Canada have a common interest in ensuring the continued relevancy and effectiveness of the OAS as the premier forum for regional consultation and collective action. This includes expending additional political capital through more regular consultations and joint action to take leadership and generate support for a more proactive approach particularly on issues (and appointments) related to democracy, human rights, and security. Canada has consistently indicated its interest in seeing the OAS take a more active role in support of democratic institutions and practices aside from electoral monitoring. Mexico's hosting of the first Forum on Latin America Democracy in October 2010 was an important start to providing a less politicized and more sober assessment of democratic challenges in the region. At the 2011 OAS General Assembly meeting in El Salvador, the Canadian minister of state for the Americas, Diane Ablonczy, called for a new focus on the "practice of democracy" suggesting that member states "share best practices" in their support of democracy.[21] Mexico and Canada should also be strategic and mutually supportive in facilitating their engagement in new regional organizations, both economic and political, like CELAC and the Pacific Alliance.

ACCOUNTABLE AND EFFECTIVE GOVERNANCE

In the decade following the signing of the NAFTA agreement, the real foundations for the Mexican/Canadian relationship were established through an extensive and wide-ranging series of visits by middle and senior level officials, technocrats, parliamentarians, and civil society leaders. They provided advice and technical assistance on a broad range of governance issues from elections to auditing and regulation and the modernization of the public service. Indeed, the extensive collaboration between Elections Canada and the Federal Electoral Institute of Mexico (IFE) during this period has been credited with contributing to the realization of real multi-party democracy with the historic defeat of the Institutional Revolutionary Party (PRI) in the 2000 election. This rich experience could form the basis for combined outreach to Central America (and potentially the Caribbean). Previous discussions with Mexican officials and academics indicated a high degree of interest in adapting some of the tools and partnerships developed with various Canadian government departments and agencies – the Canada School of Public Service, the Auditor General's Office, and Elections Canada, for example - to develop a joint program on governance that could be offered to Central America and Haiti.[22] The establishment of Mexico's first development assistance agency (AMEXCID) provides an opportune moment for Canada to partner with Mexico to respond to the very real demand for renewal and reform of democratic institutions in Central America (and possibly Haiti). Canada and Mexico would bring a very powerful combination of knowledge and experience given their complementary perspectives, their different levels of development, and Mexico's strong cultural and linguistic ties to countries in the region.

HEMISPHERIC SECURITY

Regional security issues have become an important area of mutual interest. While Mexico is itself a victim of transnational crime, it is also cognizant of the serious impact crime is having on Central America and therefore of the need for a strong and coordinated regional (and indeed global) effort. Canada is concerned with the threat transnational crime poses to Canadians and to the long-term development of the region. Canada and Mexico are already moving toward increased co-operation both bilaterally and in Central America. Morden and Benitez provide a more detailed overview and recommendations in their articles on security. We would simply underline the need for sustained, high-level, and coordinated regional engagement on security. Recent high-level meetings at the OAS and SICA have provided important steps in this direction as have new Canadian contributions.[23] Joint Mexican and Canadian co-operation can bring compelling and complementary perspectives (and hopefully resources) to the fight against crime, which may lead to a more substantive dialogue and longer-term strategy on the thornier but underlying issue of the relentless demand for drugs. Canadian and Mexican collaboration in support of US disaster relief after Hurricane Katrina and in the Caribbean offers another potential model for the Americas.

FINANCIAL STABILITY

The strong and resilient performance by Mexico and the region in the wake of the recent financial and economic crises is both welcome and historic given that the region has experienced thirty-one financial crises during the past twenty-five years. As IDB president Alberto Moreno noted, this underscores the "growing solidity of the region's fiscal and political institutions."[24] However, it remains uncertain whether the region can maintain this stability in the face of future challenges, particularly if the demand for commodities falls while energy and food prices continue to increase. A few years ago, then governor of the Central Bank of Canada, David Dodge, ruminated that the Americas needed its own version of the OECD, "around which all the economic policy makers of the Americas can gather."[25] Given Mexico and Canada's joint and active membership in the OECD and the G20 (which Mexico will host in June 2012), combined with their considerable experience and credentials on financial and fiscal management issues, they should consider developing a proposal for a Latin America OECD which would provide a depoliticized space for discussion and the exchange of best practices. Mexico and Canada could bring the prestige and resources to such an enterprise that would surely attract the engagement of many in the region.

THE REINTEGRATION OF CUBA

As the only two countries in the region which did not cut diplomatic ties with Cuba following its expulsion from the OAS, Mexico and Canada continue to be held with special regard by the Cubans. They also have considerable commercial and tourism interests in Cuba. More significantly, the Cuban government has shown an interest in acquiring a better understanding of their relationships with the US, particularly how they promote their economic interests while protecting their cultural identities. As the US moves inexorably (albeit slowly) toward normalization of relations with Cuba, Mexico and Canada could be well positioned to play a constructive role – not as mediators or even intermediaries, but as informed and trusted advisers who can help to build an atmosphere of confidence as Cuba prepares for this inevitable transition. A smooth and non-violent movement toward the normalization of relations between Cuba and the US would be in everyone's interest. Mexico and Canada could ease this transition by encouraging dialogue and facilitating the exchange of information on issues of particular interest or concern to both Cuba and the US. This could include the provision of technical assistance to help Cuban agencies responsible for important sectors such as trade and investment, health and food safety, and transportation, to undertake the changes needed to meet US regulations and standards. Additional "confidence building measures" might include discussions to address Cuban concerns about their ability to sustain their high educational and health standards or their potential

interest in participating in global economic forums like the World Bank
and International Monetary Fund (IMF).

CONCLUSION: ENHANCING THE BILATERAL THROUGH REGIONAL ENGAGEMENT

These are but a few of the many areas where Mexico and Canada could
effectively engage in the region based on their common interests, values,
and capacity. In facing the shared challenge of a declining US economy,
they should find common cause in focusing their efforts to build a stronger, more competitive, and more integrated hemisphere. By working in
tandem to improve their neighbourhood, they can build sustainable and
more equitable economic growth; enhance the security of their citizens;
and strengthen democracy by promoting the rule of law and greater
accountability and transparency in governance. Faced with both the
challenge and opportunity offered by the larger and faster growing markets of Asia, Mexico and Canada will be poised for greater success as
part of a dynamic and more competitive "Americas," rather than on
their own.

NOTES

1 The Rio Group, formed in 1986, is a smaller, political forum sometimes seen
   as a "Latin American" alternative to the OAS.
2 The Andean Community of Nations (ANDINA) was established in 1969; the
   Southern Common Market (MERCOSUR) in 1991, and the Central American
   Integration System (SICA) in 1993.
3 Edmé Domínguez Reyes, Maj-Lis Follér, Åsa Stenman, *Globalization and the
   State in Mexico*, Iberoamericana, Nordic Journal of Latin American and
   Caribbean Studies 37, 2007.
4 First established by the UN, the Friends of Haiti is a grouping of countries
   that includes the US, Canada, Mexico, France, Germany, Venezuela, Chile,
   Argentina, Spain, Norway, Guatemala, and CARICOM that supports Haiti
   reconstruction and development.
5 Mexico and Central America agreed on eight priorities for engagement: energy,
   communications, transportation, commerce, development, health,
   natural disasters, and housing.
6 Mexico currently has observer status in UNASUR and the Defence Alliance but
   has indicated an interest in becoming a full member.
7 "Mexico, Colombia, Chile and Peru Sign Pacific Accord in Lima," AFP,
   04/05/11: http://www.dialogo-americas.com/en_GB/articles/rmisa/features/
   regional_news/2011/05/04/feature-ex-2120.

8 Brian Stevenson, *Canada, Latin America and the New Internationalism* (Montreal and Kingston: McGill-Queen's University Press, 2000).

9 Speech by Prime Minister Stephen Harper, 6 February 2007, http://pm.gc.ca/eng/media.asp?id=1522.

10 See http://www.international.gc.ca/americas-ameriques/engagement.aspx?lang=eng.

11 There are also ongoing negotiations with Central America and CARICOM as well as exploratory trade talks with Brazil/MERCOSUR.

12 The Preparatory Ministerial Conference on Haiti was held on 25 January 2010 (two weeks after the earthquake) and produced the "Montreal Principles" which continue to guide reconstruction efforts in Haiti, http://www.international.gc.ca/humanitarian-humanitaire/haiti_reconstruction_haiti.aspx?view=d.

13 While Mexico has twelve FTA agreements covering over forty countries, in 2010, 8 percent of its exports were still destined for the US market.

14 Canada is the third-largest investor in Latin America and the Caribbean with over $130 billion. This far exceeds its investments in Asia.

15 See *Economist*, 9 September 2010.

16 Latin America continues to be the most "unequal region" in the world although poverty rates are declining in some countries. See UN: Millennium Development Goals Report, Latin America, 2010.

17 The IDB has reported that only one in three Latin American young people manage to obtain a secondary school education compared to 80 percent in Southeast Asia.

18 According to US Census data for 2010, there are 31.8 million Mexicans living in the United States (and an estimated 7 million illegal Mexican immigrants). The US Hispanic population (of which 66 percent is Mexican) is expected to increase from 16 percent to 30 percent of the population by 2050. Hispanic Americans: Census Facts – Infoplease.com http://www.infoplease.com/spot/hhmcensus1.html#ixzz1R9SMJux3.

19 A facility that helps manufactured goods meet the relevant rules of origin requirements.

20 The original Transpacific Agreement negotiations were launched by Chile, New Zealand, and Singapore at the APEC leaders' summit in 2002. In 2011, Japan and South Korea, along with Canada and Mexico, announced their interest in entering consultations to join the TPP.

21 "Canada suggests that member states consider the creation of a compendium of good practices where we could review and exchange information on what each member considers its national contributions to democratic practices." Address by Minister of State Ablonczy to the General Assembly of the OAS No. 2011/20, 6 June 2011.

22 Isabel Studer references the e-learning program developed for Mexican public servants – @campus – which was financed by the Canadian International Development Research Centre (IDRC) from 2000 to 2005.

23 Canada announced new contributions of $5 million for Central America
    through the Anti-Crime Capacity Building Fund and $7 million for Guatemala
    through the Stabilization and Reconstruction Task Force's Global Peace and
    Security Fund, http://news.gc.ca/web/article-eng.do?nid=607939.
24 Speech by President Luis Alberto Moreno, "The Financial Crisis and its Impact
    on the Americas," given on 1 January 2009 at the OAS, http://www.oas.org/en/
    media_center/press_release.asp?sCodigo=E-006/09.
25 Remarks by David Dodge, governor of the Bank of Canada, to the Americas
    Society and the Council of the Americas, 29 March 2007, http://www.as-coa.
    org/Newsletter/2007-April/REMARKS_Dodge-Regional%20Leaders.pdf.

Hemispheric Security:
The Canada-Mexico Conundrum

REID MORDEN

Canada's government has made it clear that re-engagement in the Americas is a critical international priority for our country ... Canada is committed to playing a bigger role in the Americas and to doing so for the long term.

Prime Minister Stephen Harper, 17 July 2007

In some respects, Mr. Harper has sought to bring welcome focus to Canada's foreign policy. But too often, that focus has lapsed. In Latin America, for instance, it consisted of words that were not followed by deeds.

Globe and Mail editorial, 18 April 2011

We will establish a common approach to security to protect North America from external threats, prevent and respond to threats within North America, and further streamline the secure and efficient movement of legitimate, low-risk traffic across our shared borders.

President Bush, President Fox, and Prime Minister Martin, Waco, Texas, 23 March 2005 on the launching of the Security and Prosperity Partnership among Canada, Mexico, and the United States

"To preserve and extend the benefits our close relationship has helped bring to Canadians and Americans alike, we intend to pursue a perimeter approach to security, working together within, at, and away from the borders of our two countries to enhance our security and accelerate the legitimate flow of people, goods, and services between our two countries. We intend to do so in partnership, and in ways that support economic competitiveness, job creation, and prosperity."

Excerpt from the joint declaration by Prime Minister Harper and President Obama in Washington, DC, on 4 February 2011[1]

If the government's actions have not lived up to the expectations created by Mr Harper's policy statement in mid-2007, neither is the *Globe and Mail's* editorial put-down at all accurate. In the security sphere alone, Canada has a good deal underway in Mexico, in Central America, and in the Caribbean. It is engaged in a variety of training, capacity-building, and information-sharing activities and programs in various security and governance-related areas. Targeted at countries and areas such as Mexico, Guatemala, El Salvador, Haiti, and the Commonwealth Caribbean, Canada is using its expertise in these sectors by adopting a whole-of-government approach.

However, the government's 2007 policy statement raises a number of issues with respect to these security-related activities or programs. Are they adequate in terms of volume in light of the statement's intentions? Are they effective in their impact on recipients and in the expenditure of public monies? With respect to Mexico, is this likely to be an area productive in enhancing the bilateral relationship, given the massive interaction between Mexico and the United States on a variety of security-related fronts? Basically, *should* something more be done to enrich this partnership? *Can* something more be done to enrich this partnership? Finally, are these programs and activities consonant with Canada's broader foreign policy goals and objectives?

The answer to the last question is yes. While some development assistance purists would argue that dollars devoted to security issues is a misuse of money better spent in other development sectors, it is safe to say that policy attitudes in Canada generally have substantially evolved over the past twenty years from a time when security was anathema to the government assistance community. However, there is now clear recognition that inadequate security has become a substantial, probably crucial, obstacle to achievement of other development or commercial objectives. That recognition has been driven home in the post 9/11 period and Canada, in its assistance programs, has on the whole responded realistically to a more dangerous and ruthless world.

The answers to the other questions are more nuanced.

Speaking specifically about Mexico, there are discrete areas in the security/judicial world where Canada can effectively collaborate with Mexicans either through individual program designs or through complementing the activities of others like the US and the European Union. In the increasingly busy security arena it will be important to minimize overlap, never mind conflicting with others, especially the United States. Achieving this objective requires a degree of frank consultation with others, above all, the Mexicans. The latter, for their part, must be prepared to identify candidly Mexican priorities and any attendant difficulties in moving forward and achieving real and substantial progress. Anything less can only lead to frustration and irritation, not to mention a waste of resources.

Can and should the relationship with Mexico be advanced? Probably, in both cases. The current set of programs and activities in a widely defined security sector defaults into the traditional aid or assistance-giving mould. There are exceptions, but usually this means that Canada gives and others take. There is nothing wrong with that, generally speaking, but it falls far short of what might be expected of efforts with respect to Canada's second-largest market in the hemisphere, a substantial investment target, and a partner in the North American Free Trade Agreement (NAFTA).

At the same time, especially in the security world where trust and confidence are paramount in a relationship, Canada should not be faulted for caution in venturing into a figurative new world. Before NAFTA, Mexico, to most Canadians was sun, sand, and margaritas. NAFTA brought about a sea change in Canadian awareness and knowledge of Mexico. At the same time, although NAFTA has been in place for over twenty years, Mexico is still a new friend and partner, and the relationship, beyond commerce and recreation, and particularly in the closed world of security, still needs to mature.

Canada has traditionally steered clear of the political issues which over the past two centuries have periodically wracked Central and South America. Over the years, Chile, Brazil, and the Commonwealth Caribbean have been targets of Canadian investment forays, sometimes, as with Brazilian Traction, with neo-colonialist overtones, but generally we have accepted that the region was the Americans' back yard. And had been since the Monroe Doctrine was enunciated in 1823.

Canada's awakening of interest in the hemisphere, and more especially in Mexico, came quite recently with two game-changing events, one, an accident of history and one a deliberate policy shift. The accident came first. After searing negotiations, Canada and the United States had reached, by 1988, a bilateral free trade agreement (FTA). Canada would have been quite happy to draw a breath and use the years immediately following to make the economic adjustments required under the FTA. Instead, faced with the prospect of a discrete US-Mexico free trade agreement which would dilute gains from the FTA, Canada was forced to push for broadening the negotiation to a trilateral agreement. Once concluded, NAFTA, after twenty years, has benefited all parties in terms of increased trade and, in Canada's case, brought about a consciousness of Mexico that probably no other event could have accomplished.

The deliberate policy shift was, of course, the Mulroney government's decision to move from observer status to full membership in the Organization of American States (OAS). Over the years, proposals to make that shift had been put forward by successive governments and then dropped as other priorities shouldered it aside. However, in 1987, driven directly by the prime minister, Canada finally, very visibly, signalled that it was prepared and ready to play a fuller role in the western hemisphere. Twenty years later, Mr Harper rededicated Canada to do just that.

Against this prime ministerial commitment, is Canada performing adequately, and, if not, what should be done? One problem is that, within the security sphere alone, there are in excess of one hundred projects in the region made up of a mix of activities with a dollar value approaching CA$100 million. At first glance this looks and sounds substantial, but it rapidly tails off with disaggregation. In fact, once disaggregated by project activity and seen as spread through the region, the individual amounts in play are derisory.

As has been demonstrated again and again in the assistance world, throwing money at a problem does not guarantee a successful or even notable outcome. That said, continuing the model of training events and teaching and coaching approaches, worthy though the individual activity may be, consigns Canada's contribution to the periphery, given the magnitude of the problems facing Mexico and others in Central America and the Caribbean.

To begin to make a real impact, expenditures should rise to at least a half billion dollars. That sounds like a lot of money, and it *is* a lot of money in Canadian terms. How then to carve out an adequate pool of money for security co-operation in Mexico and the region in a period of severe fiscal restraint and deficit reduction? Difficult, but not impossible, given sufficient political will and determination.

First, the Canadian international assistance pool totals about CA$5.3 billion,[2] all in. The government should allocate these monies where it perceives Canada's interests and political imperatives to be, leaving behind the constraints of the OECD's outmoded Official Development Assistance scorecard. For example, it should drive to its logical conclusion the process of narrowing countries of concentration for the bilateral aid program, underway in Africa. (As has been seen in Canada's last unsuccessful candidacy for a UN Security Council seat, such actions have consequences, but that does not invalidate the policy itself.) And Canada should then reallocate according to perceived Canadian interests over, say, a five-year period.

A disciplined approach along these lines would yield amounts giving real substance and heft to the Harper government's 2007 commitment to the hemisphere. In the case of Mexico, this would provide a credible sum and consequently the flexibility to contribute and co-operate in areas where the impact would be greatest. The next step, after agreeing with Mexico on its priority needs, is to find those few, very few, areas where the concentrated focus of Canada's finite resources and expertise can make and engender a difference.

With some strong cautionary words below, the menu for collaboration could range quite widely, from border security (of which more later), to defence, or to the enhancement of legal or judicial regimes. In this context, it may be worth enriching some of the bilateral subnational activities which have already yielded a variety of generally economic agreements between Canadian provinces and Mexican states. This could lead to the adoption, in agreement with the Mexican government, of twinning or partnership arrangements for security issues.

Outside Mexico, Canada should expand, again in concert with the Mexicans, its activities in promoting and strengthening the governance and security apparatus in one or more of the smaller countries south of Mexico. Here fragile infrastructures are under strain, especially as Mexican drug cartels move their operational headquarters out of Mexico in response to the pressures exerted by President Calderón's war on drugs. Trilaterally, it might be best to choose a country or countries where Canada may find it easier to operate than the US, due to baggage from past relations. At their meeting in December 2010, the foreign ministers of the three countries took a tentative step in this direction by agreeing to initiate a dialogue on these issues.

Undoubtedly, there are additional approaches. Whatever path is chosen, greater focus and ranking of priorities along with the allocation of consequent resources are at the core of any attempt to move the relationship on security issues forward on a true partnership basis.

In selecting where to focus within the broad scope of security, Canada should take one issue off the table up front. Drugs. President Calderón's robust and very bloody war on drugs has thrown up casualty rates equivalent to those suffered by the US in Vietnam. It is also almost completely centred in Mexico's northern tier bordering the US, and the degree and intensity of the two countries' involvement is massive. Take that fact and add the following considerations – that the philosophical gap in addressing the drug problem between the US and Canada is more than substantial; that the US has so far taken no serious steps to deal with its domestic demand for drugs, wherein lies the greatest single contributing factor to the problem; and that most of the weaponry in the hands of the drug cartels can be traced back to the US – and Canada would be well advised to step back from this particular *noeud de vipères*.

Another area to approach with caution is, unfortunately, a Canadian favourite – policing. No question that Canada sets good examples, gives good training, and provides good mentors. All for naught, if the "C" word – corruption – prevails. There is political pressure at various political levels in Mexico to squeeze the level of corruption in Mexico's security forces. Its success, at the moment, is moot, and without a visceral, internal commitment to noncorrupt policing, virtually all external efforts to help will largely be for naught.

All the above proposals are in the realm of what might, could, or should be done. In one specific area, something can be done by Canada and it can be done now. That something is to provide the leadership in taking forward the inclusion of Mexico within a North American security perimeter. It is clear from the Harper/Obama declaration of this past February that agreement on conditions for a security perimeter encompassing Canada and the US is a first priority and the preparatory work to give substance to the leaders' declaration is already underway.

Nothing in that declaration precludes a parallel track which broadens the discussion to assess and define the steps, processes, and circumstances which must develop eventually to bring Mexico within that perimeter. Moving forward with this inclusive approach is not only the right thing to do; it is in Canada's self interest. The increasing level of economic integration of the Canadian and Mexican economies with the US economy since the entry into force of the Canada/US Free Trade Agreement and the North American Free Trade Agreement highlights the challenges they face vis-à-vis the United States which believes that security trumps trade. Effective supply chain management alone demands that there be a seamless regime from Mexico through to Canada.

We also have an anchor-piece and basis to proceed in the recommendations of the task force on the future of North America, co-chaired by former deputy prime minister John Manley, former treasury secretary Pedro Aspé, and former Massachusetts governor William Weld, issued in 2005.[3] The report covers a broader range of issues in building a true North American community but contains a blueprint on which a truly continental security perimeter can be built. It does two other eminently sensible things. First, it recognizes up front that progress on some issues will require a "two-speed" approach. Second, it deals head-on with the concerns about loss of sovereignty noting that, "North America ... is more than an expression of geography. It is a partnership of sovereign states with overlapping economic and security interests, where major developments in one country can and do have a powerful impact on the other two."

Neither the task force report nor the agreement among political leaders in Waco even attempts to argue for the disappearance of the borders or to equate the "harmonization" of policies and procedures with the replacement of Canadian or Mexican laws, policies, and procedures with a set of laws, policies, and procedures "made in the USA." Equally, there appears to be a fairly common agreement that what the perimeter does mean is, finding the common elements of those different sets of laws, policies, and procedures and incorporating them in a common set of rules that will build the mutual trust and confidence vital to allowing goods and people to pass freely across all of North America.

The concept itself, in one form or another, has been around for a long time. In fact, one might argue that the first proposal for a North American security perimeter is essentially contained in the Monroe Doctrine which told the traditional European colonial powers to stay out of the hemisphere. Then, in a rather breathtaking reassertion of the extra-territorial application of American power in 1904, President Theodore Roosevelt created the "Roosevelt Corollary" to the Monroe Doctrine by asserting that the United States was justified in exercising "international police power" to put an end to chronic unrest or wrongdoing in the hemisphere. Canadians should remember that they are part of that hemisphere.

The same concept, but directly involving Canada's agreement, was embodied in Article V of the North Atlantic Treaty (NATO) in 1949 that an attack against one member is considered to be an attack against all members of the alliance. The North American Air (and later Aerospace) Defense agreement between the United States and Canada in 1958 created a common perimeter around the two countries against the threat of attacks by Soviet bombers or missiles. A similar perimeter exists around the two countries for purposes of controlling exports of sensitive technologies outside the perimeter. With this degree of involvement in protection outside as well as within its borders, Canada and Canadians cannot claim to be unfamiliar with the workings and benefits of the perimeter concept.

To conclude, Canada should take the lead in seeking a partnership of shared interests where trade and security go hand in hand and will continue to do so into the future. This involves political will and consequent political decisions in Canada and the determination to energize that same degree of political will in both of Canada's North American partners.

In essence, this agenda simply recognizes that the world is changing and that there is a need to be adventurous and to contemplate arrangements and institutions that will both reflect new realities and continue the construction of a true North American community. There could be no better bridge to the future well-being of the peoples of North America.

NOTES

1   Declaration on a Shared Vision for Perimeter Security and Economic Competitiveness, Prime Minister Stephen Harper and President Barak Obama, Washington, DC, 4 February 2011.
2   Canadian International Development Agency, *Statistical Report on International Assistance*, Government of Canada, 2009–2010.
3   Chairmen's Statement, Independent Task Force on the Future of North America, sponsored by the Council on Foreign Relations, Consejo Mexicano de Asuntos Internacionales, Council of Canadian Chief Executives, 17 May 2005.

Mexico and Canada: Confronting Organized Crime through Enhanced Security Co-operation

RAÚL BENÍTEZ MANAUT

AND ATHANASIOS HRISTOULAS

Before NAFTA came into effect in 1994, relations between Canada and Mexico were marginal at best. Moreover, important differences existed with respect to defence and security policies. A central aspect of the Canadian conception of security implies international co-operation, specifically with the United States and, previously, Great Britain, as well as with the United Nations and more recently the Organization of American States (OAS).[1] On the other hand, the epicentre of Mexican security and defence doctrine is internal; prior to the Fox administration (2000–06), Mexico did not have an active international security policy as did Canada.[2]

But it does not have to be that way: the central argument of this chapter is that both Mexico and Canada can work much closer together, particularly given the context of Mexico "opening up" its security agenda to the world since the signing of the Merida Initiative in 2007. This chapter first outlines the state of bilateral relations between Mexico and Canada since 9/11. Then the chapter analyses the development of organized crime in Mexico, the weakness of the security institutions, and how this affects the country's internal security as well as its international relations. The chapter describes how Mexico, for the first time in its history, has decided to confront the problem of organized crime through an international co-operation program (the Merida Initiative of 2007), which includes training and equipping Mexican armed forces. The conclusion highlights a number of areas where Mexico and Canada can further enhance security co-operation.

FROM NAFTA TO ORGANIZED CRIME

As NAFTA was being implemented between 1994 and 2000, Mexico underwent the Zapatista uprising, and the country's security policies turned inward. Many Canadian non-governmental organizations supported the Zapatista Army of National Liberation (EZLN) and the indigenous cause, and the Canadian government repeatedly stated that human rights needed to be respected. This did not please Mexican policy-makers.

With Mexico's wave of democratization in 2000, it was assumed that the country would change its autarchic and nationalistic foreign policy. This did not happen. Canada offered assistance in the area of peace-keeping operations, making the Pearson Peacekeeping Centre available to Mexican military students. Members of the Mexican military took courses there; nevertheless, the Mexican government declined to send its soldiers to the United Nations Stabilization Mission in Haiti (MINUSTAH) in 2004 as specifically requested by the United Nations.

On the matter of security, the US factor has determined the relation-ship between Mexico and Canada and has led to a rapprochement since 2001. Canada and Mexico share a common issue: border security with the United States. After the terrorist attacks in the US, Canada signed the Smart Border Agreement in December 2001; Mexico followed suit in March 2002. These very similar agreements are the first elements of what could be called a security framework for North America.[3]

At the domestic level, the United States redefined its command struc-ture and, as part of its new antiterrorist policy, it created the Northern Command, which covers Canada, Cuba, Mexico, and part of the Carib-bean. The Northern Command is based in Colorado Springs, as is the North American Aerospace Defense Command (NORAD), and the con-fluence of Canadian and Mexican military officers is leading to the development of interagency defence co-operation.

In 2005, Mexico, Canada, and the United States signed the Security and Prosperity Partnership of North America (SPP), which highlighted security co-operation in many areas, including energy security and human security. The collaboration between health ministries during the H1N1 epidemic in Mexico in April 2009, for example, proved strategic, and the relationship between Canadian and Mexican scientists was decisive.

When it comes to global issues, Canada and Mexico can be consid-ered strategic allies. At least in terms of rhetoric, both countries place strong emphasis on multilateral relations and the peaceful resolution of conflict. Both countries also consider human rights to be pillars of their foreign policies. Further, within the context of the United Nations, both countries have worked closely together to push forward the human security agenda as well as Security Council reform. Along simi-lar lines, in 2002 former Mexican president Vicente Fox "assured that

Mexico … like Canada, makes its voice heard in the most important issues on the international agenda such as the defence of multilateralism and human rights, the respect for international law, the promotion of cooperation to ensure development and peace, together with international security."

However, on a regional (North American) basis, a different reality presents itself. Here, Canada-Mexico bilateral relations have been hurt by a persistent fear on the part of Canadian decision makers that the inclusion of Mexico in the "North American" agenda is not in their country's best interests. This is not a new phenomenon in Canadian foreign policy: during the negotiations leading up to the signing of NAFTA, Canada repeatedly tried to torpedo Mexico's inclusion in the discussions.

THE 9/11 EFFECT

On the surface, things seemed to change after 9/11. Immediately after the terrorist attacks, leaders from Canada, Mexico, and the United States began talking about security perimeters, or NAFTA-Plus. Canadian foreign policy seemed to shift toward closer co-operation not only with the United States but with Mexico as well. "[T]o ensure continued prosperity and security, Canada needs a more expansive partnership with both the United States and Mexico that continues to reflect the unique circumstances of our continent."[4] More notably, Canadian decision makers argued that "Canada will engage more actively with Mexico, bilaterally and trilaterally, to ensure that the North American Partnership is truly continental in character."[5]

The apex of this co-operation frenzy was the signing of the Security and Prosperity Agreement in 2005 in Waco, Texas. The leaders declared their desire to "develop new avenues of cooperation that will make our open societies safer and more secure, our businesses more competitive, and our economies more resilient."

The terrorist attacks would serve as the event that triggered this move toward a more unified North America, but the end result would be three countries bound together not only by economic necessity but also by a desire to coordinate security, political, and perhaps even social policy. Talk of a "security perimeter" was abuzz.

Yet now, the North American agenda has changed. The SPP has failed, and nobody talks about deep integration any more. The "security perimeter" was finalized, but it includes only the United States and Canada. Mexico was excluded from the process. Very little has changed in the nature of bilateral Mexico-Canada relations since 9/11. This is partly because Canada does not see Mexico as a partner in North America and partly because Mexico's attention is almost wholly absorbed by internal problems, namely the war against drug cartels.

After 9/11, Canadian policy-makers tried to differentiate their country from Mexico, arguing that the kinds of security threats present at the Canada-US border were different from those at the Mexico-US border and should therefore be treated separately. While Canada emphasized bilateral US-Canada responses to the 9/11 terrorist attacks, Mexico pursued a trilateral approach, ironically trying to convince US policy-makers to treat the country more like Canada. A further area of contention between Canadian and Mexican decision makers was the pace of change in response to 9/11.[6] While Canada preferred an incrementalist, piecemeal approach to dealing with the terrorist threat, Mexico wanted what the Mexican foreign minister of the time, Jorge Castañeda, called the "whole enchilada," or a comprehensive renegotiation of the NAFTA agreement to include other areas such as security and migration.

In response, Canadian policy-makers argued that the issues facing Canada and the United States were (and still are) the efficient flow of legitimate goods and travellers within the context of heightened US security concerns. On the other hand, the US-Mexican border was depicted as far more complex, characterized not only by a high level of trade but also by the existence of illegal migration, drug trafficking, and corruption. The negotiation of a trilateral security mechanism would require much more time, and the introduction of a third actor – from a Canadian perspective – would unnecessarily delay the entire process or possibly stall it completely. Moreover, "smart border" technology at the Canada-US border has been in place for some time, predating the terrorist attacks by a number of years. The same was not the case along the Mexican-US border. By design, therefore, Canada chose to differentiate itself (in terms of both issues and solutions) from Mexico. While this stance could be justified on technical grounds, it also underscored important symbolic/political factors that depicted Mexico not so much as a partner but as a complicating ingredient in the neighbourhood.

THE CHALLENGE OF ORGANIZED CRIME
AND THE WEAKNESS OF SECURITY
AND DEFENCE INSTITUTIONS

Since President Felipe Calderón took office in December 2006, Mexico has reported approximately 42,000 casualties in the war against drugs (up to June 2011), 90 percent of whom have been drug traffickers, 5 percent government officials, and 5 percent innocent bystanders. These figures have alarmed the Mexican people and the international community. When Mexicans hear reports about these violent crimes on television, radio, and in the newspapers, they are shocked and they fear that the government is incapable of controlling the country. In this context, the national security debate has been focused on whether the war on drug trafficking is being won or lost, a discussion that is far from the recognition that Mexico is a failed state or that it is leaning that way.[7]

Criminal organizations are taking advantage of the weaknesses of Mexican national security structures for their own benefit. One of the most significant dimensions is the lack of co-operation and coherence among the police, the military, and the judiciary. The Mexican government's critics argue that the constitutional and legal structure – particularly the division of federal, state, and municipal powers – is the central weakness of the Mexican state. For this reason, two of the main policies being implemented aim to transform the federal government's capabilities. The first seeks to reform the sub-systems of national security, defence, intelligence, justice, and the police at the federal, state, and municipal government levels. The second, by accepting US assistance to start up these structural reforms, seeks to acquire technology that is unavailable in the local market. Consequently, controlling violence and murder have, surprisingly, become new indicators of governability and government efficiency, indicating the real reason why President Felipe Calderón took the unprecedented step of recognizing the Mexican state's inability to fight big drug cartels alone and asked for help from the United States and other countries.

Political life is usually free from military interference, except when matters directly involve the armed forces. The military holds silent political power that gives it a veto over decisions that could affect it. For instance, the military has successfully opposed attempts by different presidents to appoint a civilian minister of defence and every effort to allow Mexico's eventual participation in United Nations peacekeeping operations. It has not published a White Book,[8] now common practice in other Latin American countries, and until recently it was able to avoid public scrutiny of its annual reports. Notwithstanding, the public has confidence in the military: it ranks second in public opinion polls with 71 percent of respondents asserting confidence in the institution.[9]

Among the police forces there is total dispersion and decentralization. There are two federal police agencies: the Federal Police (mostly preventive, created at the end of the 1990s) and the Ministerial Police (mostly investigative, created at the beginning of this century). Additionally, every state, as well as the Federal District, has at least two police agencies, and many municipalities have their own police corporations. Consequently, in 2006 there were 1,661 police bodies in Mexico. Dispersion hampers professionalism and induces corruption. The legislatures and the citizenry have little control over the police. In practice, police forces are subordinated only to their corresponding executive authority. However, it is well known that among the police forces there are "brotherhoods" that in part manage them, and in so doing disengage them from institutional control. In some cases, organized crime has infiltrated police agencies, with corrupt police officers working for drug traffickers. Recently, in some states and at the federal level, supervisory bodies have been set up to monitor police activities, but these bodies are embryonic and mainly symbolic. Due to corruption and ineffectiveness, the police rank last in surveys exploring the people's confidence in institutions.

However, the main problems in the area of extra-legal violence are organized crime and drug-trafficking cartels, which have been able to build paramilitary-type organizations with great firepower. To confront them, President Calderón has engaged the military. This move has raised concerns about protection of human rights.

In the arena of national and public security there is little communication between civil society and government. Reforms in these areas are usually conducted without consulting the public. Consequently, no significant measures to remedy the critical situation in matters of public security are being publicly discussed.

The future of the war on drugs in Mexico will depend on whether state institutions can be rebuilt; whether corruption – the drug traffickers' main weapon in weakening the state – can be eliminated; whether all mechanisms of international co-operation such as the Mérida Initiative, can be successfully articulated; and whether the fight against drugs can be demilitarized by implementing parallel programs against addiction on the demand-side, as well as preventive social and economic measures on the supply-side.

THE MERIDA INITIATIVE

In Mexico, public opinion has increasingly looked inward for threats to security: public insecurity, the spread of petty crime, and the increasing presence of organized crime. Thus, the paradigm of the 1980s and 1990s has returned: drug trafficking and its offshoots (in other words, organized crime) have become the new threat. This blight, unlike that of terrorism, is real for Mexico, exists in other countries, and is gaining strength. Mexico does not have efficient instruments with which to fight it. Laws are inconsistent, if indeed there are laws, and Mexico has not managed to develop the human and material resources and structures required to successfully combat the problem. This is not a military issue, as a simplistic view would suggest.

Organized crime is invisible and has considerable capacity to penetrate into the state itself via corruption. Military personnel are equally susceptible to being corrupted by the lure of money. The intelligence services have yet to develop the special (or more sophisticated) investigative capacities needed to combat this problem, and the armed forces cannot be deployed efficiently if they do not work in partnership and coordination with other state institutions and with broad international co-operation.

Organized crime takes advantage of the different legal systems and the vacuums and inconsistencies they create. First and foremost, organized crime takes advantage of porous borders – Mexico-Guatemala and Mexico-US. Second, the crime syndicates use the lack of transparency in the control of civil servants' salaries, the lack of professionalism on the part of police corps, and the lack of adaptation of military doctrine and training systems to their advantage. Third, they contribute to a massive informal economy which by its very nature is difficult if not impossible to tax, thus reducing the government's ability to function properly. Finally, they divert intelligence services' attention away from other priorities. Added to this is the mistrust between Mexican and US authorities. Few, if any, mechanisms for co-operation and communication exist, and little communication and information sharing takes place between the authorities of these countries. "U.S. law enforcement officials often find themselves in frustrating situations, unable to deal with the inefficiency that often characterizes Mexican officials, while Mexican authorities are overly sensitive to U.S. unilateralism, and lack the technical expertise to form the kinds of cooperative mechanisms that exist along the Canada-U.S. border."[10] The end result is that no "security confidence" exists along the US-Mexican border, and as David Shirk argues, "bi-national cooperation is typically focused on reducing cross border interagency irritants and misunderstandings rather than on coordinated operations."[11]

The shift in the policy of co-operation with Latin America and the de facto abandonment of the focus on terrorism to concentrate more on organized crime have paved the way for more realistic bilateral relations. The new threat is everywhere, all-corrupting, and justifies a new, integrated co-operation policy. The problem lies at the very top of the pyramid, especially with the large drug cartels and their leaders, since governments' capacity to tackle this threat is very limited. Strengthening institutional security structures is a priority. This can be done with internal resources or external aid. The Merida Initiative is the first experiment in hemispheric co-operation of its kind.

The Merida Initiative is considered a turning point in bilateral US–Mexico relations. It is the first time the US has provided such a substantial amount of military and police assistance to Mexico. Moreover, the level of co-operation between Mexican and US authorities, specifically in the area of training, is unprecedented. Indeed, more than an assistance package, "the Merida Initiative should be seen as a central element in a broader strategy of growing cooperation between the United States and Mexico to address a shared threat presented by organized crime."[12] Along similar lines, others have argued that the initiative "can serve as an important element in building confidence and cooperation between the two countries." [13]

The agreement is designed to provide Mexico with $US1.4 billion over a three-year period beginning in 2008. The initiative provides assistance in equipment, technology, and training for Mexico. Forty percent of the money will be used to purchase fixed and rotary wing aircraft designed to facilitate interdiction and rapid response. The rest is for inspection equipment.

Both the promoters of the Merida Initiative and its critics have raised the level of expectation of Mexico in combating organized crime. However, anyone who believes that US$1.4 billion over three years (2008–10), with US$500 million in the first year, will eradicate or reduce drug trafficking is unquestionably wrong. It is an insignificant amount in relation to the requirements for an integrated plan to combat organized crime and the big cartels. Similarly, the plan's critics in Mexico overestimate the capacity of the US to "violate sovereignty" by actively participating in the war against drugs. Whoever believes that this small sum can impact on Mexican independence seriously underestimates sovereignty.

A country's sovereignty is an intangible, qualitative reality that is developed at the level of perceptions. For those who support the plan, it is organized crime that violates sovereignty in order to undermine the state and dismantle social cohesion, so that help, however modest, can contribute to reinstating the state's weakened authority in imposing the rule of law. From this perspective, the serious consideration is that the Mexican state has still not devised, on its own and using its own resources, an efficient strategy after twenty years of countless failed attempts at fighting drug trafficking. In other words, the problem is the absence of a real national security strategy.

WHAT CAN CANADA DO?

Strengthening security and the military in Mexico has been an urgent priority since the government of Felipe Calderón took power in 2006. The increase in aid from the US via the Merida Initiative can have two effects: one positive and one negative. The positive side is that the Mexican government recognizes the need to modernize its military equipment, to update the technology used in its intelligence systems, and to modernize the systems for training people who are involved in defence and national security institutions. The negative side is that there could be an unwanted increase in the militarization of the strategy for fighting organized crime, and this could impact human rights and also result in military control of police security forces which should, by their institutional nature, be civilian. The Merida Initiative, therefore, could have the collateral effect that decision-making processes in defence matters are not modernized, and this could undermine the process to fully democratize the state.

Another factor to take into account is the collateral effect on markets. Drug trafficking is a global phenomenon and should be tackled globally through multinational co-operation. If the amount of cocaine entering the US is reduced, then the traffickers will seek to tap European markets. And there is already evidence that the drug routes between the Andes and Africa and Europe are being consolidated.[14] Accordingly, these co-operative efforts must be transformed into a multinational strategy and not focused only on bilateral programs. Drug traffickers are successful business people and have shown considerable flexibility and capacity to adapt to the various strategies that have sought, and failed, to control and remove them.[15]

The perception in Ottawa is that Canada and Mexico have very different security concerns. Canada's North American security focus does not extend south of the Rio Grande, and to a great extent the country's decision makers are preoccupied with the war in Afghanistan, Arctic sovereignty, etc. For its part, Mexico believed that the trilateralization of the war against terror would lead to other benefits, such as North American deep integration, but given the failure of that project for reasons discussed above, Mexico has re-energized its bilateral security relationship with the United States within the context of the Merida Initiative process.

Co-operation between Canada and Mexico should go beyond the Merida Initiative and focus on those areas where Canada has depth of experience, namely security sector reform and professionalization. For example, Canada participates in co-operative mechanisms between the Royal Canadian Mounted Police (RCMP) and various civilian police forces in Mexico. But Canadian policy-makers should extend this co-operation to include assistance in technical capacity, intelligence gathering, and professionalization. Canada could also increase co-operation on social security through assistance in community building and drug rehabilitation, share its model of working in conjunction with civilian populations in order to manage violence in inner cities, provide the expertise of the RCMP in confronting organized crime, and co-operate in intelligence and training for the military forces and civilian diplomats to take part in future UN peace missions.

Another important area of co-operation between Canada and Mexico is the social, for example, health and the social integration of youth. At the local level, many Canadian cities promote co-operative programs between public security forces and the education system to help manage crime principally perpetrated by marginalized and immigrant youth. Mexico has little experience in this area and would benefit tremendously from co-operation with Canada.

Further, there is very little interaction between government and civil society in Mexico. Such interactions tend to broaden the options available to decision makers with respect to the management of delinquency beyond simply the public security response. The Canadian experience in this regard – whereby dialogue and co-operation between government and society is encouraged – is desperately needed by Mexico. Unfortunately, since the crisis in Mexico, the Canadian government has implemented certain measures that both Mexican authorities and Mexican citizens view as going against the spirit of NAFTA. The visa program stands out as an example. Stephen Harper's government has not proposed any substantial mechanisms for enhanced co-operation, with the result that very little assistance is afforded to Mexico in comparison to that coming from the United States. Indeed, the perception in Mexico is that Canada is not an ally precisely at the moment when Mexico needs friends.

CONCLUSION

Co-operative efforts between Mexico and Canada should include mechanisms to strengthen the security relationship between Mexico and Canada. Canada is well positioned to help Mexico build a better institutional framework and improve the training of its military and security units. Hemispheric relationships could be strengthened. Further, Canada's experience in promoting the interaction between civil society and government could go a long way in helping Mexico manage its social problems. Finally, the departments of Foreign Affairs could co-operate in launching hemispheric agreements and supporting the OAS in meeting the terms of its agreements on justice, defence, security, and preventive diplomacy.

Mexican decision makers recognize that Canada has limited resources and cannot mirror the US's contribution through something similar to the Merida Initiative. Nevertheless, Canada's international co-operation experience, where resources and information are shared between different nations, could be very useful to Mexico. Canada's vast experience in the management of military justice and respect for human rights through decades of peacekeeping activity can also serve to professionalize and train Mexican military and police forces. In sum, there is much work to be done in Mexico, and Canada can make a significant contribution.

Therefore, Canadian decision makers need to recognize that Mexico matters. And Mexico *does* matter. Colin Robertson, the vice-president of the Canadian Defence and Foreign Affairs Institute, argues that

> Mexico is Canada's third-largest trading partner and our fourth-largest export market, and its economic prospects are positive. The World Bank's 2010 annual report, *Doing Business*, declared Mexico

the easiest place in Latin America to run a company. Goldman Sachs predicts that in 40 years, Mexico will be the world's fifth-largest economy, bigger than Russia, Japan or Germany. More than 2,500 Canadian firms are active. Walk down any of Mexico City's main streets and you will spot a Bank of Nova Scotia, now the sixth-largest bank in Mexico. Shop in the supermarket and you are likely to find Canadian products ... If we can provide 1,000 trainers in Afghanistan, then surely we can do more for Mexico, where our interests are vastly more important.[16]

NOTES

1 Public Safety. *Securing an Open Society: Canada's National Security Policy* (2009), www.publicsafety.gc.ca/pol/ns/secpol04-eng.aspx, 2009-07-30.

2 Raul Benitez-Manaut, *Mexican Security and Defense Doctrines: From the 19th to the 21st Centuries* Woodrow Wilson Center Update on the Americas (Washington, 2002).

3 Jordi Diez, ed., *Canadian and Mexican Security in the New North America. Challenges and Prospects* (Montreal and Kingston: McGill-Queen's University Press, 2006).

4 Department of Foreign Affairs and International Trade (DFAIT), Canada. *Revitalizing Our North American Partnership*. Canada's international policy statement: A Role of Pride and Influence in the World (10 June 2006), http://www.international.gc.ca/cip-pic/documents/IPS-EPI/partnership-partenariat.aspx?lang=eng&view=d.

5 Ibid.

6 Loretta Bondi, *Beyond the Border and Across the Atlantic: Mexico's Foreign and Security Policy Post-September 11th* (Washington: SAIS, 2004).

7 Jorge Garay, Eduardo Salcedo, and Isaac De Leon, *Illicit Networks Reconfiguring States: Social Network Analysis of Colombian and Mexican Cases* (Bogotá: Metodo Foundation, 2010).

8 Beginning in the 1990s Latin American countries such as Chile and Argentina began to produce military White papers specifically designed to make defence policy transparent and therefore open to public debate.

9 CASEDE, IPADE, SIMO, USAID, "Encuesta: efectos de la violencia asociada al narcotráfico en los comportamientos sociales y políticos de la ciudadanía," México (July 2011).

10 David Shirk, "Law Enforcement and Security Challenges in the U.S.-Mexican Border Region," *Journal of Borderlands Studies* 18, no. 1 (Fall 2003):1–24.

11 Ibid.

12 Andrew Selee, *Overview of the Merida Initiative* (Woodrow Wilson Center, May 2008).

13 Eric Olson, *Six Key Issues in United States-Mexico Security Cooperation* (Woodrow Wilson Center, July 2008).

14 Francisco E. Thoumi et al. The Impact of Organized Crime on Democratic Governance in Latin America (Berlin: Friedrich Ebert Stiftung, 2010). http://www.fes.de/lateinamerika.

15 Juan Carlos Garzón, *Mafia & Co. The Criminal Networks in Mexico, Brazil, and Colombia.* (Washington: Woodrow Wilson International Center for Scholars, 2008)

16 Colin Robertson, *Put Mexico at the top of Canada´s aid list, Globe and Mail* (18 May 2011).

PART FIVE

A Global Agenda

Making the Case for Multilateral Co-operation between Canada and Mexico

ENRIQUE BERRUGA-FILLOY

A rules-based international system is the arrangement of choice for both Mexico and Canada. Historically, neither country has advanced its interests through the threat or actual use of force or through economic sanctions or trade embargoes. The North American region has enjoyed peace for many decades and likely will continue to do so for years to come. Thus, it is increasingly apparent that Canada and Mexico will be concerned primarily with issues that are beyond their national or bilateral control, such as climate change, migration, food supplies, disease, human rights, nuclear proliferation, ideological and religious clashes, energy regulations, and global monetary arrangements. In dealing with these matters, a predictable and widely accepted set of global governance rules is of the essence for the present and future well-being of these two nations.

Fortunately, Mexico and Canada can fall back on a sound track record in multilateral forums. By and large, they enjoy a solid reputation as bridge builders, as proponents of valuable initiatives, and as active participants in facing challenges of global scope. It is very rare to see any special grouping or debate at the United Nations in which neither Canada nor Mexico is invited to join – except, perhaps, on regionally focused or narrow issues. Whether it is the reform of the UN at large or special working groups to create and enhance institutions, Canada, Mexico, or both, are common fixtures in crafting the rules under which the international community works.

The value that Canada and Mexico usually bring to the table, the legitimacy that stems from having both on board, has provided an advantage in moving international negotiations forward. But, paradoxically, Ottawa and Mexico City have seldom deliberately used this advantage as a policy tool to push their national interests and viewpoints. Both are seen as valuable players by the rest of the world. However, Mexican and Canadian delegations do not commonly present themselves as part of a joint effort, letting the rest of the membership know that they are together in pursuing certain goals. A more strategic approach and an enhanced multilateral cooperation could yield increased leverage to both countries' foreign policies and, quite likely, add dynamism to stalled international negotiations.

In short, the question is whether Canada and Mexico should decide to become partners beyond trade and investment, beyond NAFTA, to join forces in the multilateral arena.

CHANGING STRATEGIES FOR A DIFFERENT WORLD

For the first time since the end of the Cold War, a new balance of power is emerging in the international scene. While changes in the power structure take longer to become apparent and relevant, over the last two decades the world has clearly witnessed a rapid shift in the international division of labour. China has consolidated as the manufactures supplier of the world and is rapidly moving to other fields, including military equipment, financing, and technologically advanced goods. India is becoming a value added, outsourcing, and engineering hub. Brazil is increasing its share in the oil market, aviation, and renewable energies. Financial liquidity is moving to the Persian Gulf, while Russia increasingly competes as a supplier of natural gas, oil, and high tech items.

Turning economic might into political power is the next big thing in this rapidly changing international environment. India and Brazil are actively seeking a permanent seat at the UN Security Council (UNSC) as proof that their charging economies carry a political weight that should be acknowledged by the rest of the international community. Whether an expansion of this nature would actually improve the capacity of the Security Council to meet issues of peace and security is a different conversation. However, holding a permanent seat is one clear signal that these countries belong to a higher and more distinguished group of nations.

Within this shifting balance of power, India managed to get United States support for its bid for a permanent seat at the UNSC. Brazil, on the other hand, got less than clear support from Washington for its aspirations, signalling perhaps that the South American giant has a smaller impact on slowing down the drive of the Chinese in global affairs. Japan and Germany, two of the largest contributors to the United Nations' budget, remain committed to fulfilling their aspirations of becoming permanent members of the Security Council, and thereby receiving full recognition of their position in the world. However, Germany's bid has stumbled on the problem of an over-represented Europe – with France and the UK already permanent members – while Japan needs to overcome the hurdle of a Chinese veto to become a permanent member.

Because of the need for a two-thirds majority at the General Assembly and all five votes from the current permanent members, the possibility of seeing reforms in the composition of the UNSC any time soon is unlikely. For political reasons, it is likely that such aspirations will remain on the table regardless of the slim chances they have of becoming a reality. However, the sheer fact of being named and recognized as a legitimate aspirant carries additional clout for those countries seeking permanent membership. In this complex reform, Mexico and Canada's role need not focus on endorsing any particular country for permanent membership, but should push for a Security Council structure that best serves the goals of preserving peace and security in the world – again, working on the rules, rather than favouring any specific aspiration.

As a trusted partner of Mexico, Canada could have a positive impact on Mexico's reluctance to engage in peacekeeping operations (PKOs). Although this is increasingly discussed by politicians, the military, and diplomats, Mexico City has not yet chosen to participate in a single PKO. As the largest Latin American contributor to the United Nations' budget, Mexico deems that that covers its participation on peace and security matters. However, other UN members as well as many Mexican diplomats and scholars believe that Mexico ranks among a handful of countries that could make a meaningful contribution to PKOs on the ground. Indeed, Mexico's experience – assisting the electoral processes (along with Elections Canada) of newly independent Timor-Leste and, later, Iraq, and sending a police contingent to El Salvador to help with disarmament of former guerrilla groups and institution building – makes the case for a deeper Mexican involvement in PKOs. In this field, Canada is in a unique position to help Mexico allay concerns about the implications and management of PKO participation. Canada has a vast experience in this regard as well as an increasing collaboration with Mexico on security matters. The exposure that the Mexican military would gain to other armies' practices and the UN's prevention of conflict skills could be a most valuable asset in dealing with Mexico's domestic security concerns, as it combats drug gangs and organized crime.

Beyond the realm of the UN, the slow but steady decline of American power poses a real challenge to the international community. This issue carries major implications for the world in the future. There are already some recognizable signals and more to come. The US dollar is no longer the swing currency and stabilizing force that it was for decades. Monetary negotiations are ever more hazardous for lack of a hegemonic currency. Military power is not so easily used as a credible threat, insofar as it has to gain a large domestic consensus and international legitimacy. Iraq was a painful example of the significance of these two features. Where and why the United States may wield its military power is an increasingly larger question and therefore military power has much narrower scope as a foreign policy tool. American domestic indebtedness is also a source of concern, which may imply that the US will be in need of tightening its budgetary belt and will look inward, rather than displaying an active and far-reaching foreign policy. Its security and economic concerns may create barriers to migration and trade, hit domestic consumption and, most importantly, highlight rivalries and competition with China.

American worries and fortunes will certainly impinge on the national policies and conditions of America's only two neighbours – Canada and Mexico. The two borders, air traffic, migration flows, and trade expediency have already changed in the wake of 9/11. As the US struggles to preserve its lead vis-à-vis China and other emerging powers, unilateralism will have to give way to negotiations within the G20, the WTO, the Conference of the Parties (COP), and other forums on global environmental issues and other matters. A question will immediately re-emerge: Are Mexico and Canada just accidental, geographical neighbours? Will they strive to have coordinated policies on issues of common concern? Will they develop a regional approach beyond NAFTA or will the two neighbours simply react to American policies that are intended for other parts of the world but that have an impact on the immediate vicinity?

As if in concentric circles, Mexico and Canada need to assess the behaviour and trends of the United States in the years to come. Frustration and political division in Washington may lead to erratic and more difficult-to-read policies and more blurred terms of engagement with the troubled superpower. Trilateral communication needs to be enhanced. An in-depth conversation on the role and possibilities of the North American region in the emerging international scene is an increasing necessity.

A growing number of regions and nations are actively working to reposition themselves on the world stage, be this China, the Association of Southeast Asian Nations (ASEAN) countries, South America and Southern Africa, Russia, India, or the Persian Gulf States. Against this background, North America needs to get its act together.

NEW TOOLS FOR GLOBAL NEGOTIATIONS

For the eighth year in a row, Canadians ranked first on the level of appreciation Mexicans have for foreigners. In the 2010 survey conducted by the Centro de Investigación y Docencia Económicas (CIDE), the Mexican general public gave Canada 68 points (out of 100) and

Mexican opinion leaders 82 points on the international scale.[1] This indicates that Mexicans would be more willing to pair with Canada than with any other country on international initiatives. It does not imply that Canada or Mexico's global agendas need to have the same set of priorities or that their viewpoints may not differ. But it does imply that Mexicans would feel comfortable in teaming up with Canada on pushing ahead a number of issues of global importance. What are those issues and what forums are the most relevant?

The short answer is those issues discussed and approved by both governments. Indeed, governments are supposed to lead in the crafting of common strategies and in establishing agendas. Unfortunately, neither government has been sufficiently forthcoming in communicating the extent of their agreements, and bilateral mechanisms to discuss and search for common ground are not working properly. Bilateral dealings – such as trade, tourism, security, and investment – seem to work reasonably well (except for the major step backward taken by Ottawa when it imposed a visa requirement on all Mexicans). However, on the global and multilateral front, a more active and noticeable partnership is of the essence.

Over the next decade, the most salient areas of regional and global co-operation will be environmental negotiations, regional security arrangements, migration, energy, and financial and fiscal rules.

On the environmental front, the UN Framework Convention on Climate Change (COP) is no doubt a top priority for Mexico, Canada, and the world at large. As neighbours to the largest greenhouse gas emitter, these two countries ought to push for a regional and global agenda that engages the United States to ensure that the emerging environmental system includes American participation and therefore counts. On a worldwide scale, Canada and Mexico are in an enviable position to call on the international community to move such negotiations ahead. Their room for manoeuvre within the G20, the successful outcome Mexico brokered at the COP-16 in Cancún, the fact that Mexico is one of the eight mega-diverse countries of the world, the fact that Canada's northern regions are already experiencing the damages of global warming as are Mexico's coastlines and, finally, that both Ottawa and Mexico City have played a long-standing committed role in trying to craft a workable world agreement to substitute and enhance what the Kyoto protocol achieved; all these elements strengthen their bargaining position to deal with environmental issues. Perhaps the most significant missing element is that the international community needs yet to know that Canada and Mexico are together, working in tandem to reach a positive outcome on these negotiations. Perceptions in this and other fields are as important as the subject matter under discussion.

A lack of progress in international negotiations often leads to frustration and, more worrisome, to strained and unco-operative relations. Luckily, once in a while it also leads to more pragmatic approaches to spare the world from stalled agreements. A case in point in setting up alternative forums is the G20, spearheaded by then Canadian prime minister, Paul Martin. The G20 has often been criticized for being a *self-appointed* mechanism – an accurate description applied mainly by those who do not belong to it. Its decisions are not compulsory, not even for the group's members, let alone for the international community at large. Many even question the legitimacy of such group, calling for a more prominent role of established institutions such as the UN General Assembly or UN subsidiary bodies. Such criticism is oblivious of the fact that global negotiations – by all 193 UN members – have proved to be as ideal as they are ineffectual. On the other hand, at universal forums it is normally the rule that a handful of countries influence their respective regional groupings enough so as to make them their own.

In light of these dynamics and the pressing need to address and move forward the international agenda, a group such as the G20, which comprises 85 percent of global GDP and 80 percent of world trade, may muster the necessary influence to speed up change. One salient feature of the G20 is that it "seeks to address issues that go beyond the responsibilities of any one organization" – that is, fill the vacuums left by traditional multilateral forums. Thus, the G20 should be seen as an alternative and a catalyst, rather than a substitute for universal bodies. The G20 composition² effects a combination of pivotal countries and regional balance, allows for an important role on the new international division of labour, and represents the leading cultures, political systems, and religious beliefs globally. Although many countries do not feel represented within this group, most could identify a natural partner or a participant who is willing to bring a specific concern to the G20's table. And perhaps most important, the G20 can be more agile in drawing conclusions and turning them into national public policies.

The G20 should become a turf of choice for Canada and Mexico. What matters is not only how well they perform within the G20 itself, but their capacity to reach out to and engage other countries. On monetary matters, for example, the critical agreements will be those obtained within the G20, since their currencies' strength is unmatched. However, on issues such as the environment, it will be fair and necessary to keep in mind the concerns of small island states, nations prone to natural disasters, and countries with high deforestation rates due to dire economic conditions.

CAESAR'S PARTNERSHIP

In the Roman Empire it was not enough that Caesar's wife was chaste; she also had to appear to be chaste. In modern international affairs, those who sponsor a particular initiative are often as important as the contents of the proposals. Suspicion is an inevitable part of international life, which is compounded by the fact that most professional diplomats are good at spelling out their national position but laconic when it comes to explaining the rationale behind the position.

By and large, Canada and Mexico are perceived as constructive players in the international arena. They are also seen as too preoccupied with dealing with their giant neighbour. In most corners of the world (including our own), it is taken for granted that North America will not go further in its integration arrangements, nothing beyond free trade. This may be so for the foreseeable future.

Canada and Mexico's standing in the world could be properly capitalized if both countries were to decide to work closer together and let it be known that they are indeed in tandem. As in the case of Caesar's wife, perceptions matter; the world will react differently to Canadian or Mexican overtures depending on whether they are presented in isolation or as a joint endeavour. Thus, within the G20, at the OAS, or at the United Nations itself, Canada and Mexico should polish their bilateral mechanisms so as to spot key issues for both countries and then tailor a strategy to increase the chance of success.

Mexico and Canada, as visible partners in multilateral issues, may hold the middle ground, may become a hinge on selected international negotiations. This pattern allowed for Mexico's success at the COP-16 and Canada's institution-making at the inception of the G20. It is time for both governments to build on that reputation and work together on issues critical to humankind.

NOTES

1 Guadalupe González, Jorge Schiavon, David Crow, and Gerardo Maldonado, *Mexico, Las Américas y el Mundo 2010* (México: CIDE, Marzo 2011).
2 South Africa for Africa; Canada, Mexico, and the United States for North America; Argentina and Brazil for South America; China, Japan, and South Korea for the Far East; India and Indonesia for the South of Asia; Saudi Arabia for the Arab World; Russia; Turkey; France, Germany, Italy, the UK, and the European Union for Europe; and Australia.

will begin to fade

Collaboration on Global Issues –
A Democratic Dividend
for Canada and Mexico?

PHILIP OXHORN

In 2000, with the election of opposition candidate Vicente Fox as president, Mexico finally joined the club of democratic nations. This important political milestone might have been expected to lead to greater collaboration between Canada and Mexico on a number of global issues in which they have shared interests. The two countries were already part of the largest free trade area in the world, the North American Free Trade Agreement (NAFTA). NAFTA came into force in 1994 when the prospects for truly competitive elections still seemed remote and uncertain at best. After six years of growing economic and concomitant political ties, it would seem only reasonable to expect both countries to reap some kind of "democratic dividend" in terms of greater collaboration internationally once Mexico shed its overtly authoritarian character. Yet this did not happen. As NAFTA approaches its twentieth anniversary, the potential for such collaboration has only grown, as have the potential advantages for both Canada and Mexico in trying to realize that potential.

AN IDEAL PARTNERSHIP?

Canada and Mexico are in many respects ideally suited for jointly promoting important shared interests at a global level. The mere fact that they share a continent with the United States means that Canada and Mexico have sought to counteract the preponderance of US economic, political, and military power by adopting a value-based foreign policy, with a particular emphasis on human rights and multilateralism. Now that Mexico is a democracy, the overlap between their foreign policy

value-based / policy

values has never been greater. The flip side of this is that the United States' greater international weight has allowed it to pursue a variety of interests that have created a history of mistrust and tarnished its credibility on a number of fronts internationally, particularly in Latin America. This means that both Canada and Mexico have a certain credibility in attempting to lead on a number of global issues that the United States, and in some respects many European countries as well, cannot match. In particular, both countries can play an important role in helping to broker consensus on difficult issues. As a result of NAFTA, Canada and Mexico now have substantial experience in working together; their leaders and senior officials know one another through the growth of intergovernmental relations since 1994, and mechanisms are in place to help avoid conflicts and develop common interests at the bilateral level. No global partnership would risk being seen as artificial or some sort of marriage of convenience, even if such strategic partnerships have been rare and not something the leadership of either country seems to consider seriously.

It is important to emphasize that any global leadership potential that Canada and Mexico might possess will be enhanced only if they work in tandem. This is because both are essentially middle powers, even if Canada is much more economically developed than Mexico. Canada, given its historically close ties with the United Kingdom and the US, has consistently been able to "punch above its weight" at the international level. While it certainly aspires to continue doing so, Canada must now confront the fact that its reputation will begin to fade as a number of emerging countries gain in economic and political influence, at the same time that its close ties with the United Kingdom and the US need to be leveraged in a new context in which the UK is now part of the European Union and the US is the sole remaining superpower in a global environment with a number of contending powers – including Mexico.

Mexico, on the other hand, has generally tended to punch below its weight internationally. With a few notable exceptions, particularly when it exercised a genuine leadership role in attempting to broker peace in Central America during the 1980s despite US opposition, Mexico has generally refrained from asserting the level of influence internationally that its regional economic and political clout might otherwise afford it. Whereas Canada has been largely successful in leveraging its close relationship with the United States to enhance its international presence, Mexico's geographic proximity to the behemoth to its north seems to have relegated Mexico to relative obscurity. A closer alliance between Mexico and Canada on the world stage could help pull Mexico more firmly out from under the shadow of the US while contributing to Canada's continued ability to remain in the international limelight.

This fundamental complementarity of interests between Canada and Mexico is reflected in other ways that would suggest greater collaboration between the two countries could have a powerful impact on the global scene. As an "old" democracy with ties to Western Europe and the Commonwealth, Canada offers an important bridge to the global North's developed economies. Mexico's relationship with Latin America and its history of engagement with the global South, as well as Mexico's status as a relatively "new" democracy and emerging market, mean that it provides important links with the developing countries and the issues that deeply concern them. This potential for global influence is only magnified by the fact that Mexico and Canada share a unique relationship with the United States, which makes them potentially compelling interlocutors on a variety of issues, particularly when US engagement is problematic.

INTERNATIONAL DEVELOPMENT POLICY AND GLOBAL GOVERNANCE REFORMS

There is no dearth of opportunities for forging such alliances. As members of the OECD and the G20, for example, Canada and Mexico are uniquely well positioned to lead on a variety of economic fronts. Follow-up on the 2002 United Nations International Conference on Financing for Development, which Mexico hosted in Monterrey, provides what could perhaps become a template for future Canada-Mexico joint initiatives. The so-called Monterrey Consensus has become a cornerstone of development policy. It encapsulates key issues revolving around the need for private finance, domestic economic resources, and trade to supplement official development assistance, as well as the need for greater international policy coherence in promoting economic development and the need to control corruption, among other issues. These goals also reflect the strongly held national positions in both Canada and Mexico. It is a classic example of how the two countries independently came to support similar goals at the highest levels of international governance with minimal prior coordination. One could only imagine the potential synergies and leverage that could emerge if Canada and Mexico together worked to ensure adequate follow-up on the Monterrey Consensus, which continues to be problematic, especially in the aftermath of the 2008 international economic crisis.

The example of a post-Monterrey alliance between Canada and Mexico also underscores their potential roles at the level of international governance more generally. Canada and Mexico are uniquely poised to work in tandem on such key issues as the need to reform, if not replace, the Bretton Woods institutions for international economic governance in order to better accommodate rising economic powers, like Mexico, and develop more effective policies that can address the myriad of economic problems dramatically exposed by the 2008 economic crash. Going further, what better champions of United Nations reform than Canada and Mexico? With their combined ties to important constituencies and their proven records of support for multilateralism, together Mexico and Canada would have a convening capacity second to none. This is particularly true for Security Council reform, given that both have served on it as elected members and neither has expressed a strong interest in becoming a permanent member in an expanded council.

INTERNATIONAL ORGANIZED CRIME AND NARCO-TRAFFICKING

In terms of specific issues that Canada and Mexico not only can but should take the lead on, the most important is international organized crime, particularly narco-trafficking. The devastating effects this has had on Mexico are well known, but Canada is not immune either. As a result of both its legal and illegal economic and migratory linkages with Mexico, it cannot ignore the severity of the problem in Mexico. At the same time, both Canada and Mexico are deeply affected by US policies. This creates yet another source of common interest in trying to forge a counterbalance to US policies, working to fill the void created by the limitations of US policy through a search for more effective, integrated solutions to the problem that go beyond criminalization and interdiction.

Fundamentally, however, any medium- or long-term solution to organized crime and narco-trafficking has to be global; regional solutions simply will not suffice. Globalization means that even regions have lost their centrality in delimiting criminal networks and their victims. The decades-long war on drugs has clearly demonstrated that policies focusing on a single country merely force organized crime to move to more propitious national contexts, often further weakening already fragile states and precarious institutions for enforcing the rule of law. This was, after all, a key reason that Mexico (as well as Peru and Bolivia) became so vulnerable to international organized crime when the United States and the Colombian government "successfully" targeted the Colombian cartels. Today, history is repeating itself as the crackdown in Mexico forces the drug trade into Central America, compounding the consequences for the poor of weak states and rampant violence dating back to the 1990s. And the problem is not limited to the Americas. The market for cocaine in Europe is now almost as large as that of the United States because organized crime has been able to reroute supplies, actually bringing down street prices despite Europe's increasing emphasis on the same policies of criminalization and interdiction that the United States has pioneered since the 1970s. As the example of Europe clearly shows, if we still do not know what policies are most likely to succeed at a global level, current policies at best have not succeeded, at worst are counterproductive, and truly global policy alternatives – both geographically and in terms of multidimensional solutions – are desperately needed.

It is hard to imagine a more ideal pair of countries to lead a serious global rethinking of policies toward narco-trafficking and organized crime more generally. For Mexico, which is dramatically experiencing the consequences of such criminal activity firsthand, such leadership would provide an opportunity to explore innovative policy alternatives that can convince its increasingly frustrated domestic population that it is on the right track in dealing with the problem; at the same time, Mexico can ensure that the interests of countries that have borne the brunt of the costs associated with organized crime are taken into account. For Canada, it provides a potential avenue for highlighting what it does so well in terms of the establishment of a democratic rule of law with low levels of societal violence, particularly when compared to the United States; at the same time, Canada can give voice to the interests of countries that similarly have relatively large markets for illicit drugs but have supported at least isolated experiments for more effectively dealing with the demand-side of the problem – something of great concern to all countries affected by narco-trafficking, including Mexico. Both countries' unique relationship to the US similarly offers better prospects for finding a new consensus that might avoid the severe limitations of current policies.

GLOBAL IMMIGRATION REFORM

A second area in which Canada and Mexico are ideally suited to take a lead is immigration. This has been an ongoing source of tension between Mexico, the US and, to a lesser extent, Canada. Yet immigration is complex and not simply a North American problem. Not only does Mexico increasingly receive immigrants from other Latin American countries, particularly Central America, but migration (legal and illegal) is a growing problem throughout the world, including South-South migration. Such migration among developing countries has led to growing tensions, often ethnically based, while transnational migration throughout the world has had significant negative consequences for the respect of basic human rights, particularly for women and the young. These issues have become increasingly notorious in Europe and have a long, problematic history in the United States.

Canada and Mexico's exceptional capacity to jointly lead efforts to create a more robust global regime for resolving migration issues should be apparent. Canada, a country increasingly dependent on immigrants, has avoided the extreme reactions found in much of Western Europe and the United States. Mexico, as a major country of origin for immigrants and increasingly the host to new waves of immigrants from poorer countries, is in a unique position to help ensure that the interests of the most vulnerable are represented in global discussions. Mexico's particular experience has already led it to attempt to assume a lead role internationally on immigration reform, so this might even be an area in which Canada would initially be following Mexico's lead. The potential for synergy between the two countries cannot be ignored, particularly in supporting a new, wide-ranging critical dialogue on this increasingly sensitive issue.

DEMOCRACY PROMOTION

Given Mexico's relatively recent democratic transition, a third issue on which Mexico and Canada can jointly take a lead internationally is democracy promotion, particularly electoral monitoring. This has long been a core element in Canada's foreign policy, so Canada would contribute considerable experience and credibility in this area. Yet Mexico's prolonged (it lasted well over a decade), largely peaceful, and negotiated transition to electoral democracy provides it with a unique perspective. Civil society played an active role in leading the transition through successful mobilizations and, in particular, the establishment of citizen oversight of the actual electoral process to ensure its fairness. This experience was complemented by the active participation of the country's three principal political parties leading to the creation of a series of important institutions designed to ensure the political neutrality of elections oversight. The Federal Electoral Institute stands out as a model for administering fair elections in a large territory, insulated from excessive partisan influences.

The need for clear international policies for democracy promotion remains as timely as ever. In 2011 the dichotomy of authoritarian versus democratic rule that characterized Mexico throughout the 1990s was brought to the fore by popular mobilizations in often spectacular, albeit ambiguous, ways. There is still much that we do not understand about such processes, and the international community urgently needs to be able to provide useful assistance in negotiating transitions, constructing an appropriate infrastructure for administering elections, and supporting the formation of political parties or other actors that can successfully compete in elections by aggregating interests in a way that channels citizen participation effectively (and peacefully) in order to establish representative and accountable governments. Canada, as an "old" democracy with years of accumulated practice in these areas, along with Mexico as a "new" democracy that has garnered invaluable experience through its own prolonged but largely successful democratic transition, can play a vital role in spearheading international efforts to fill these needs.

GLOBAL CLIMATE CHANGE

Following on the heels of the disappointing Copenhagen Agreement, the Cancún Agreement that came out of the 2010 summit sponsored by Mexico helped restore some credibility to global climate change negotiations but still fell far short of any definitive longer-term commitments to finding actual solutions to the dislocations climate change now seems destined to generate. The seemingly intractable issues involved in addressing global climate bring to the fore not only historic North-South tensions but also the new tensions created by the growing economic weight of emerging market economies. While Mexico has already demonstrated its leadership potential in hosting the Cancún summit, Canada's leadership seems to have faded since it originally signed the Kyoto Accords well over a decade ago. This both complicates the possibility of a Canada-Mexico alliance on climate change and raises its potential should the two countries agree on a common front for realistically addressing global climate change that they could champion together. As important petroleum producers that are necessarily impacted by any climate change strategy adopted by the United States, Canada and Mexico are in a unique position to help broker a global consensus. At the same time, they can help bridge the North-South emerging market divides, recognizing that there is an obvious void that has to be filled because, at least to date, there are no clear potential leaders on climate change.

TODAY'S MOST DIFFICULT CHALLENGES
REQUIRE INNOVATIVE APPROACHES

If the idea of Canada and Mexico working together in the search for global consensus on important issues seems dubious today, the fact is that when one takes the time to think about it, Canada and Mexico often seem to have independently adopted quite similar positions on a number of difficult issues at the international level. The potential synergies from such an alliance, stemming from shared interests, their geographical proximity to the US, and the fact that they are both middle powers at different levels of economic development in a rapidly changing global context, may prove to be precisely what is needed to begin to make more rapid progress in areas of vital interest not only to Canada and Mexico but to the world as a whole. In many ways, their differences – including culture, geography, and language – are as much a part of the promise of such an alliance as they are impediments to its success. The very novelty of such an alliance almost by necessity would likely generate the kind of innovative approaches that are required to meet pressing challenges, and that same novelty may represent the best prospects for winning the support any new consensus requires. Canada and Mexico obviously cannot solve the globe's problems, but together they may be able to play a catalytic role in finding effective solutions.

Lessons from Cancún for North America

AMBASSADOR LUIS ALFONSO DE ALBA AND BERENICE DÍAZ CEBALLOS

INTRODUCTION

The adoption of the Cancún Agreements on 11 December 2010 was the cornerstone of a new era of international co-operation in the fight against climate change. Despite divided opinions and dissimilar approaches to how states could deal with climate change, consensus was reached on a broad, comprehensive, and balanced package of actions. The results obtained in Cancún placed the international community on the path to stabilizing global temperature while enhancing co-operation for climate change; they therefore represent a major achievement for multilateralism and Mexican diplomacy.

This article attempts to derive lessons from the COP-16 experience in order to enhance North American environmental co-operation. The multilateral climate change negotiations will carry on in Durban, South Africa, and Mexico will continue to play a key role in the fight against this global challenge. At the same time, from a regional perspective, Mexico could strengthen co-operation with the United States and Canada by building on the key factors leading to the success of Cancún.

The article is divided into three sections. The first describes the negotiation process resulting in the Cancún Agreements. The second assesses the COP-16 legacy. The final section suggests ways to strengthen the regional environment regime based on key features of the COP-16 success story.

North American integration has made significant progress since NAFTA came into effect, but it has also experienced setbacks. Enhanced environmental co-operation could offer a new opportunity to energize and diversify regional co-operation, set high goals, and deliver significant results to our citizens.

I PREPARING AND NEGOTIATING
THE CANCÚN AGREEMENTS

The Cancún achievements are even more relevant when one considers that the negotiation process had been in crisis for some time. Divided opinions and dissimilar approaches on how states could deal with climate change produced a very complex environment for negotiations. There was a major gap between developed and developing countries and even among developing countries themselves. The COP also dealt with the fact that there are developing countries with high greenhouse gas emissions and developing countries with no significant emissions but who are severely affected by climate change.

It is important to remember that mistrust and accusations abounded. Civil society and public opinion criticized the outcome of the Copenhagen Conferences in 2009 and denounced the inability of governments to reach agreements and their role in putting the UN Framework Convention on the edge of inoperability. The Convention Secretariat was going through a severe credibility crisis for not overcoming the inflexibility of many actors involved in the process, bringing the UN process as a whole into question. Given these circumstances, a number of analysts considered it almost impossible to reach further agreements in Cancún.

As the Cancún Conference approached its deadline, no one knew what the outcome would be, even twenty-four hours before its conclusion. There were multiple unresolved aspects and opposing interests. Many countries were not willing to cede on their national concerns or to find formulas for compromise. Furthermore, working group chairs and facilitators designated by the presidency were having difficulty eliminating the text of proposals on which there was no agreement. There was a need for a balanced agreement between the two negotiations tracks (long-term co-operation under the UN Framework Convention on Climate Change and the Kyoto Protocol) and within each track as well. External pressure and the fatigue of negotiators heightened the differences among countries, but the possibility of not reaching an agreement implied that countries would have to assume a higher cost.

Given this complex scenario, openness, leadership, creativity, responsibility, and above all, courage were required. And these were the qualities and skills that the Mexican presidency proved to possess. Nevertheless, Cancún's success was also the result of a series of wise decisions and the good management of a complex negotiation in a methodical, transparent, and inclusive consultation process.

First, diplomacy was a key element in a negotiation process that had previously been conducted mainly by technical experts. Previous COPs had shown that climate change was a global problem that could not be addressed solely in a technical way. Consequently, new working methods were needed to add further flexibility. Mexican president Felipe Calderón designated Foreign Affairs Minister, Ambassador Patricia Espinosa Cantellano as chair of the conferences, to be supported by the Ministry of the Environment and other ministries.

Second, Mexico assumed both a host and a facilitator role a year in advance of officially assuming the COP presidency. Denmark, the chair of COP-15 until the opening of COP-16 in Cancún, understood that the preparatory process of a COP is the responsibility and concern of the next host country. Denmark's position enabled Mexico to prepare its own working plan and carry it out with no limitations or restrictions. Some parties openly questioned Mexico's resolve to plan the conference in terms of both logistics and the substantive aspects of the organization. Nonetheless, we decided to act cautiously in order to start rebuilding trust among stakeholders.

The development of informal consultations demonstrated the particular complexities of this multilateral process and allowed us to overcome procedural obstacles. Attachments to "tradition" and "rules" were frequently used to filibuster initiatives. There was also a resistance to take successful lessons from other multilateral processes, mainly because the vast majority of delegates had no further diplomatic experience.

Third, the action plan proposed by the Mexican presidency privileged openness, inclusiveness, and transparency as crucial elements for consensus building. It was important to show that we were patient and open enough to take into account all positions, and that we had both a clear idea of our direction and the resolve to succeed. We kept direct contact with the largest possible number of delegations, with special focus on delegations that felt most excluded. We also called for several informal consultations throughout the year, including some at the ministerial level.

Mexico's emphasis on diplomacy, a broad preparatory process, and open and transparent consultations brought about the Cancún Agreements, surpassing all expectations. Among the most important results are the goal to keep the temperature two degrees below the global average and the possibility to review progress toward achieving this goal in the near future; the commitment of developed countries to mitigation; and the commitment of developing countries to actions that derive from their common but differentiated responsibilities. Equally important, a green fund was created as the major financial mechanism of the convention, to mobilize long-term financial resources. With regard to the Kyoto Protocol, the agreements ensure the continuity of the work for a second stage of commitments; the first commitment period ends in December 2012 and it is imperative not to have a gap between commitments. In addition to formalizing unilateral mitigation measures, we reinforced the system to monitor, report, and verify (MRV) mitigation actions.

Significant progress was also achieved in enhancing adaptation plans and technology access through the creation of dedicated committees and the commitment to allocate greater resources to these activities. These steps included an important boost to the fight against deforestation.

2 THE COP-16 LEGACY

Beyond the success that the COP-16 represented for Mexican diplomacy and for the fight against climate change, Cancún made a considerable contribution to the multilateral system: it showed that it is possible to work within the UN and achieve consensus among the 190 states participating in the climate change process – in other words, that there is a common interest and a collective responsibility. This may sound trivial but it is important to recall that the credibility of previous COPs had been widely questioned. Another significant lesson refers to the "consensus" concept. After Cancún, it is important to interpret the word "consensus" correctly so as not to confuse it with "unanimity." To do so would be highly undemocratic and would be equivalent to the veto power in the Security Council.

A more important achievement of the Cancún process was our ability to broaden our approach to climate change. Before Cancún, climate change was dealt with in multilateral settings as a purely environmental issue. The long-term contribution of the Cancún Conference was the possibility of rethinking climate change as not only an environmental but also a social, political, and economic challenge. The language of the Cancún Agreements reflects this new vision, which demands a profound transformation of our consumption and growth patterns in order to harmonize them with environmental sustainability. This could be interpreted as a change of paradigm in the multilateral assessment of climate change, and certainly constitutes a hallmark of the success of the Cancún Conference.

This profound change in the way we think about climate change was only possible through the incorporation of a larger number of actors and stakeholders into the consultation process. Indeed, climate change has become a matter of interest not only to the Ministries of the Environment but also to the Ministries of Finance, Energy, Economy, Agriculture, Foreign Affairs, and Development, among others at the federal or national level. Other levels and branches of government are increasingly involved, including legislators and local governments in countries around the world. Moreover, civil society has gained a more important role in advocating a climate change regime. Strong voices are being heard not only from NGOs but also from the business sector, unions, academia, and increasingly organized interest groups such as indigenous peoples and women. This has clearly set the stage for a comprehensive, multi-disciplinary approach to climate change.

This level of ambition and inclusiveness could inspire environmental co-operation at the regional level, particularly in North America, the region with the highest level of carbon emissions in the world.

THREE LESSONS FOR NORTH AMERICA

North America is responsible for about one quarter of global greenhouse gas emissions. The region emits twice as much carbon dioxide as Europe, over five times as much as Asia, and over thirteen times as much as Africa. Per capita emissions are several times higher in Canada and in the US than in almost any other country. This rate has already produced severe social, economic, and environmental damage in the region through weather-related events, such as hurricanes, floods, droughts, heat waves, and wildfires, thus raising the costs in property damage and loss of economic activity to billions of dollars a year.[1]

Even though Canada and the US were strong political supporters and had very fluid communication with the Mexican presidency of the COP-16, their level of commitment to reducing greenhouse gas emissions is strikingly low for advanced countries and is modest even when compared to some developing countries. This is particularly evident at the regional level. These salient differences can be explained in terms of domestic politics. Whereas in Mexico we have widespread support for climate change action across party lines and within the civil society, in Canada and even more in the US there is widespread skepticism within the political class and in public opinion. The preference is for "business as usual." Political conditions in Mexico are clearly more favourable to setting higher goals against climate change.

In preparation for the Cancún Conference, Mexico did not wait for the "heavyweights" to move forward before starting to act. Later on, Cancún proved that climate change agreements can be pushed forward through a "bottom-up" process in which all countries, not only the largest emitters, were willing to contribute to fight climate change. I believe the same strategy could apply in the North American context. In the words of Mexican president Felipe Calderón, "climate change is not something only developed nations should fight. This is not true. Every country has to fight it, certainly in a different proportion, but every country has to."[2] Mexico has adopted a mitigation goal to reduce 51 million tons of CO2 emissions per year until 2012, and up to 30 percent of its emissions toward 2020 in relation to its current trends, if the international community provides financial and technological support. We believe developed countries should define mitigation commitments between 25 percent and 40 percent under the 1990 levels by 2020, and of at least 80 percent by 2050.

Because of these commitments, it is important that the United States and Canada work hard with their business sectors, legislators, unions, political parties, NGOs, and the forum of public opinion in order to persuade them of the importance of fighting climate change and of the dramatic consequences of inaction. Only through an active campaign of dialogue and persuasion will we be able to raise the level of ambition in the region. President Barack Obama has marked a clear difference with the Bush administration in terms of climate change policy. But partnerships with key actors and stakeholders in the United States remain a challenge.

Some progress is being made at the local government level in both Canada and the United States. The state of California and the province of Quebec have put forward legislation to address climate change in a way that surpasses the goals of their national governments. This could gradually lead to a favourable legislative process at the federal level to enhance emission reduction goals.

CONCLUSION

The attempt to transfer the Cancún lessons to the North American region is a challenging task; the actors involved and the actual institutional framework are strikingly different. Nevertheless, some suggestions can be derived from Cancún to enhance regional co-operation on the environment.

The first is to raise our level of ambition. The current regional environmental architecture is moving in the right direction, but the three countries could be more ambitious. Mexico has shown its resolve to act. We have literally helped produce an international change of paradigm regarding climate change, one that frames the discussion in the broader context of political, social, and economic transformation to attain sustainability. Our northern neighbours should follow Mexico's lead.

Second, because domestic political conditions are unfavourable to climate change action in the US and Canada, the governments of both countries should actively engage their parliaments, NGOs, business sectors, local governments, and interest groups in the discussion. Their sensibility and mobilization are key factors in enhancing greenhouse gas emission targets.

Third, Mexico needs to boost economic growth and development. We could benefit from investment, experience, technology transfer, and capacity building from the US and Canada. As a developing country, we need to strengthen our national capacity to combat climate change and poverty at the same time.

Fourth, just as the success of the Cancún Conference breathed new life into multilateralism by proving that the diverse community of the UN can reach agreements and deliver, enhanced environmental co-operation at the regional level could give North American integration a fresh push. At a time when the region has greatly benefited from trade and investment, but has disagreed on migration, human rights, and arms trafficking, ambitious climate change collaboration could well infuse a new impetus into the North American project of greater convergence, coordination, prosperity, and integration. This could also reinforce North American co-operation with other countries in their environmental efforts.

Climate change continues to affect an increasing proportion of the world's population. After Cancún there is still much to be done, and we now have to face the challenge of coordinating efforts for implementation. The international community must sooner than later adopt more rigorous mitigation measures. Mexico will participate in this work in the constructive spirit that characterizes us. As a responsible global actor, Mexico must continue to demonstrate its leadership and skill in other multilateral and regional settings. It is now time for North America to step in with resolve to fight climate change.

NOTES

1 Commission for Environment Cooperation, *The North American Mosaic: An Overview of Key Environmental Issues*, 2001, 2, http://www.cec.org/Storage/32/2354_SOE_Climate_en.pdf.
2 Speech by President Felipe Calderón on the International Day of the Environment, 6 June 2011, http://www.presidencia.gob.mx/2011/06/el-presidente-calderón-en-el-dia-mundial-del-medio-ambiente-2011.

Climate Change
and North America

DAVID RUNNALLS

Dealing with climate change may be the biggest single economic challenge for North America over the next fifty years. I say economic rather than environmental because coping with the challenges posed by climate change implies wholesale changes in the energy system. And energy is at the heart of the North American economy. Canada, Mexico, and the United States collectively produce about 25 percent of the world's emissions of CO_2 with approximately 7 percent of the world's population. The US alone accounts for almost 20 percent of the world total.

Fossil fuel production is a lucrative and powerful part of the politics and economics of all three countries. Mexico and Canada are both major oil and gas exporters, with Canada being in the fortunate position of having the second or third largest oil reserves in the world. All three countries have energy intensive and rather energy inefficient economies.

The science of climate change is clear. In Copenhagen, all governments who signed the accord (including the three North American economies) acknowledged that any average global temperature rise beyond 2C would constitute dangerous interference with the world's climate system. This translates into a concentration of CO_2 in the atmosphere of 450 parts per million (ppm) at most. Many scientists are skeptical and pressure is growing for a lowering of that figure to 350 ppm or so. We are now above 280 ppm. It is therefore certain that the developed countries are looking at reductions of 70 to 80 percent of their emissions by 2050 and of 25 to 30 percent by 2025–2030. Neither the United States nor Canada is remotely prepared to meet those targets.

All three countries have been active participants in the international climate negotiations. In the initial stages leading up to the 1992 Earth Summit and beyond, Canada was a leader in the negotiations. In fact, former prime minister Brian Mulroney actively tried to persuade President Bush to agree to national reduction targets in the original UN agreement on climate change. He failed. The result was a "framework convention" with exhortatory targets only. It was signed in Rio. Five years later a significant negotiation in Japan led to the adoption of the Kyoto Protocol. The negotiations were stalled until the last-minute intervention of Vice President Gore, among others. In the end, the protocol called for reductions in the 1990 level of emissions by all developed countries. Canada and the United States agreed to reduce their emissions by 6 percent below 1990 levels.

This began a significant period of hypocrisy on the part of both the United States and Canada. Although the United States had signed the protocol, the Clinton administration made no serious attempt to present it to the senate for ratification. Nor did it vigorously pursue any domestic climate policy. When George W. Bush came to power, he announced that the United States would not ratify Kyoto at all. In Canada, the policy was significantly more opaque. It is well known that the Canadian delegation to Kyoto was instructed by the prime minister to agree to nothing less than the United States targets, despite a national consultative process which had agreed on stabilization as the most ambitious target and despite Australia, a similar economy, making off like a bandit from Kyoto, with an allowable increase in its emissions of 11 percent over 1990 levels. The delegation returned from Kyoto to a drumbeat of criticism, especially from the private sector.

This began a period of acrimony and mistrust between the provinces (who are responsible for natural resources under the Canadian constitution) and the federal government and between the fossil fuel industry and much of civil society, a period that continues to this day. Canada has become the "black hat" of the international negotiations. This stance reached its apogee when Prime Minister Harper announced that Canada had no intention of fulfilling its international legal obligations under the Kyoto Protocol and would formally withdraw from the treaty. This is the first instance anyone can remember of a Canadian government repudiating an international obligation in this way.

Despite the five or more (depending on how you count) attempts to produce a national climate change strategy, both Liberal and Conservative governments have failed to produce a credible plan. Yet concern for climate change remains high among Canadians. One recent poll shows that about twice as many Canadians are concerned with climate change as Americans.[1] Canada is also one of the few countries to fight an election in which climate change became a major issue. The Liberal leader,

Stéphane Dion, made the "green shift" to propose taxes on pollution the centrepiece of his campaign and lost by a considerable margin.

Since then Canada has become an obvious policy taker from the United States on this issue. Canada entered the Copenhagen negotiations with a target of reducing emissions by 20 percent over 2005 levels by 2020. When they heard that the US was committing to 17 percent, that figure became the Canadian target overnight as well.

President Obama made climate change one of his major election issues. Once he became president, however, the issue soon became lost in the struggle to avoid worldwide depression and to cure the American health care system. A half-hearted attempt to move a bill through Congress proved a failure and the mid-term election produced a whole horde of Republican climate change deniers who even blocked a House resolution pointing out that climate change is real and is largely caused by human activity.

As a result, US national climate policy has become a patchwork of incentives for renewable energy production, tightened standards for auto fuel efficiency, and an attempt by the Environmental Protection Agency (EPA) to regulate greenhouse gas (GHG) emissions through old-fashioned command and control legislation. In the United States, this route has been chosen by the Obama administration because congressional opposition to carbon taxes or cap and trade schemes has left it little choice.

The very conservative Canadian government has chosen the same route in the face of opposition from civil society and most of industry. Environment Canada is currently drawing up rules to regulate GHG emissions, this despite the fact that most research concludes that the use of market-based instruments is both cheaper and more efficient. The defeat of Mr Dion's green shift undoubtedly played a major role in the decision to shift to command and control, but it is still a curious move.

Throughout this period, Mexico played an active role with a well-briefed and staffed delegation at the UN negotiations. But since developing countries are not required to reduce emissions under Kyoto, it was not called upon to take action domestically. Mexican policy changed dramatically in 2009 with the publication of a national plan to combat climate change. During the Poznan meeting of the parties to the convention, Mexico announced its intention to reduce emissions by 50 percent from 2002 levels by 2050. In Copenhagen in 2010 the country added a commitment to reduce emissions 51 percent below business-as-usual estimates by 2012 and 30 percent by 2020. These targets will be difficult for Mexico to meet. In fact, the whole idea of a national energy strategy is made doubly difficult by the iconic status of Pemex, a state-owned petroleum firm, which successive Mexican governments have treated as a cash cow.

Mexico deserves credit for rescuing the international negotiating process from the swamp into which it had fallen in Copenhagen. Masterful diplomacy by Foreign Minister Espinosa and timely interventions by President Calderón reversed the downward slide begun the year before.

So we have one national government with an active, clearly defined policy for the reduction in CO2 emissions, one which is faced with determined opposition from its Congress, resulting in essentially no national climate policy, and a third which seems determined to follow the lead of the second. Not a particularly promising basis for collaboration.

STATES AND PROVINCES TAKE THE LEAD

It would be misleading to assume that nothing is happening in either the United States or Canada on climate change issues. Although the current political and economic turbulence in the US makes the future of some of these arrangements shaky, the US has developed three regional initiatives to deal with climate change.

The most ambitious programs have been developed in California. Former governor Arnold Schwarzenegger also took the initiative to construct the Western Climate Initiative (WCI). WCI was composed of eleven US states and four Canadian provinces. Two Mexican states were observers to the process. The initiative was bold, planning for 15 percent reductions in 2005 emissions levels by 2015. Originally each of the signatories promised to develop cap and trade systems by 2012 for electricity, industrial, and commercial combustion sources and industrial process emissions. For various reasons, only California seems on track to produce the cap and trade system by 2012.

California has a number of additional programs to reduce GHGs, which are too numerous to document here. One that has the potential to develop into a hot NAFTA issue is the low-carbon fuel standard. This is a graduated tax that increases with the carbon content of the fuel. It is largely aimed at fuels produced from Canada's oil sands. It has been adopted by a number of other states and by portions of the US government. Canada worries that it will result in unfair non-tariff barriers to Canadian trade in energy.

A less ambitious scheme was put in place in the northeastern states. Under the Regional Greenhouse Gas Initiative there are mandatory caps on electricity generators that are designed to stabilize emissions from 2009 to 2014 and reduce them by 2.4 percent per year between 2015 and 2018. At least one-quarter of permits have to be auctioned and half the states have auctioned off all the permits. The system is in operation and working effectively.

In addition to these multistate initiatives, there are a host of plans from municipal governments, and individual states have adopted a series of measures designed to move toward smarter grids and much greater reliance on renewable power through renewable portfolio standards and feed-in tariffs.

Less helpfully, many states have joined with the federal government to prop up the corn ethanol industry. According to virtually every study, the effects of ethanol use on GHG emissions is marginal at best. But the programs have resulted in almost 40 percent of the US corn crop being used to produce motor fuel. According to the World Bank, this is one of the major contributors to the spike in world food prices.[2]

Canadian provinces have also been active. Four provinces, representing 75 percent of Canada's GDP, remain as members of the WCI, although none is likely to meet the 2012 deadline for cap and trade systems.

British Columbia has moved the furthest, with a carbon tax in place which will price carbon at $30 a ton by 2012, higher than the current European price. Most revenues from the carbon tax are used to reduce income taxes. A provincial election was fought largely on this issue and the government was re-elected, casting doubt on the thesis that carbon taxes are merely a form of political suicide. British Columbia has also adopted a whole series of flanking policies from requiring LEED (Leadership in Energy and Environmental Design) Gold standard buildings at the provincial and municipal level, to making its largest university carbon neutral by 2015.

Ontario will phase out its coal-fired electricity plants that at one point produced almost 30 percent of the province's electricity and will move to a mix of renewables and nuclear power in the medium future. It has become the first jurisdiction in North America to install "smart meters" in every household and has developed an extensive program to subsidize renewable energy through a series of feed-in tariffs. This program has now been challenged by Japan in the WTO and perhaps by T. Boone Pickens's company through NAFTA. The continuation of many of these programs is contingent on the results of the October 2011 election.

Quebec has instituted a carbon tax. It plans to have its WCI cap and trade system in operation by the deadline and it has a whole series of very ambitious targets for sustainable development and greenhouse gas reductions. In contrast to Ontario, there is almost universal support in Quebec for emissions reduction programs, sustainable development, and green growth.

FUTURE AVENUES OF CO-OPERATION

Although the three national governments are at very different stages in the development of climate policy, eventually both Canada and the US will have to produce more realistic programs, so it is essential that contact among the three continue in advance of the G20 meeting in Mexico.

An expansion and rejuvenation of the Clean Energy Dialogue established between Canada and the United States is in order to continue a dialogue at the highest level. Climate policy is energy policy and energy policy is a big-ticket item in each of the countries.

It would make sense to create more electricity linkages between the US and Mexico to provide markets for renewable energy from Mexico as that country moves to maximize its comparative advantages in wind and solar.

Canada and the United States, perhaps through the North American Electricity Reliability Council, need to talk regularly as plans for smart grids develop. A smart system is only as smart as its weakest link.

States and provinces need to talk with each other about such things as harmonizing standards for renewable energy programs (for example, is large-scale Canadian hydroelectricity a renewable resource?), renewable portfolio standards, and feed-in tariffs or we will have a crazy quilt of conflicting rules and regulations for producers to navigate.

The trade community needs to become involved in the discussions about potential border tax adjustments and non-tariff barriers to trade in energy at least within North America. This could provide a role for the NAFTA Commission on Environmental Cooperation. And as the climate debate begins to mature internationally, all these issues of level playing fields, compulsory purchases of allowances, and the like may well become major constraints to trade and the subject of WTO disputes.

Both the United States and Canada have pledged money through the various funding options that have opened since Copenhagen, although US support seems less certain in the current climate. The other North American governments should be talking with Mexico about support for energy efficiency and for renewable and conservation programs in Mexico. In particular, Mexico stands to be a major beneficiary of funding for REDD (Reducing Emissions from Deforestation and Forest Degradation in Developing Countries) programs.

Finally, it seems likely that we will be seeing an international shift in climate negotiations from "top-down" multilateral initiatives to "bottom-up" and plurilateral initiatives. North America could provide the same kind of advantages as the EU system has provided to its members. Although the politics of this issue are by no means ripe, there are many cross-border initiatives that have been developed by provinces, the private sector, and civil society in the three countries. We need to find a way to nurture these relationships so that when the time comes for more concerted North American action, we will be ready.

NOTES

1   "Climate compared: Public opinion on climate change in the United States & Canada," Public Policy Forum and Sustainable Prosperity, February 23, 2011.
2   Mitchell, Donald, World Bank Policy Research Working Paper 4682, 2008/07/31

Conclusion:
Canada and Mexico –
Moving the Agenda Forward

AMBASSADOR GUILLERMO
E. RISHCHYNSKI

As outgoing Ambassador of Canada to Mexico, I am honoured to have been asked by the editors of *Canada Among Nations* to offer some final comments on this impressive volume, as well as a few thoughts on where our bilateral partnership has been, and may lead us, over the medium and longer term.

In the early 1990s, I served as deputy director for Mexico and Latin America at the (then) Department of External Affairs, which provided me with a unique vantage point from which to observe the debate within Canada about a possible North American Free Trade Agreement (NAFTA). The 1990s were a pivotal period in Canada's engagement with Mexico, and with Latin America as a whole. Our entry into the Organization of American States (OAS) as a "full member" in 1990, and the decision to pursue a trilateral trade agreement with the United States and Mexico, changed the course of Canada's foreign policy priorities in dramatic fashion.

I had the good fortune to be one of the "drafters" of the many memorandums to ministers at that time advocating Canada's pursuit of NAFTA. We made the case for trilateralism by arguing that it would boost the competitiveness of all three North American partners and would ensure preferential access to our most important market – the United States. During visits to Mexico, I learned that the same arguments were being put forward by my Mexican counterparts, focusing on the US as the *sine qua non* for the pursuit of this seminal agreement. There were some references in both our countries to Canada-Mexico relations, and the potential for stronger economic (obviously) and political ties, but these were not seen to be the principal considerations for our leaders and policy-makers when examining the potential benefits of greater North American economic integration.

The real prospects for the expansion of Canada-Mexico relations was made manifest to me during the 1992 "Canada Expo" in Monterrey, Nuevo León, far from the epicentres of policy-making. This trade initiative brought over 450 Canadian firms to Mexico – many for the first time – and it remains the most successful trade promotion initiative I have witnessed in thirty years in the Canadian Foreign Service. As I watched Mexican and Canadian entrepreneurs engage with one another in Monterrey, it was clear that a trilateral trade agreement would undoubtedly open previously unexplored commercial opportunities for both countries and underpin a rapid expansion of two-way trade between us.

The events I witnessed in Monterrey were, however, much more than "just business." I realized that I was participating in the coming together of two countries, in the discovery by Canadians and Mexicans that, differing histories and determining factors notwithstanding, we had much more in common with each other than we had ever realized, and that we were embarking on a new journey of discovery and engagement whose prospects offered previously undiscovered benefits that would reach well beyond trade and commerce.

The rest, as they say, is history. As has been well documented in previous chapters, our economic partnership expanded at a blistering pace: two-way trade has grown by over 500 percent since 1994. NAFTA has spurred direct investment by Canadian companies in Mexico, which now exceeds $10.5 billion in asset value, and over 2,600 Canadian companies are present in the Mexican market. For Mexico, Canada is now the third most important market for its products. In manufacturing, services, financial services, tourism, and food and agriculture – the list goes on – Canadians and Mexican are working together as never before. Today, these exchanges go well beyond the import and export of finished products, to integrated supply chains central to the ability of Mexican and Canadian firms to compete internationally. We are making things together, both for the North American market and for the world. Few imagined this in 1990 (I admit, readily, that these results far exceeded my modest expectations at that time). Regrettably, it is a story overlooked by media in both countries and remains a "silent benefit" of what free trade has brought to both our countries; we still tend to measure NAFTA from the perspective of the "centrality" of the US for both our economies.

The burgeoning economic linkages of the early 1990s were accompanied by a flurry of political and diplomatic initiatives that also took Canada-Mexico bilateral relations to new heights. I recall with fondness the initial Joint Ministerial Meetings of the 1990s, which sometimes brought together up to one-third of the respective cabinets of both governments and which created the basis for more extensive bilateral engagement. Mexican presidents and Canadian prime ministers met bilaterally at least once a year – sometimes more frequently – and engaged directly in the discussions between ministers in guiding a relationship valued highly in both capitals. The co-operation in these years between Elections Canada and the Mexican Federal Electoral Institute (IFE) provided an important contribution to the strengthening of democratic governance in Mexico at a defining time in its history. We continue to see the impact to this day.

The notion of Mexican and Canadian "common cause" in our North American and global interaction was the leitmotif for expanded dialogue and interaction across an impressive array of issues. Even the financial crisis of 1994, a deep and searing experience for Mexico, did not impede this accelerated level of engagement. Canadians looked to the long term, betting on Mexico's ability to recover and on the internal dynamism of its society and economy to bolster further our growing bilateral partnership. In Ottawa and Mexico City, the "third pillar" of NAFTA – the Canada-Mexico pillar – was seen as a strategic underpinning for both countries.

As has been pointed out in preceding chapters, much has happened in Canada, Mexico, and the world since those initial heady days of discovery. The political agendas in both our countries have since come to be dominated by global threats (i.e., security, migration, and transnational crime) and a "regional agenda" in respect of North America, and our incipient bilateral engagement has, perhaps, become a secondary priority.

This is not to say that the last decade has been bereft of important bilateral interaction between Canada and Mexico. During the administration of President Vicente Fox, important new joint initiatives were brought forward on the protection and expansion of human rights, privacy, and access to information to which Canadian experts contributed to great effect, particularly in the drafting of new legislation. The Canada-Mexico Partnership (CMP) came into being in 2005 and represents a unique platform for bilateral dialogue, bringing together government and private sector representatives from both countries to consider key bilateral issues such as labour mobility, trade, technology and innovation, energy, human capital development, environmental and forestry protection, agribusiness, and even a highly productive exchange of experiences in housing technologies and policies. If the strength of a bilateral relationship is ultimately measured by the substance and depth of the agenda being pursued by the partners, the CMP is testament to the strong desire by Mexico and Canada to work more closely together on the range of issues that affect economic competitiveness and citizen security, to deepen and expand the contact between our peoples, and to project this partnership at the regional and global level. These are the central tenets that have guided the Canada-Mexico Joint Action Plans endorsed by President Calderón and Prime Minister Harper since 2007.

During my four years as Ambassador in Mexico (2007–11), I have witnessed growing bilateral collaboration in a number of new endeavours: a bilateral civil-military political dialogue, which is a highly innovative forum for both countries. Canada's active participation as a partner in Mexico's security and judicial reform efforts since 2008 has brought our police and justice officials together to help address Mexican priorities as never before. Bilateral co-operation in anti-crime capacity building and crime prevention strategies has opened new horizons for joint action, with both sides finding useful actions and experiences to share.

A new Youth Mobility Agreement and a bilateral Rapid Reaction Consular Mechanism have provided a strong underpinning in facilitating people-to-people linkages, as has the continued expansion of the Seasonal Agricultural Worker's Program (SAWP) which now provides access for 18,000 Mexican workers to travel to Canada each year under a legal, secure, and orderly framework in response to labour market needs. Our newly minted Bilateral Air Services Agreements (2011) makes real a liberalized market for air connections between Canadian and Mexican cities, supporting the movement of tourists, business people, workers, and students (which will soon exceed 2 million per year) in a spirit of "open skies" between both countries. These are significant bilateral "deliverables," which reflect the breadth and scope of a bilateral partnership that has grown substantially in a very short time.

The above developments notwithstanding, there is very real sentiment in many government, business, academic, and media circles in both countries that Canada and Mexico have but scratched the surface of the potential of even closer bilateral engagement. It is an undercurrent reflected in many of the contributions contained in this volume, and one which I have confronted on an almost daily basis in interactions with Mexicans and Canadians during my tenure as ambassador. Why is this? Permit me to proffer a few personal observations.

First, I believe that Canada and Mexico both continue to define our bilateral relations perhaps too narrowly through the prism of NAFTA. As the North American agenda has stalled somewhat from its initial promise in the 1990s with "thickening borders," red-tape, and bureaucratic inertia, the Canada-Mexico relationship has been tarred with the same brush. I would argue that the evidence is otherwise.

In a mere decade-and-a-half, a correct but distant, and low decibel, relationship between our two countries has been utterly transformed. I know of no other bilateral partner – save the United States – with whom Canada pursues the same range and scope of bilateral agenda and dialogue as we do with Mexico. The fact that nine federal Canadian departments and agencies, as well as three provincial governments (Quebec,

Ontario, and Alberta), maintain active, full work programs in Mexico via resident representation in the country speaks for itself. I would submit that the partnership that has been forged over these years has been propelled by our growing trade and investment levels and the importance of our respective markets to the bottom-line health of our business communities.

Second, as in any long-term relationship, we have seen the initial glow of "something new" give way to a feeling of comfort, that all is proceeding reasonably well. We both may be guilty of taking each other for granted as new priorities have inserted themselves into our national agendas. We continue to see incremental, "under the radar" expansion of the scope of our bilateral engagement. However, the political priority to further accelerate our interaction, coordination, and integration – bilaterally and beyond – may not seem to carry the imprimatur of the audacious and bold vision set out twenty years ago.

Contributors to this volume have set out a blueprint for many areas of enhanced engagement that we could readily pursue to rekindle the "spark" that made Canada-Mexico relations unique and promising in the past. In my judgment, these objectives can and should be pursued by stakeholders in both countries, and they do not depend on a North American agenda to be attainable. It is in our individual interest as countries to do so.

Third, while we have become much closer as societies, we still have much to learn from each other about the "real" Canada and Mexico. Although the level of interaction among our citizens – be it as visitors, students, workers, or in business – has grown at an unprecedented rate, we still remain hostage to stereotypical characterizations of each other. We have also been unable to create a more broad-based understanding of our complementarities and the benefits we bring to the table as true allies. Our knowledge of each other's societies, values, and culture require a level of renewed investment commensurate with the "strategic" nature of the partnership we have constructed. This is, from my point of view, the most critical element required in a reinvigorated bilateral agenda.

The preceding chapters offer important guideposts for how a new, twenty-first century Canada-Mexico agenda might be structured, and the key priorities we can address as partners in forging even closer relations in the future. Like the inuksuit in Canada's Far North, these chapters point the way for like-minded stakeholders in both countries to move discussion, debate, and consideration toward this goal. As Canadians and Mexicans, we have enjoyed an unprecedented period of engagement. We know the issues, we understand the priorities, and we have seen what can be achieved when government, business, academe, and civil society in both countries join forces in pursuit of a singular vision to create a basis for a deeper and more compelling bilateral partnership.

This is the journey we began in those heady days when, as a young foreign service officer, I ruminated about what Canada and Mexico might be to, and for, each other in a generation. In returning to Mexico twenty years later, I remain in awe of the progress we have made together. We have the foundation to go forward. If we have the will to do so, I have no doubt that those reflecting on our progress twenty years hence will be equally struck by how far we have come.

Contributors

OLGA ABIZAID (oabizaid@focal.ca) is coordinator of the Canadian chapter of the Canada-Mexico Initiative. She is former director of the Research Forum on North America at the Canadian Foundation for the Americas (FOCAL).

AMBASSADOR LUIS ALFONSO DE ALBA (ladealba@sre.gob.mx) has served as a Mexican diplomat since 1983. He was promoted to the rank of ambassador in 2001, has served as special representative on Climate Change and permanent representative of Mexico to the Office of the United Nations and other international organizations in Geneva. He was president of the Human Rights Council from 2006 to 2007.

JON ALLEN (jon.allen@international.gc.ca) is assistant deputy minister for the Americas at the Department of Foreign Affairs and International Trade (DFAIT) in Canada. He served as ambassador to Israel (2006–10) and minister (Political Affairs) at the Canadian Embassy in Washington (2004–06).

THE HONOURABLE JOHN BAIRD (bairdj@parl.gc.ca) was first elected federally in 2006. He has held several high-profile cabinet portfolios and has travelled to Mexico on official business several times. Mr Baird was appointed Foreign Affairs Minister by Prime Minister Stephen Harper in May 2011.

RAÚL BENÍTEZ MANAUT (manaut@servidor.unam.mx) is professor and researcher at the North America Research Center of the National University of Mexico (UNAM) and president of the Mexican NGO Colectivo de Análisis de la Seguridad con Democracia (CASEDE). He lectures in Political Science and International Relations at UNAM and the Instituto Tecnologico Autonomo de Mexico(ITAM).

ENRIQUE BERRUGA-FILLOY (enriqueberruga@hotmail.com) is president of the Mexican Council on Foreign Relations (COMEXI) and former vice-president of Corporate Relations and Communication of Grupo Modelo. He has served as permanent representative of Mexico to the United Nations, ambassador of Mexico to Costa Rica, personal representative of the president of Mexico for the United Nations Reform Process, and deputy foreign secretary at the Ministry of Foreign Affairs.

STEPHEN BLANK (sblank5642@aol.com, www.stephenblank.info)is director of the Portal for North America, an online network linking main centres on North American research and teaching. He is a senior fellow at the Center for North American Studies at American University and at the Macdonald-Laurier Institute in Ottawa; senior research analyst at Arizona State University's North American Center for Transborder Studies; and adjunct research scholar, Center for Energy, Marine Transport and Public Policy at Columbia University.

ALEX BUGAILISKIS (Alexandra_Bugailiskis@carleton.ca) is a senior official at the Canadian Department of Foreign Affairs and International Trade with extensive experience on Latin America and the Caribbean. She is a former assistant deputy minister for the region and has served as Canadian ambassador to Cuba and as a senior distinguished fellow at the Norman Paterson School of International Affairs.

JOSÉ CARREÑO FIGUERAS (carreno.jose@gmail.com) is a researcher at the Centre for Dialogue and Analysis on North America at the Tecnológico de Monterrey, correspondent for publications such as *El Universal* in Washington, DC, and a collaborator with Univision, CNN, NBC, CBC, World Net, and Deutsche Welle, among others.

LUIS DE LA CALLE PARDO (ldelacalle@cmmsc.com.mx) is managing director and founding partner of De la Calle, Madrazo, Mancera, S.C. (CMM). He has served as undersecretary for International Trade Negotiations in Mexico's Ministry of the Economy, board member at Pemex Exploration and Production and at the National Forest Commission, executive secretary of the National Foreign Investment

Commission, and Trade and NAFTA minister at the Mexican Embassy in Washington, DC.

ED DOSMAN (edosman@yorku.ca)is senior research fellow at the Centre for International and Security Studies, York University and founding director of FOCAL (the Canadian Foundation for the Americas). He was professor of Political Science at York University and is the author of *The Life and Times of Raúl Prebisch* (McGill-Queen's University Press, 2008).

GRAEME DOUGLAS (Graeme.s.douglas@gmail.com) is an independent researcher and writer. He served as the coordinator of research for FOCAL's Canada-Mexico Initiative. Prior to his work with FOCAL, Graeme worked as a Balsillie Student Fellow at the Centre for International Governance Innovation's Portal for North America, where he wrote on economic and political issues linking Mexico with its North American neighbours. His work focuses on Canada-Mexico relations and the foreign policy of the United States.

JOSEPH M. DUKERT (dukert@verizon.net) is senior associate with the William E. Simon Chair in Political Economy at the Center for Strategic and International Studies in Washington, DC and an independent energy analyst focusing on North America's energy market and policies. He was formerly International Energy Agency consultant and senior adviser to the North American Commission for Environmental Cooperation.

JOSÉ NATIVIDAD GONZALEZ PARÁS (jngonzalezp@primercirculo.com) is president of ANDAAP (Academia Nacional de Derecho Administrativo y Administración Pública) and former federal deputy for and governor of Nuevo León where he also served as the secretary general of the state of Nuevo León.

THE HONOURABLE BILL GRAHAM (Patricia.Fortier@international. gc.ca) is chancellor of Trinity College at the University of Toronto, chair of the Atlantic Council of Canada and co-vice chair of the Canadian International Council. He has served as a Liberal member of Parliament, as chair of the Standing Committee of the House of Commons on Foreign Affairs and International Trade from 1995 to 2002, as minister of Foreign Affairs, and as minister of National Defence.

HER EXCELLENCY SENATOR ROSARIO GREEN (rgreen@senado.gob.mx) is a senator (2006–12) and president of the Foreign Affairs Commission in the Mexican Senate. She has served as secretary of Foreign Affairs and deputy foreign minister for Mexico, as secretary general of the

Institutional Revolutionary Party (PRI and as ambassador to East Germany and Argentina. She is former executive secretary of the National Human Rights Commission and subsecretary for Political Affairs at the United Nations

FEN OSLER HAMPSON (fen_hampson@carleton.ca) is Chancellor's Professor and the Director of The Norman Paterson School of International Affairs (NPSIA), Carleton University, Ottawa and a fellow of the Royal Society of Canada. He is also a senior advisor to the United States Institute of Peace, a member of the Board of Directors of the Pearson Peacekeeping Centre, the Parliamentary Centre, and the Social Science Foundation Board at the University of Denver. Dr Hampson is the author/co-author of nine books and editor/co-editor of more than twenty-six others. He has written numerous articles and book chapters on international affairs and is a frequent contributor to the national and international media.

PAUL HEINBECKER (paul@heinbecker.ca) is senior distinguished fellow, Centre for International Governance Innovation, and professor, Sir Wilfrid Laurier University. His early diplomatic career included postings to Ankara, Stockholm and Paris. He then served as director of the US division in the External Affairs Department and head of policy planning, and was subsequently appointed to the Canadian embassy in Washington. After serving as Prime Minister Brian Mulroney's chief foreign policy adviser and speechwriter and assistant secretary to cabinet for foreign and defence policy, he was named ambassador to Germany. In 1996, he became deputy minister for global and security policy, led the Canadian delegation to the Kyoto climate change negotiations, and headed the interdepartmental task force on Kosovo. In 2000, he was appointed permanent representative of Canada to the UN. Paul has authored, edited, and contributed to a number of books and articles on international relations

CARLOS HEREDIA ZUBIETA (carlos.heredia@cide.edu) is chair and professor in the Department of International Studies of the Centre for Research and Teaching in Economics (CIDE) in Mexico City. He is a former member of the Mexican Congress. Mr Heredia is a graduate of McGill University and also attended the Université Laval.

ATHANASIOS HRISTOULAS (ahristoulas@itam.mx) is professor of International Relations, director of Canadian Studies, and the coordinator of the diploma course on National Security at the Instituto Tecnologico Autonomo de Mexico. He is a regular lecturer at the Mexican army's College of National Defence and at the Mexican navy's Center for Superior

Naval Studies. He held the position of Military and Strategic Fellow at the Norman Paterson School of International Studies in Ottawa. He has written extensively on North American security issues.

JENNIFER JEFFS (jjeffs@onlinecic.org) is president of the Canadian International Council (CIC), a member of the editorial board of *Foreign Affairs Latinoamérica* (previously *Foreign Affairs en Español*), a director of the Canadian Council of the Americas, and a director of the Centro de Estudios y Programas Interamericanos in Mexico City. She sits on the Advisory Council of the Canada-Mexico Initiative.

MARINA JIMÉNEZ (MJimenez@globeandmail.com) is a journalist specializing in immigration and Latin American issues. She has covered stories on Haiti, Chile, Mexico, Brazil, Panama, Colombia, and Venezuela. She is a member of the *Globe and Mail's* editorial board and teaches a course in Media Studies at the University of Toronto.

LOURDES MELGAR (lourdes.melgar@gmail.com) is founding director of the Center for Sustainability and Business at the EGADE Business School and an independent energy consultant. A former career diplomat and director general for International Affairs at SENER (Secretaría de Energía de México), she has held the positions of Mexico Public Policy Scholar at the Woodrow Wilson Center for International Scholars and visiting scholar at the Center for International Energy and Environmental Policy of the University of Texas.

REID MORDEN (reidmorden@rogers.com) is president of Reid Morden & Associates. He served as director of the Canadian Security Intelligence Service, deputy minister of Foreign Affairs, and president and CEO of Atomic Energy of Canada Ltd. He was the executive director of the Independent Inquiry Committee into the United Nations Iraq Oil-For-Food Program (Volcker Inquiry).

PHILIP OXHORN (philip.oxhorn@mcgill.ca) is professor of Political Science at McGill University, founding director of the Institute for the Study of International Development, editor-in-chief of the *Latin American Research Review*, and author of *Sustaining Civil Society: Economic Change, Democracy and the Social Construction of Citizenship in Latin America* (The Pennsylvania State University Press, forthcoming).

DAVID PARKS (davidparks@eastlink.ca) is a consultant on governance issues related to North American integration and manager of the Mexico program at the Forum of Federations since 2001.

ROBERT PASTOR (rpastor@american.edu) is professor of International Relations and director of the Center for North American Studies at American University. He has served as the director of Latin American Affairs on the National Security Council and was vice chair of the Council on Foreign Relations Task Force on North America. Dr Pastor is the author of seventeen books, most recently *The North American Idea: A Vision of a Contintental Future.*

CARLOS E. REPRESAS (cer@amskap.com)has been chair of the Advisory Board of Bombardier Mexico since 2007. He served as chair of the Board of Nestlé Group Mexico from 1983 to 2010. He is a member of the Board of Directors of Bombardier Inc., Merck & Co., Inc., Swiss Re Group, and a member of the Latin American Business Council (CEAL) and of the Board of Dean's Advisors of the Harvard School of Public Health. He is chair of the Board of Trustees of the National Institute of Genomic Medicine of Mexico, and of the Mexico chapter of the Latinamerican Chamber of Commerce in Zurich, Switzerland. From 1994 to 2004, he was Executive Vice President and also President of the Americas of Nestlé, S.A. in Switzerland.

AMBASSADOR GUILLERMO E. RISHCHYNSKI (Guillermo.Rishchynski@international.gc.ca) served as Canada's ambassador to the United Mexican States from September 2007 to September 2010. He joined the Canadian Foreign Service in 1982 after a career in marketing and project management in Africa and Latin America. He has served at the Canadian Consulates General and Canadian embassies in several countries, as Canadian ambassador to Colombia in 1999, as vice-president for the Americas at the Canadian International Development Agency (CIDA), and as Canadian ambassador to Brazil from 2005 to 2007. In Ottawa, he has held a number of senior positions, including deputy director, Mexico, Latin America, and Caribbean, director of the Team Canada Task Force, and inspector general of the Department of Foreign Affairs.

AMBASSADOR ANDRÉS ROZENTAL (rozental@consejomexicano.org) is a member of the international board of governors of Canada's Center for International Governance Innovation and a board member at the Migration Policy Institute. He served as deputy foreign minister, Mexican ambassador to the United Kingdom and Sweden, and as the permanent representative of Mexico to the United Nations in Geneva.

DAVID RUNNALLS (drunnalls@iisd.ca) is distinguished fellow at the International Institute for Sustainable Development, a member of the Advisory Committee on Partnerships to the Minister for International

Cooperation, a member of the Environment Canada Cross-Cutting Issues table, a member of the Advisory Council for Export Development Canada, and former co-chair of the China Council Task Force on the WTO and Environment.

ISABEL STUDER (isabel.studer@itesm.mx) is founding director of the Center for Dialogue and Analysis on North America at the Tecnológico de Monterrey in Mexico City and former assistant director general for Canada at the Mexican Ministry for Foreign Affairs.

JULIÁN VENTURA (jventura@sre.gob.mx) is undersecretary for North American Affairs; former director-general for Asia-Pacific Affairs; the chief of cabinet to the secretary of External Relations; and the chief of cabinet to the undersecretary for Africa, Asia-Pacific, Europe, and United Nations Affairs.

OSCAR VERA (oscarhvera@prodigy.net.mx) is economic consultant and board member with several Mexican companies. He has lectured at various universities and was visiting professor at the University of Alberta, Canada. He has published four books and numerous articles on economic issues both in Mexico and abroad.

JOHN WEEKES (WeekesJ@bennettjones.com) is a senior business adviser at Bennett-Jones LLP, former Canadian ambassador to the WTO from 1995 to 1999, and former chair of the WTO General Council. He served as Canada's chief negotiator for the North American Free Trade Agreement (NAFTA) and as Canadian ambassador to the GATT (General Agreement on Tariffs and Trade) during the Uruguay Round of multilateral trade negotiations.